THE INKLINGS
HANDBOOK

To
Ben Duriez
Ellie Porter
Emilia Duriez
Lauren Porter

THE INKLINGS HANDBOOK

A comprehensive guide to the lives,
thought and writings of
C.S. Lewis, J.R.R. Tolkien, Charles Williams,
Owen Barfield and their friends

COLIN DURIEZ
and
DAVID PORTER

First published in Great Britain in 2001 by Azure,
1 Marylebone Road, London NW1 4DU.

© Copyright 2001 Colin Duriez and David Porter

North American edition published 2001 by Chalice Press,
P.O. Box 179, St. Louis, MO 63166–0179.

Visit Chalice Press on the World Wide Web at
www.chalicepress.com

10 9 8 7 6 5 4 3 2 1
01 02 03 04 05

Library of Congress Cataloging-in-Publication Data

Duriez, Colin.
    The inklings handbook : a comprehensive guide to the lives, thought and writings of
C.S. Lewis, J.R.R. Tolkien, Charles Williams, Owen Barfield and their friends / Colin Duriez
and David Porter.
        p. cm.
    ISBN 0-8272-1622-X
    1. Inklings (Group of writers)—Handbooks, manuals, etc. 2. Oxford
(England)—Intellectual life—20th century—Handbooks, manuals, etc.
3. Authors, English—20th century—Biography—Handbooks, manuals, etc.
4. English literature—20th century—Handbooks, manuals, etc. 5. Fantasy
literature, English—Handbooks, manuals, etc. 6. Lewis, C. S. (Clive Staples),
1898–1963—Handbooks, manuals, etc. 7. Tolkien, J. R. R. (John Ronald Reuel),
1892–1973—Handbooks, manuals, etc. 8. Williams Charles, 1886–1945—Handbooks,
manuals, etc. 9. Barfield, Owen, 1898–.—Handbooks, manuals, etc. I. Porter, David. II.
Title.
    PR478.I54 D87 2001
    820.9'00912—dc21
2001003306

Contents

Preface

Recent readers' polls in Britain put Tolkien's *The Lord of the Rings* at the top of the popular books. One poll – conducted by a leading bookshop chain – put it at the top of readers' choices as the book of the twentieth century. The trilogy has comparable popularity in the United States and throughout the English-speaking world. It is also prominent in translated form in bookshops and book stands in numerous non-English-speaking countries. It was secretly translated into Russian long before the end of the Cold War and today has massive popularity there. C.S. Lewis' *Chronicles of Narnia* also have wide international appeal, an appeal that continues to grow. As we write he is probably the subject of far more doctoral theses in process in the non-English-speaking world than in the whole of the United Kingdom.

Though there are a number of Christian writers who have impacted the wider world – a world Lewis would call post-Christian – Lewis and Tolkien are perhaps unique in their popularity. Another main Inkling – Charles Williams – has been neglected, but his day may yet come. As this book tries to demonstrate, his themes are of great interest to the contemporary world, and to Christians relating their faith to this world. He is also a writer of great power, whose interests have been taken up by other, mainstream, writers. He also had a dramatic impact on Lewis.

The continuing appeal of the Inklings raises fascinating questions about the relevance of Christian faith and its virtues in a modern, war-torn, secular and increasingly global culture. The group of writers also explored the insights of pagan and pre-Christian belief, particularly as expressed in myth and story. Another main Inkling – Owen Barfield – is better known in the United States than his native Britain. His solution to the challenge of modernism was different from his friends in kind as well as degree – he combined Christian and esoteric doctrines in a powerful critique of contemporary thought. Lewis and Tolkien (particularly Lewis) owed a great deal to Barfield's insights, even though, like Williams, they found their sufficiency within orthodox Christian faith.

The Inklings expanded from the deep friendship between Tolkien and Lewis, a remarkable association comparable to that between Wordsworth and Coleridge in literary significance. The group enlarged organically to take in more and more people, notably Williams and Lewis' old friend Barfield. Lewis, in his book, *The Four Loves*, explains the process by which friendship, the least jealous of loves, expands. Here he refers to Tolkien as 'Ronald' and to Williams as 'Charles':

> In each of my friends there is something that only some other friend can fully bring out. By myself I am not large enough to call the whole man into activity; I want other lights than my own to show all his facets. Now that Charles is dead, I shall never again see Ronald's reaction to a specifically Caroline joke. Far from having more of Ronald, having him 'to myself' now that Charles is away, I have less of Ronald. Hence true Friendship is the least jealous of loves. Two friends delight to be joined by a third, and three by a fourth, if only the newcomer is qualified to become a real friend ... Of course the scarcity of kindred souls – not to mention practical considerations about the size of rooms and the audibility of voices – set limits to the enlargement of the circle; but within those limits we possess each friend not less but more as the number of those with whom we share him increases.

It is clear from our study that the group of men enhanced rather than subdued each other's particular natures. In this Handbook we have tried to open up both the distinctive and the unifying features of the Inklings. We have carefully sought to avoid imposing artificial patterns and unities. Yet there were undoubtedly qualities in each that were brought out in, and sometimes perhaps only in, the context of the remarkable friendships that made up the Inklings.

There were of course important friendships outside the Inklings which were significant – Williams' with his wife, Michal, and with Phyllis Jones ('Celia'), as well as with Dorothy L. Sayers and T.S. Eliot; Tolkien's with his wife, Edith, and with his schoolboy friends cut down in the First World War; Lewis' with Joy Davidman, Arthur Greeves, and Mrs Janie Moore; and so the list could go on.

Our Handbook tries to capture the elusive complexity of these friendships and these individuals who made up the Inklings as an entity. The Handbook is designed to encourage exploration and discovery by suggesting links and cross-connections, or by highlighting central themes in the main writers, themes which surprisingly often overlap. There is a mystery at the heart of all friendships as there is at the heart of all persons, and we have tried to respect this reality. At the same time we remain convinced that there is a real, defining essence – a quiddity – to the Inklings, making it one of the most remarkable associations of writers in the last century of the second millennium. Their themes and concerns are strikingly relevant to the beginning of the third.

The Handbook is divided into two parts. Part One provides a kind of map or overview, with key biographical and thematic sections, including a detailed chronology as a reminder that the association of friends had a context in their times, which included intellectual ferment, great changes even in cloistered Oxford University, bereavement and the impact of human evil embodied in a modern world war. It also included the unique homeliness of a British pub where, amid choking tobacco smoke, beer and cider lubricated creative theology and writing, and indirectly, the growth of the Christian church. Part Two provides a simple dictionary format to give easy access to the writings, themes, ideas and people associated with the Inklings.

To allow our readers to follow through themes and subjects that capture their interest, we have used asterisks within the articles and sections in this book to show other references. If a significant cross-reference is not included, we give it at the article or section end. Where appropriate we have added suggestions for further reading. For an expanded treatment of two of the central Inklings, the reader is referred to Colin Duriez's *The C.S. Lewis Encyclopedia* (2000) and *Tolkien and The Lord of the Rings* (2001).

The writers of this book have many debts to acknowledge, not least to each other. The book itself is the fruit of a friendship that goes back many years to before we were university students of English Literature (and concurrently Philosophy, in Colin Duriez's case, and previously librarianship and bibliography, in David Porter's). In preparation of this book Colin Duriez was the grateful recipient of the 1994 Clyde S. Kilby Research Grant from the Marion E. Wade Center, Wheaton College, Wheaton, Illinois, USA. The kindness of Marjorie L. Mead and the library staff was deeply appreciated. He also wishes to thank friends in the Tolkien Society for opportunities to speak on and explore the relationship between Tolkien and the other Inklings. He is particularly grateful for the honour of twice being invited to give the Annual Banquet Speech, in Hull in 1992 and in Chepstow in 1997, and to experience TS room parties. He is also grateful for the friends made through Tolkien- and Lewis-related conferences in Wheaton, Illinois; Turku, Finland; Oxford; Cambridge; Belfast, Northern Ireland; Granada, Spain; and Warsaw, Poland. There are many others to thank, all of whom have helped in the talking-through of this book.

David Porter's prolific writing activities have been less directly focused on the Inklings than have Colin's, but he is grateful for the input and friendship of a large circle of Inklings-loving 'virtual friends' on the Internet, particularly those in alt.books.cs-lewis; to Andrew Rilstone, who in this as in other subjects amply demonstrates that great learning is fully compatible with great wit; to Douglas Gresham for keeping the flame burning bright; to Janine Goffar and Walter Hooper, for their C.S. Lewis *Index* and *Companion and Guide* respectively (how warmly future readers will thank them!); to

Iron Crown Enterprises for their Middle-earth games series – a constant, authentic joy; and to the editors at Oxford University Press and a number of other publishing houses and periodicals, for the opportunity to contribute material on C.S. Lewis and the Inklings to a number of reference works, books and journals.

COLIN DURIEZ and DAVID PORTER
Leicester, and Greatham, Hampshire

Abbreviations

OB   Owen Barfield

CSL   C.S. Lewis

JRRT   J.R.R. Tolkien

CW   Charles Williams

Part One

ONE

The Life and Times
of the Inklings

Once upon a time there was a group of male friends, all people of talent, who met together at least once a week to talk about ideas, to read to each other for pleasure and criticism pieces they were writing, and to enjoy a good evening of 'the cut and parry of prolonged, fierce, masculine argument'. 'The Inklings' embodied CSL's ideals of life and pleasure. In fact, he was the life and soul of the party. The literary group of friends was held together by his zest and enthusiasm. JRRT was also a central figure in the Inklings, who cast them fictionally in his unfinished 'The Notion Club Papers'*. Their important years as a literary group were from around 1933 to about 1949, especially during the war when another key member, CW, was resident in Oxford*. In these years they met in CSL's rooms in Oxford, as well as in the Eagle and Child* and other pubs. CW wrote poetry, novels, plays, literary criticism, and off-the-beaten-track theology. He powerfully influenced CSL, though JRRT was not so taken with him. JRRT played a vital role in CSL's conversion to Christianity – the latter was for many years an atheist, then a pantheist.

Though the two most celebrated members of the group – JRRT and CSL – are sometimes considered out of touch with the real world, the fact is that their values have captured an audience of numerous millions around the globe. If they are unconnected with real modern life, why have so many of their contemporaries and more recent readers responded to them? The Inklings undoubtedly represent an important part of twentieth-century cultural history, in which literature still has a high place. What is remarkable, and perhaps unique, is that they were Christians. Much of their work, especially JRRT's, explored pre-Christian paganism, the idea of what CSL called the *anima naturaliter Christiana*, a kind of natural theology. Their pre-modernism has a remarkable appeal to our post-modernist culture. It seems that in their apparently foolish preoccupation with myth* and fantasy, a Christian voice was in preparation that would still speak at the beginning of the twenty-first century to the wider world. The literary critic, George Watson, points out that CSL's literary critical works largely belong to the age of modernism, and he was a lifelong anti-modernist. Paradoxically,

Watson remarks, CSL's 'mingling of formalism and fantasy – a critical and analytical interest in the forms that fantasy takes – was something which, when he died in 1963, was on the point of becoming fashionable'.

Other key members of the informal group making up the Inklings included CSL's brother (Major W.H. 'Warnie' Lewis*), OB* (a brilliant thinker, follower of Rudolf Steiner's* anthroposophism*, and author of a key book in CSL's and JRRT's thinking, *Poetic Diction**), H.V.D. 'Hugo' Dyson*, and others. CSL describes a typical meeting in a letter to an absent member – his brother – in 1939. The 'new Hobbit book' is a reference to the first volume of *The Lord of the Rings*.

> On Thursday we had a meeting of the Inklings … we dined at the Eastgate. I have never in my life seen Dyson so exuberant – 'A roaring cataract of nonsense'. The bill of fare afterwards consisted of a section of the new Hobbit book from Tolkien, a nativity play from Williams (unusually intelligible for him, and approved by all), and a chapter out of the book on the Problem of Pain from me.

JRRT described the Inklings in a letter as an 'undetermined and unelected circle of friends who gathered around C.S.L[ewis], and met in his rooms in Magdalen … Our habit was to read aloud compositions of various kinds (and lengths!) …'

CSL himself gives an insight into the Inklings almost incidentally in his preface to *Essays Presented to Charles Williams**, to which JRRT contributed. CSL points out that three of the essays in the collection are on literature, and specifically, one aspect of literature, the 'narrative art'. That, CSL says, is natural enough. CW's *'All Hallows' Eve* and my own *Perelandra* (as well as Professor Tolkien's unfinished sequel to *The Hobbit*) had all been read aloud, each chapter as it was written. They owe a good deal to the hard-hitting criticism of the circle. The problems of narrative as such – seldom heard of in modern critical writings – were constantly before our minds.'

JRRT occasionally refers to the group in his *Letters**. Writing approvingly to his publisher about CSL's science-fiction story, *Out of the Silent Planet**, he speaks of it 'being read aloud to our local club (which goes in for reading things short and long aloud). It proved an exciting serial, and was highly approved. But of course we are all rather like-minded.'

JRRT points out that 'the Inklings had no recorder and C.S. Lewis no Boswell'. However, glimpses of meetings can be seen in the letters of JRRT and CSL, and in the diaries of CSL's brother, Major Warren Hamilton Lewis. There also exists a lively and vivid description of the group by someone who was once a member of it, but who gradually realized that the aims and sympathies of his life and writings were out of keeping with it. There is a convincing overlap between this description of the group of an 'outsider', and the insights into the Inklings given by those heartily in favour of its aims, however informal.

The novelist and poet John Wain's* description of the Oxford group occurs in his autobiography, *Sprightly Running*. He remembers that, though admiring CSL and his friends tremendously, 'already it was clear that I did not share their basic attitudes. The group had a corporate mind, as all effective groups must'. He defined it like this: 'Politically conservative, not to say reactionary; in religion, Anglo- or Roman Catholic; in art, frankly hostile to any manifestation of the "modern spirit".'

He admits however that he would be giving quite a false picture of CSL and his friends if he presented them as merely reactionary, as if they were putting all their energies into negatively being *against* things. This is far from the truth, he says. As he put it: 'this was a circle of instigators, almost of incendiaries, meeting to urge one another on in the task of redirecting the whole current of contemporary art and life'.

According to Wain, after CW's death in 1945, the two most active members of the group became JRRT and CSL. Wain writes that 'While C.S. Lewis attacked on a wide front, with broadcasts, popular-theological books, children's stories, romances, and controversial literary criticism, Tolkien concentrated on the writing of his colossal "Lord of the Rings" trilogy. His readings of each successive installment were eagerly received, for "romance" was a pillar of this whole structure'. Writers admired by JRRT and CSL ('the literary household gods' of the group, Wain calls them) included George MacDonald*, William Morris ('selectively'), and E.R. Eddison. They all had in common the fact that they *invented*. According to Wain, 'Lewis considered "fine fabling" an essential part of literature, and never lost a chance to push any author, from Spenser to Rider Haggard, who would be called a romancer'. John Wain points out that, during the time he was involved with the Inklings (around 1944 or 1945 to 1946), he was surprised by the 'unexpected alliances' it was capable of forming. (Wain tends to describe the group of friends in martial terms.) Yet he felt that the key to this unexpectedness lay in CSL's character: 'Lewis . . . is basically a humble man. While he will fight long and hard for his beliefs, he is entirely free of the pride which refuses reinforcement for the sake of keeping within its hands the sole glory of conquer or, if need be, of heroic defeat.' The 'unexpected alliances' included Dorothy L. Sayers*, the children's author Roger Lancelyn Green, and the right-wing poet Roy Campbell*. Wain concludes, 'Lewis, during these years, had very much the mentality of a partisan leader: anyone who would skirmish against the enemy – the drab, unbelieving, sneering, blinkered modern world – should be his brother, be he ne'er so vile.'

The group was no mutual admiration society. They mainly felt deeply the truth of the poet Blake's aphorism: 'Opposition is true friendship'. CSL himself was 'hungry for rational opposition'. His friend Professor John Lawlor thinks that to attack CSL in this way was probably the first step towards friendship with him. JRRT remembered how much CSL felt at home in this kind of company. 'C.S.L. had a passion for hearing things read aloud, a power of memory for things received in that way, and also a facility in extempore criticism, none of which were shared (especially not the last) in anything like the same degree by his friends.'

It is clear from JRRT's letters that the Inklings provided valuable and much-needed encouragement as he struggled to compose *The Lord of the Rings*. Indeed, without the encouragement of CSL in particular, he would never have completed it.

A letter to his son Christopher, away with the RAF in South Africa, is typical, written in 1944:

> Monday 22 May... It was a wretched cold day yesterday (Sunday). I worked very hard at my chapter – it is most exhausting work; especially as the climax approaches and one has to keep the pitch up: no easy level will do; and there are all sorts of minor problems of plot and mechanism. I wrote and tore up and rewrote most of it a good many times; but I was rewarded this morning, as both C.S.L[ewis]. and C[harles]. W[illiams]. thought it an admirable performance, and the latest chapters the best so far. Gollum continues to develop into a most intriguing character...

Other members not so far mentioned were J.A.W. Bennett*, Lord David Cecil*, Nevill Coghill*, Commander Jim Dundas-Grant*, Adam Fox*, Colin Hardie*, Dr 'Humphrey' Havard*, Gervase Mathew*, R.B. McCallum*, C.E. ('Tom') Stevens*, Christopher Tolkien*, and Charles Wrenn*.

For their habitual Tuesday meetings one of the favourite haunts of the Inklings was 'The Eagle and Child' public house in St Giles (known more familiarly as 'The Bird and Baby'). Many a discussion or friendly argument was washed down with beer. The Thursday evening meetings had a literary focus, and the men tended to meet in CSL's rooms in Magdalen College. In fact, the meetings that centred around reading aloud for criticism and enjoyment took place in the important years of the Inklings (see Chapter 2, *The Inklings: A Chronology*). As a group of friends the Inklings continued to meet until the year of CSL's death, 1963.

W.H. Lewis, CSL's brother, was sceptical of the idea of the Inklings representing a school of literature or theology. He is probably right to be so in view of the diversity of its members at one time or another. However, CSL hankered for others who shared his core beliefs, and certainly the main Inklings like CW, JRRT and even OB did, though OB never became an orthodox Christian. Even though he was baptized into the Anglican Church he remained committed to anthroposophism.

Speaking in America in 1969, OB tried to define the Inklings as an entity. He wondered if something was not happening to 'the Romantic Impulse' during its life. He could discern four important strands, each mainly identified with CSL, JRRT, CW, or himself:

1 The yearning for the infinite and unattainable – CSL's *sehnsucht* or joy*.
2 In OB's own words, 'The conviction of the dignity of man and his part in the future history of the world conceived as a kind of progress towards increasing immanence of the divine in the human' (OB's own position).
3 The idealization of love between the sexes, as in CW's thought and writings.
4 The opposite of tragedy, the Happy Ending, JRRT's idea of the eucatastrophe.

FURTHER READING

Humphrey Carpenter, *The Inklings: C.S. Lewis, J.R.R. Tolkien, Charles Williams and their Friends*, George Allen and Unwin: London, 1978.

Gareth Knight, *The Magical World of the Inklings*, Elements Books, 1990.

Rand Kuhl, 'Owen Barfield in Southern California', *Mythlore*, vol. 1, no. 4, 1969.

Diana Pavlac, *The Company They Keep: Assessing the Mutual Influence of C.S. Lewis, J.R.R. Tolkien, and Charles Williams*, PhD thesis, University of Illinois at Chicago, 1993.

John Wain, *Sprightly Running: Part of an Autobiography*, Macmillan, 1962.

TWO

The Inklings: A Chronology

'Of course there was no reading on Tuesday, and the talk often veered to College and English School politics; but whatever the topic one could rely upon its being wittily handled'.
(W.H. Lewis' MS Biography of C.S. Lewis, Wade Center, p. 270)

1917 – JRRT begins writing the tales which will become *The Silmarillion**.

Autumn 1919 – CSL and OB first meet as undergraduates and survivors of the war.

1920 – JRRT is appointed Reader in English Literature at Leeds University.

1925 – JRRT is elected to the Chair of Anglo-Saxon at Oxford* University.

23 January 1926 – CSL gives his first lecture in the Oxford English School on 'Some Eighteenth-Century Precursors of the Romantic Movement'.

11 May 1926 – the first recorded meeting between JRRT and CSL.

18 September 1926 – CSL's narrative poem, *Dymer**, is published.

1928 – OB's *Poetic Diction** is published, the ideas of which have an enormous impact, first on CSL then JRRT.

17 October 1928 – CSL begins lectures on 'The Romance of the Rose and its Successors'.

1929 – by this year JRRT and CSL are meeting on a weekly basis, usually on Monday evenings in CSL's rooms at Magdalen College.

7 December 1929 – CSL writes in warm response to being lent JRRT's poetic version in progress of 'The Lay of Leithian' (The tale of Beren and Lúthien* from *The Silmarillion*): 'I can quite honestly say that it is ages since I have had an evening of such delight: and the personal interest of reading a friend's work had very little to do with it . . . The two things that came out clearly are the sense of reality in the background and the mythical value: the essence of a myth being that it should have no taint of allegory to the maker and yet should suggest incipient allegories to the reader' (*The Lays of Beleriand*, 1985, p. 151).

1929 – in an undated letter to OB, possibly written in 1929, CSL observes: 'You might like to know that when Tolkien dined with me the other night he said *à-propos* of something quite different that your conception of the ancient semantic unity had modified his whole outlook and that he was almost just going to say something in a lecture when your conception stopped him in time. "It is one of those things", he said, "that when you've once seen it there are all sorts of things you can never say again."'

1930 – JRRT begins to write *The Hobbit**.

19 September 1931 – After talking with JRRT and 'Hugo' Dyson, CSL becomes convinced of the truth of Christian belief.

22 November 1931 – CSL writes to Warnie about his meetings with JRRT: 'This is one of the pleasant spots in the week. Sometimes we talk English School politics: sometimes we criticize one another's poems: other days we drift into theology or "the state of the nation": rarely we fly no higher than bawdy and "puns".'

1932 – CSL reads the incomplete draft of *The Hobbit*.

18 January 1932 – CSL begins lectures on 'Prolegomena to Medieval Poetry'.

25 May 1933 – CSL's *The Pilgrim's Regress** published. That year an undergraduate club called 'The Inklings' disbands, and the title is transferred to CSL's immediate circle of friends.

1935 – In the early part of the year CSL's GP, Dr Havard, later dubbed 'Humphrey', attends him for influenza, and they discuss Aquinas. Soon after he is invited to join the Inklings circle. This is because of his evident interest in 'religio-philosophical discussion'. The Inklings are described to Havard as a group who meet on Thursday evenings, read papers they have written, and discuss them. The group is made up of friends of CSL's, and it is only later he learns their names.

Wednesday, 11 March 1936 – CSL first writes to CW, in appreciation of his novel, *The Place of the Lion**: 'A book sometimes crosses one's path which is . . . like the sound of one's native language in a strange country . . . It is to me one of the major literary events of my life – comparable to my first discovery of George MacDonald, G.K. Chesterton, or Wm. Morris . . . Coghill of Exeter put me on to the book: I have put on Tolkien (the Professor of Anglo Saxon and a papist) and my brother. So there is three dons and one soldier all buzzing with excited admiration. We have a sort of informal club called the Inklings: the qualifications (as they have informally evolved) are a tendency to write, and Christianity. Can you come down some day next term (preferably *not* Sat. or Sunday), spend the night as my guest in College, eat with us at a chop house, and talk with us till the small hours?' (Letter in possession of the Wade Center).

28 June 1936 – CSL writes to OB: 'I lent *The Silver Trumpet* to Tolkien and hear that it is the greatest success among his children that they have ever known.' He signs the letter 'The Alligator of Love'.

Thursday, 9 September 1937 – CSL refers to CW's novel, *Descent Into Hell**, in a letter to him, as 'a thundering good book and a real purgation to read'.

Friday, 18 February 1938 – JRRT writes to his publisher, Stanley Unwin, concerning CSL's science-fiction story, *Out of the Silent Planet*. It had been, he says, read aloud to the Inklings ('our local club'), which went in for 'reading things short and long aloud'. He records that it proved to be exciting as a serial, and was highly approved by all of them. JRRT reveals that he and CSL each planned to write an excursionary thriller into space or time, each encountering myth. *Out of the Silent Planet* was the space story. His own, of time, was only a fragment (this was *The Lost Road*). Later he was to explore the same theme in the also unfinished, *The Notion Club Papers**, loosely based on the Inklings gatherings.

4 July 1938 – CSL meets CW in London. Later, in *Essays Presented to Charles Williams* (1947), CSL remembers the meeting as 'a certain immortal lunch' which was followed by an 'almost Platonic discussion' in St Paul's church-yard which lasted for about two hours.

4 September 1939 – Warren Lewis recalled to active service the day after Britain declares war on Germany.

7 September 1939 – CW moves with OUP to Oxford. Later CSL arranges for him to lecture at the university. CSL remarks that from September 1939 'until his death we met one another about twice a week, sometimes more: nearly always on Thursday evenings in my rooms and on Tuesday mornings in the best of all public-houses for draught cider' (Green and Hooper, *C.S. Lewis: A Biography*, Collins, 1974, p. 157).

Thursday, 2 November 1939 – At an Inklings gathering attended by CSL, CW, JRRT and Charles Wrenn* the discussion turns over the issue of God's goodness and the damned.

Thursday, 9 November 1939 – After dining at Oxford's Eastgate Hotel, the Inklings listen to JRRT reading an early part of *The Lord of the Rings**, CW reading a nativity play, and CSL reading a chapter from *The Problem of Pain**. The group feel that the extracts form almost a logical sequence, and this gives rise to a wide-ranging discussion. CSL describes the ever talkative Dyson as 'a roaring cataract of nonsense'.

Thursday, 30 November 1939 – There is no Inklings meeting, as CW and Gerard Hopkins (of the Oxford University Press) are both away. CSL goes around to JRRT's house in Northmoor Road, where they read chapters from *The Problem of Pain* and *The Lord of the Rings*.

Thursday, 25 January 1940 – Writing to his brother, CSL records that 'the usual party assembled on Thursday night, heard a chapter of the new Hobbit, drank rum and hot water, and talked'.

Thursday, 1 February 1940 – Dr 'Humphrey' Havard* reads a short paper on the clinical experience of pain, prepared as an appendix for CSL's book, *The Problem of Pain*. CSL writes to his absent brother: 'We had an evening almost equally compounded of merriment, piety, and literature.'

5 February 1940 – CW celebrates the theme of chastity in Milton's *Comus* in a lecture.

Wednesday, 14 February 1940 – T.S. Eliot* writes to CW, commenting that 'one of your most important functions in life (which I tried to emulate in *The Family Reunion*) is to instill sound doctrine into people (tinged sometimes with heresy, of course, but the *very best* heresy) without their knowing it . . .'

Thursday, 15 February 1940 – Unusually, OB attends an Inklings meeting.

Thursday, 29 February 1940 – Dyson visits the Inklings meeting from Reading, so all are present except for Warren Lewis and OB, CSL reports to his brother. Adam Fox* reads a poem on Blenheim Park in winter. On being told of CW's lectures on Milton and the doctrine of virginity Dyson remarks that CW is 'becoming a common *chastitute*'.

Thursday, 25 April 1940 – Writing to his absent brother, CSL refers to Dr 'Humphrey' Havard reading the group a straight account, in plain language, of a mountain climb he had participated in. CSL describes it as making their hair stand on end. JRRT makes reference to his son, John, at college in Rome.

Thursday, 2 May 1940 – Writing to Warnie Lewis, CSL recounts an unusually good Inklings at which CW 'read us a Whitsun play, a mixture of very good stuff and some deplorable errors in taste'.

Thursday, 16 May 1940 – CSL, writing to the absent Warnie, recalls sitting in the north room in Magdalen College, looking out on the hawthorn in the grove, as he awaits the arrival of the Inklings. He much regrets the fact that his brother 'had passed from the status of a sense-object to that of a mental picture'. He notes that Dr Havard came first, then CW, and then JRRT. As he went into the south room with them he notices 'the exquisite smell of the wisteria pervading the whole room'. Charles Wrenn turns up after that and they walk in the extensive grounds of the college.

14 October 1940 – CSL's *The Problem of Pain* is published. It is dedicated to the Inklings.

Tuesday, 7 January 1941 – Dr Havard drives JRRT and the CSL brothers to a pub out at Appleton, some miles west of Oxford. It is a snowy night, and the roads slippery. JRRT's offer of snuff, a recent gift, is taken up by several locals, and Major Lewis recounts an amusing story about visiting Blackwell's Bookshop in Oxford with the irrepressible 'Hugo' Dyson.

Monday, 23 June 1941 – 'Lord David was very agreeable last night; sorry he missed you; looks forward to meeting you; has ordered *The Descent of the Dove*; didn't know of the novels' (letter from CW to Michal Williams, 24 June 1941).

Thursday, 7 August 1941 – CW refers, in a letter to his wife Michal, to CSL as the person out of all in Oxford who understands his thinking.

Sunday, 21 December 1941 – In a letter to Dom Bede Griffiths, CSL describes CW and lists the Inklings: 'He is an ugly man with rather a cockney voice. But no one ever thinks of this for five minutes after he has begun speaking. His face becomes almost angelic . . . CW, Dyson of Reading, & my brother (Anglicans) and JRRT and my doctor, Havard (your church) are the "Inklings" to whom my *Problem of Pain* was dedicated.'

1942 – CW's *The Forgiveness of Sins* is published, dedicated to the Inklings.

18 February 1943 – Sheldonian Theatre, Oxford. An honorary MA is awarded to CW, with many of the Inklings in attendance.

Wednesday, 5 May 1943 – CW, in letter to Michal, mentions Havard turning up in a naval lieutenant's uniform. Havard, JRRT, the Lewis brothers, and CW have dinner at the George Hotel at lunchtime.

28 September 1943 – *Out of the Silent Planet* is published in the USA. CSL writes for the dust jacket: 'My happiest hours are spent with three or four old friends in old clothes tramping together and putting up in small pubs – or else sitting up till the small hours in someone's college rooms talking nonsense, poetry, theology, metaphysics over beer, tea and pipes.'

Friday, 15 October 1943 – CW writes in a letter to Michal: 'To-night Gervase Mathew is to take me to meet a clergyman called Austin Farrer, a philosopher and theologian – whose books are far too learned for me. But *Beatrice* has allured him, I am told.'

Thursday, 28 October 1943 – At a meeting of the Inklings in CSL's rooms in Magdalen, CW reads some of his novel in progress, *All Hallows' Eve**. CSL exclaims that it is much the best thing that CW has done. Some months later CW records in a letter to Michal that Magdalen (i.e. the Inklings group) 'thinks it "tender and gay" among all the melodramatic horrors'.

Tuesday, 11 November 1943 – CW's lecture on *Hamlet* fills the lecture hall, while his friend JRRT's students have all but deserted him to hear CW. The only student who remains for the Anglo-Saxon lecture is one who has been sent to take notes. JRRT is left to lecture to the single student, but he magnanimously has a drink with CW afterwards.

Thursday, 9 December 1943 – CSL hears CW read more of his novel in progress, *All Hallows' Eve*, probably at an Inklings meeting at Magdalen College.

Tuesday, 14 December 1943 – CSL makes a point of inviting CW over to Magdalen College in order to meet 'Hugo' Dyson, who is over from Reading, where he teaches at that time.

1944 – CW continues reading *All Hallows' Eve* to CSL and JRRT as it is being written. JRRT later remembered: 'I was a sort of midwife at the birth of *All Hallows' Eve* read aloud to us as it was composed, but the very great changes in it were I think mainly due to C.S. Lewis' (letter to Anne Barrett, 7 August 1964).

Wednesday, 5 January 1944 – CW mentions in a letter to Michal about a *Time* magazine journalist writing on CSL. Having interviewed CSL he wants the view of CW, as a friend. The cover feature eventually appears in 1947 and helps to ensure CSL's popularity in the United States.

5 February 1944 – CW writes to Michal, his wife: 'I have found myself thinking how admirable it would be if I could get a Readership here when I retire. I know it may only be a dream; on the other hand, C.S.L. and Tolkien are only human, and are likely to take more trouble over a project which would enable them to see a good deal more of me than over anything which didn't.'

1 March 1944 – In a letter, JRRT comments on the *Daily Telegraph*'s description, the 'ascetic Mr Lewis'. 'I ask you! He put away three pints in a very short session we had this morning, and said he was "going short for Lent".'

Tuesday, 11 April 1944 – JRRT spends two hours with CSL and CW, during which time he reads a recently composed chapter from *The Lord of the Rings* – to the pleasure of the others.

Thursday, 13 April 1944 – In a letter to his son Christopher, in South Africa, JRRT writes that he is going to Magdalen College that night for an Inklings meeting. He anticipates that those attending will be the Lewis brothers, CW, David Cecil*, and probably Dr Havard ('the Useless Quack', who was 'still bearded and uniformed'). He mentions that Warnie Lewis is writing a book, adding that this activity 'was catching'. In the event all turn up except David Cecil, and they stay until midnight. The best part of it, according to JRRT, is Warnie's chapter on the subject of the court of Louis XIV. He is not so partial to the concluding chapter of CSL's *The Great Divorce*.

Wednesday, 19 April 1944 – JRRT reads his chapter on the passage of the Dead Marshes from the unfolding *The Lord of the Rings* to an approving CSL and CW that morning.

Monday, 8 May 1944 – JRRT reads a new chapter of *The Lord of the Rings*, in which Faramir, a new character, comes on the scene. It receives 'fullest approbation' from the listeners, CSL and CW.

Monday, 22 May 1944 – After an exhausting previous day writing a new chapter of *The Lord of the Rings*, JRRT is rewarded by its enthusiastic reception by CSL and CW that morning.

Thursday, 25 May 1944 – JRRT records, in a letter to his son Christopher, a long, very enjoyable Inklings. 'Hugo' Dyson attends from Reading. JRRT thinks him tired-looking, but still 'reasonably noisy'. Warnie Lewis reads another chapter from his book on the times of Louis XIV, and his younger brother reads extracts from *The Great Divorce* (then going by the title of 'Who Goes Home? – which JRRT quips should rather be called 'Hugo's Home').

Monday, 29 May 1944 – JRRT reads the latest two chapters from *The Lord of the Rings* to CSL in the morning, 'Shelob's Lair' and 'The Choices of Master Samwise'. CSL approves of them with unusual fervour, according to JRRT, and is moved to tears by the second chapter.

Thursday, 8 June 1944 – The Inklings assemble in CSL's rooms at Magdalen College, those present being JRRT, the Lewis brothers, CW and E.R. Eddison, author of a fantasy approved by the Inklings, *The Worm Ouroborous*. There is three and a half hours of reading, including a long chapter from Warnie Lewis' book on Louis XIV, a new extract from *The Lord of the Rings*, an unrecorded piece from CSL, and a new chapter from Eddison of a work in progress, *The Mezentian Gate* (which remained incomplete at his death in 1945). Eddison has previously attended an Inklings meeting in February 1943.

Wednesday, 12 July 1944 – CW records visiting CSL in a nursing home with JRRT. CSL has had a minor operation to his arm.

Monday, 14 August 1944 – In a letter to Michal, CW refers to an ideal life, which includes 'a Tuesday drink with the Magdalen set and a sometimes Thursday evening'.

1944 – During this year CW reads the first two chapters of a work never completed, *The Figure of Arthur**, to JRRT and CSL. In *Arthurian Torso** (1948) CSL invites his reader to imagine the scene: 'Picture to yourself . . . an upstairs sitting-room with windows looking north into the "grove" of Magdalen College on a sunshiny Monday Morning in vacation at about ten o'clock. The Professor and I, both on the Chesterfield, lit our pipes and stretched out our legs. CW in the arm-chair opposite to us threw his cigarette into the grate, took up a pile of the extremely small, loose sheets on which he habitually wrote – they came, I think, from a twopenny pad for memoranda, and began . . .'

Thursday, 31 August 1944 – An Inklings evening is attended by CSL, CW and others. CSL reads a long paper on Kipling, and CW reads his essay on Kipling from his book *Poetry at Present*.

Thursday, 21 September 1944 – An Inklings at Magdalen College is attended by the Lewis brothers, JRRT and CW. Warnie Lewis reads the final chapter of his book in progress on Louis XIV, and they hear from CSL an unnamed article and a long extract from his translation of Virgil's* *The Aeneid* (never published). JRRT walks part of the way home afterwards with CW, discussing the concept of freedom, and its misuses. The Inklings agree that, if they are spared to have one, their victory celebration will consist of hiring a country inn for at least a week, spending the time entirely in beer and talk, totally ignoring any clock.

Tuesday, 3 October 1944 – At noon JRRT and CW look in at the Bird and Baby (Eagle and Child) pub. Surprisingly the Lewis brothers are already there (records JRRT in a letter to Christopher). The conversation becomes lively. JRRT notices a 'strange gaunt man' rather like Strider at the inn in Bree. He doesn't have the usual 'pained astonishment of the British (and American) public' on encountering the Lewises and Tolkien in a pub, but rather has an attentive interest in the conversation. Eventually he interjects a comment on Wordsworth. The stranger turns out to be the right-wing poet and soldier Roy Campbell*, recently lampooned by CSL in the *Oxford* Magazine. He is promptly invited to the next Inklings on Thursday.

Saturday, 14 October 1944 – Writing to Michal, CW refers to the Inklings as the 'Tolkien–Lewis group'.

Tuesday, 14 November 1944 – After dining out, the Inklings meet at Magdalen College. Colin Hardie* gives a paper, which is followed, in CW's words, by a 'learned discussion of dates and texts'. The meeting breaks up at 10.30p.m., after which CW goes back with CSL to his rooms for an hour.

Thursday, 23 November 1944 – JRRT, CW and Dr Havard (dubbed 'the Red Admiral' because he returned from the Navy with a red beard) eat at the Mitre before joining CSL and OB, who have dined at Magdalen College. JRRT considers OB the only person who can tackle CSL when in full flood of argument, 'interrupting his most dogmatic pronouncements with subtle *distinguo*'s'. Writing about the evening to his son Christopher, JRRT describes it as 'most amusing and highly contentious'. Items they hear include a short play by OB concerning Jason and Medea, and two sonnets that have been sent to CSL. They discuss ghosts, the special nature of hymns (following CSL's involvement with the revision of *Hymns Ancient and Modern* for the Church of England), and other subjects.

24 December 1944 – In a letter to his son Christopher, JRRT relates CW's comment on the unfolding chapters of *The Lord of the Rings*: 'C. Williams who is reading it all says the great thing is that its *centre* is not in strife and war and heroism (though they are understood and depicted) but in freedom, peace, ordinary life and good living' (letter 93, *The Letters of J.R.R. Tolkien*).

1945 – JRRT takes up the Chair of English Language and Literature at Oxford University.

Tuesday, 15 May 1945 – Warnie Lewis records in his diary the sudden, unexpected death of CW: 'And so vanishes one of the best and nicest men it has ever been my good fortune to meet. May God receive him into His everlasting happiness.'

20 May 1945 – CSL writes to a former pupil, 'I also have become much acquainted with grief now through the death of CW, my friend of friends, the comforter of all our little set, the most angelic man' (*Letters of C.S. Lewis*, rev. ed. 1988, p. 377).

December 1945 – There is a walking party of the Inklings to celebrate the war's end. The group includes the Lewis brothers and JRRT, with Dr 'Humphrey' Havard in attendance some of the time.

Thursday, 28 March 1946 – Warnie Lewis records that an Inklings gathering included himself, CSL, Christopher Tolkien, Humphrey Havard, Colin Hardie, and Gervase Mathew*. Among other things they discussed the possibility of dogs having souls.

Thursday, 8 August 1946 – In his diary, Warnie notes an Inklings attended by himself, his brother, Hugo Dyson, Dr Havard, JRRT, Gervase Mathew and a visitor, Stanley Bennett of Cambridge. It is not, he writes, the sort of evening he enjoys: 'mere noise and buffoonery'.

1946 – Novelist John Wain, a member of the Inklings for a time, recalls this period: 'I can see that room so clearly now, the electric fire pumping heat into the dank air, the faded screen that broke some of the keener draughts, the enamel beerjug on the table, the well-worn sofa and armchairs, and the men drifting in (those from distant colleges would be later), leaving overcoats and hats in any corner and coming over to warm their hands before finding a chair. There was no fixed etiquette, but the rudimentary honours would be done partly by CSL and partly by his brother, W.H. Lewis, a man who stays in my memory as the most courteous I have ever met – not with mere politeness, but with a genial, self-forgetting considerateness that was as instinctive to him as breathing. Sometimes, when the less vital members of the circle were in a big majority, the evening would fall flat; but the best of them were as good as anything I shall live to see' (*Sprightly Running*, 1962, p. 184).

Thursday, 22 August 1946 – An Inklings attended by JRRT, his son Christopher, and the Lewis brothers. Warnie Lewis records his brother reading a poem on Paracelsus' view of gnomes, and 'Tollers' (JRRT) reading 'a magnificent myth which is to knit up and conclude his Papers of the Notions Club' – on the downfall of Númenor.

Tuesday, 10 September 1946 – Dr Humphrey Havard picks up the Lewis brothers and Christopher Tolkien from Magdalen College, and drives them out to a favoured inn, the Trout at Godstow, near Oxford. They sit in the garden, records Warnie, and discuss the views Dr Johnston probably would have had on contemporary literature. They also talk about the nature of women.

8 September 1947 – A *Time* magazine cover feature on CSL, 'Don v. Devil', described his growing influence, Oxford life, and conversion from atheism, where he 'found himself part of a small circle of Christian Oxonians who met informally each week or so to drink and talk'. *Time* described 'his handsome, white-panelled college room overlooking the deer park' and 'his tiny, book-crammed inner study'.

13 November 1947 – Warnie Lewis, in his diary, records an Inklings at Merton (JRRT's college). There 'Tollers' reads 'a rich melancholy poem on autumn, which J[ack] very aptly described as "Matthew Arnold strayed into the world of Hobbit"'.

27 November 1947 – Warnie Lewis' diary notes the topics at an Inklings that night, attended by JRRT, CSL, Stevens*, Havard and himself: 'We talked of B[isho]p. Barnes, of the extraordinary difficulty of interesting the uneducated indifferent in religion: savage and primitive man and the common confusion between them: how far pagan mythology was a substitute for theology: bravery and panache.'

Septuagesima 1948 – JRRT writes to CSL about often, in fact, wanting noise: 'I know no more pleasant sound than arriving at the B.[ird] and B.[aby] and hearing a roar, and knowing that one can plunge in' (letter 113, *Letters of J.R.R. Tolkien*).

20 October 1949 – The final Thursday night Inklings is recorded in Warnie's diary. 'No one turned up' the following week. This essentially marks the end of the Inklings as a writing group, though the friends continue to meet in The Eagle and Child and other pubs (such as the King's Arms) until the year of CSL's death in 1963. Chad Walsh recalls, in the first study of CSL, 'Only in retrospect did I realize how much intellectual ground was covered in these seemingly casual meetings. At the time the constant bustle of Lewis racing his friends to refill empty mugs or pausing to light another cigarette (occasionally a pipe) camouflaged the steady flow of ideas. The flow, I might add, is not a one-way traffic. Lewis is as good a listener as talker, and has alert curiosity about almost anything conceivable.' (*C.S. Lewis: Apostle to the Skeptics*, 1949, pp. 16–17).

13 February 1951 – Roger Lancelyn Green, a frequent visitor to the Inklings at this time, records in his diary: 'To "Eagle and Child" to meet C.S.L.: a grand gathering – Tolkien, McCallum, Major Lewis, Wrenn, Hardie, Gervase Mathew, John Wain, and others whose names I didn't catch. Discussion on C. Day Lewis (who was elected Professor of Poetry last week, beating C.S.L. by 19 votes): C.S.L. praised his *Georgics* but considered his critical work negligible' (*C.S. Lewis: A Biography*, Green and Hooper, 1974, p. 158).

1954 – Publication of first two volumes of *The Lord of the Rings*. This first edition JRRT dedicates to the Inklings.

9 November 1954 – Roger Lancelyn Green notes in his diary: 'To 'B.[ird] and B.[aby]' to meet Lewis; his brother, McCallum, Tolkien, Gervase M. there as well. Very good talk, about Tolkien's book, horror comics, who is the most influential and important man in various countries: decided Burke for Ireland, Scott for Scotland, Shakespeare for England – but there difficulties arose, Pitt and Wellington also being put forward' (*C.S. Lewis: A Biography*, pp. 158–9).

1955 – Publication of the final volume of *The Lord of the Rings*.

1959 – JRRT retires from his teaching at Oxford.

17 June 1963 – In his diary Roger Lancelyn Green notes, in perhaps the last record of the Inklings: 'To "Lamb and Flag" about 12, there joined Lewis. Several others – Gervase Mathew, Humphrey Havard, Colin Hardie, and a young American, Walter Hooper, who is writing some sort of book or thesis about Jack' (*C.S. Lewis: A Biography*, p. 159).

22 November 1963 – CSL dies at home.

9 April 1973 – Warnie Lewis dies, still mourning his beloved brother.

2 September 1973 – JRRT dies.

14 December 1997 – OB dies, a few months short of his century.

In retrospect Warnie Lewis writes of the Thursday evening Inklings: 'The ritual of an Inklings was unvarying. When half a dozen or so had arrived, tea would be produced, and then when pipes were well alight Jack would say, "Well, has nobody got anything to read us?" out would come a manuscript, and we would settle down in judgment on it – real unbiased judgment, too, since we were no mutual admiration society: praise for good work was unstinted, but censure for bad work – or even not-so-good work – was often brutally frank. To read to the Inklings was a formidable ordeal, and I can still remember the fear with which I offered the first chapter of my first book – and my delight, too, at its reception' ('Memoir of C.S. Lewis', in *Letters of C.S. Lewis*, 1966, pp. 13–14).

THREE

The Making of Narnia

Narnia is the fantasy land in which CSL's children's stories are set, a land in which events reflect several themes of Christian theology just as the presiding image of his adult science-fiction trilogy echoes the motif of fall, incarnation, redemption and restoration. CSL, however, argued strongly that the Chronicles of Narnia should not be viewed as an allegory like Bunyan's *Pilgrim's Progress*, though he acknowledged the intentional parallels between the main features of Christian teaching and the Chronicles, not least in the unambiguously supernatural Christ-symbol, Aslan* the Lion.

By the time CSL began to publish the seven Chronicles of Narnia, he was well known as a literary critic and a lay theologian, and had a discerning audience for his poetry. His science-fiction writings were admired by leading writers in the field, and he was a popular broadcaster. For a bachelor whose life revolved round the mainly male environment of Oxbridge, embarking on a fiction series for children was a surprising change of direction. But CSL liked children and had got to know a number of evacuees very well when his Oxford home, the Kilns, was made available immediately before the start of the Second World War. (The best known of the Narnia Chronicles, *The Lion, the Witch and the Wardrobe*, begins with evacuees arriving at the home of an elderly professor in the country.)

The Chronicles were published in the following order: *The Lion, the Witch and the Wardrobe* (1950), *Prince Caspian* (1951), *The Voyage of the 'Dawn Treader'* (1952), *The Silver Chair* (1953), *The Horse and His Boy* (1954), *The Magician's Nephew* (1955), and *The Last Battle* (1956). The order in which CSL preferred them to be read is still debated, and as published they do not follow Narnian chronology: such an order would be created by reading in the sequence *The Magician's Nephew*, *The Lion, the Witch and the Wardrobe*, *The Horse and His Boy*, *Prince Caspian*, *The Voyage of the 'Dawn Treader'*, *The Silver Chair* and *The Last Battle*. For individual plot summaries, see the entries for each novel elsewhere in this Handbook.

Sources

Though there are obvious similarities between Narnia and JRRT's Middle-earth, there are also considerable differences. Of the two, Middle-earth is much the more consistent and academically coherent, drawing for example on extensive linguistic scholarship (as in the creation of the Elvish language), and recognizably using the literature of ancient Europe as its background. The elaborate appendices to *Lord of the Rings**, the mass of detail in *The Silmarillion**, and the series of large volumes compiled by JRRT's son Christopher from JRRT's Middle-earth notebooks, all have the stamp of the working professor's notes and are quite different from the discursive, rambling detail of Narnia.

Narnia, by contrast, is an amalgamation of many influences and is drawn from many periods of CSL's life. In part it is related to the worlds of the great animal story classics such as Kenneth Grahame's *Wind in the Willows*. On the other hand Aslan, the central lion-figure, is unique. There is simply no character in animal fiction possessing the same degree of holiness, and it is to George MacDonald* one must turn to for comparison, and then mainly in his human characters. Another influence is the English Common Man as seen in Langland's *Piers Plowman* (whom CSL originally planned to portray in *The Last Battle*); many of the characters speak with the earthy common sense and sturdy values that CSL, entirely unpatronizingly, often admired in his non-academic acquaintances. His child-characters tend to be drawn from an adult's perspective, and the books contain some arch jokes (for example about thermal underwear in *The Voyage of the 'Dawn Treader'*) that reflect the fact that CSL's rapport with children came as he approached middle age. It is when they become kings and queens in Narnia that they become completely convincing, adopting the high language of chivalry and a natural, authentic heroic manner. Even then the attitudes of his day are always evident; there is a fair amount of gender stereotyping; CSL would for example have had no truck with those who today argue for the right of women to fight in the front line of battle.

The earliest hints of Narnia come very early in CSL's life, long before he became a Christian; the common assumption that he wrote the whole series as an extended allegory* of the Christian faith, with a strong evangelistic motive, is one that CSL always denied and which is not borne out by the facts. In a number of essays he mentions that the first stirrings of the Chronicles were mental images (*The Lion, the Witch and the Wardrobe* began with an image of a faun in a snowy wood carrying an umbrella and parcels). He explained that these images began to cohere into themes and story-lines, most notably when 'Aslan came bounding into it'.[1]

The actual writing began with various notes made by CSL in about 1939; comments he made to various people over the next decade; and readings of parts of the manuscript to, among others, Roger Lancelyn Green (1949). He read Green two chapters now known as the Lefay Fragment, most of which can be recognized in the later Chronicles. The seven books, published annually from 1950 to 1956, were written at even greater speed, five of them within the space of less than two years (summer 1948–March 1950). *The Magician's Nephew* (which he found difficult to complete) and *The Last Battle* took him until early 1954, though his major work *English Literature in the Sixteenth Century** was also completed during that period.

The sources of the Narnia Chronicles are literature, legend, fairy story, folklore, religion and many more genres. At the heart of the series is the Christian myth* (in the technical sense) which generates the dramatic events at the heart of *The Lion, the Witch and the Wardrobe* – the death and resurrection of Aslan on the stone table – and the New Heaven/New Earth theme at the close of *The Last Battle*. There are plentiful references to biblical narrative – for example, Susan and Lucy tending Aslan's body on the shattered stone table evoke memories of the women at Christ's tomb, and in *The Last Battle*, medieval imagery of Christ as warrior is evoked. In the American editions of the Chronicles, CSL made significant changes, for example in the characters' names, which emphasize the Norse background to much of the story; CSL's deep attachment to Scandinavian myth and the landscape of the Norse sagas was formed when he was very young. And the theme of the suffering wounded redeemer, as found in the Arthurian* myth of the Dolorous Blow and the Wounded Knight, may have been in CSL's mind when he describes Digory's quest for the magical apple in *The Magician's Nephew* that will heal his dying mother.

One of the Chronicles' best-loved characters, Reepicheep the courageous mouse, has obvious roots in fairy stories and folk tales; indeed he probably shares a common ancestry with Peter Pan. The various witches, ogres, dwarves and other stock characters of folklore and children's fantasy (Queen Prunaprismia in *Prince Caspian* might have come straight out of Hans Andersen) are embroidered with classical allusions; Tumnus the faun is a kind of intellectual dwarf; Professor Kirke chides the children for not having been taught Plato*. Sometimes the different worlds of CSL's imagination collide with splendid results, as when Father Christmas appears, and also Silenus, in *The Lion, the Witch and the Wardrobe*. But there is a serious purpose here, very similar to that of Milton's 'On the Morning of Christ's Nativity' (1629). The incarnation, if it is to be redemptive at all, must be redemptive of all the old religious symbols, drawing them into a Christianized fullness, as what they foreshadowed illuminates them.

The history of Narnia

Narnia is a land in which time runs independently of time in our world; to spend many years there can often mean only an absence of brief hours from 'normal' time. CSL, after completing the Chronicles, drew up an 'Outline of

Narnian History so Far as it is Known'. The creation of Narnia, with its talking animals, as witnessed by Polly and Digory in *The Magician's Nephew*, is located in 1900, as is the entrance of the White Witch Jadis and the coronation of Frank (a cab driver from Earth) as King Frank I of Narnia. The next visit by human children takes place 40 English years later (in *The Lion, the Witch and the Wardrobe*) but in Narnian time 1,000 years have gone by; Archenland, Calormen, the Lone Islands, Telmar and other territories have been settled and ruled, and, somewhere around 1936 English-time, the White Witch has come from the far North and cast Narnia into a long, frozen winter.

The Lion, the Witch and the Wardrobe recounts the arrival in Narnia of four English children – Peter, Susan, Edmund and Lucy Pevensie – who break the Witch's power and initiate a Golden Age, during which the events of *The Horse and His Boy* (set largely in the lands of Narnia's enemy Calormen, and Archenland) take place; a sub-narrative within the main narrative of the Chronicles, it sheds much light on Narnian geography, culture and politics.

A year after the events of *The Lion, the Witch and the Wardrobe* it is 1942 in England and 1,300 years have passed in Narnia. The reign of the four Pevensie children (led by Peter, the High King) that is celebrated there has long passed into Narnian history. The magic horn owned by Peter's sister Queen Susan is in the possession of Prince Caspian, of the Telmarine dynasty now ruling Narnia. Caspian is on the run from his uncle Miraz, the usurper. He uses the horn to summon back the Pevensies, who help him to overcome Miraz and put Caspian on the throne as rightful ruler (*Prince Caspian*).

The years pass both in Narnia and in England. In *The Voyage of the 'Dawn Treader'* Caspian sets out on a great voyage to the end of the world. But though only a year has passed in England, the children are growing older. Only the youngest of the four, Edmund and Lucy, are allowed to go back to Narnia to join Caspian's great enterprise; a third child, their cousin Eustace Scrubb, who is cynical and disbelieving about Narnia, is drawn in as well. He undergoes a profound character transformation which CSL uses as an effective image of Christian conversion. Eustace's 'education', at a progressive school called Experiment House, is the cause of most of his original scorn for Narnia; he returns with a school friend, Jill Pole, later the same English year, to help Caspian search for his son Prince Rilian. Many years have passed meanwhile in Narnia, and Caspian is now an old man. The quest is described in *The Silver Chair*, which contains some memorable characters, such as Puddleglum, the Marshwiggle – a character who rivals A.A. Milne's Eeyore, and was reputedly based on Fred Paxford, the gardener at the Kilns.

CSL's chronology is very sketchy, and Narnian history from 2356 (*The Silver Chair*) to 2555 (*The Last Battle*) is barely covered in his 'Outline' apart from a suggestion of increasing lawlessness in Narnia. Throughout Narnian history, and crucially in the Chronicles, the figure of Aslan the lion presides over history, appearing at the point of greatest need to those who believe in him, functioning as protector of his people as individuals and also as the protector of a largely unbelieving nation. The Golden Age of Narnia, when the talking trees and beasts were abroad and the High Kings and Queens ruled, is long past when *The Last Battle* opens. Narnia is in decline, but it is not the heroic villainy of the Long Winter but rather a loss of faith and conviction, the slow deterioration that sets in as cultures grow morally weak and complacent. Aslan has not been seen in Narnia for 200 years, and some are openly questioning whether he ever existed. Thus the spark that sets the Last Battle in motion is not a clash between tyrants but a squalid attempt by Shift the ape to pass off a crude replica of Aslan as the lion king, and himself as Aslan's spokesman. Narnia's long-standing enemy Calormen sees the ape's foolishness as an excellent opportunity to make trouble and joins Shift's cause. King Tirian the last Narnian king refuses to believe that the new regime is of Aslan's making, with its destruction of the talking trees and enslaving of talking animals. The final chapters of *The Last Battle* describe Tirian's stand, aided by Eustace and Jill, who are drawn into Narnia while on a train journey, in response to the king's desperate prayer for help.

As the culmination of the Chronicles, *The Last Battle* makes much clear, bringing together pointed references to the Last Days, the New Heaven and the New Earth, the final destruction of the devil (in the person of Tash, the evil god), and much more. As the children join in the great procession higher up and further in, and the great reunion with Peter, Edmund and Lucy Pevensie, and with all the kings and queens of Narnia (Susan, we discover, is 'no longer a friend of Narnia'), they discover – as does the reader – that the train in which they had been travelling crashed into the station. They had been journeying to a reunion, organized by Professor Kirke, of all who knew Narnia. Thus all were killed together, and all are reborn in the new Narnia; the term time is over, says Aslan, and the holidays have begun. *The Last Battle* is probably the only children's novel ever written in which the two principal characters are dead before the book begins.

The geography of Narnia

JRRT created a lovingly detailed map and history of Middle-earth, so detailed that many who came after him have been able to suggest completions of the parts he left incomplete, without violating the coherence and consistency of the whole.[2] By contrast Narnia is sketched in broad strokes; whole regions are barely described, while the seas and islands of, for example, *The Voyage of the 'Dawn Treader'*, are described in often meticulous detail.

Where JRRT supplied large folding maps of Middle-earth in the appendices to *Lord of the Rings* and *The Hobbit* was clearly mapped, the maps supplied in the Narnia Chronicles give a very patchy idea of Narnia. In *Prince Caspian* Pauline Baynes provides 'A Map of Narnia and Adjoining Lands'. It shows Narnia as a large province on a land mass bounded on the east by sea, on the west by a mountain range and the Lantern Waste in the north-west, and in the north by the 'Wild Lands'. To the south lies Archenland, given by Aslan as part of the territory of the kings and queens of Narnia.

The land mass resembles eastern Scotland around Inverness; somewhat to the north of the peninsular corresponding to Scotland's Black Isle is Cair Paravel, at the mouth of the Great River that leads past Aslan's How up to its source in the north. An even more convincing case can be made for resemblances between CSL's native Ulster and the landscapes of Narnia (just as there are resemblances between the Shire and the West Midlands of JRRT's childhood). In *The Voyage of the 'Dawn Treader'* (where we are quite sensibly given instead of a general map of Narnia a plan of Caspian's ship), there is a small map of the Lone Islands, far to the east of Narnia, though their location is not pinpointed and Caspian himself does not know their history. The sparse map in *The Horse and His Boy* (which is, admittedly, mainly of a desert) shows Archenland, the desert to its south and Calormen beyond. In *The Silver Chair*, we are given a map of the Wild Lands of the North, showing the Great River rising in the Lantern Waste, Ettinsmoor on Narnia's northern border, and a few locations in a mountainous region beyond. (Ettinsmoor's mountains resemble the range in JRRT's Mordor.)

In the 'Narnia Solo Games' books, suppressed by the CSL estate because of an inadvertent infringement of copyright by the publishers Iron Crown Enterprises,[3] a map by Elissa Martin adds little to what we are given in the Chronicles.

But Narnia is not only a map of a territory. It is a spiritual and imaginative landscape, redolent with associations: the Northern Wastes are not only politically dangerous, they echo the cold bleak Scandinavian otherness that CSL cherished as a boy. Reepicheep's passionate desire to know what lay beyond the eastern rim of the world has resonances with much of CSL's correspondence and conversation. A medieval scholar by profession, in his Chronicles he created a land that drew heavily on medieval literature. JRRT's meticulously crafted Middle-earth draws on Old English Anglo-Saxon literature, and its characters, heroes and monsters are recognizably of that period. CSL is more eclectic, though his primary focus is medieval.

As a boy, around 1906, he had written stories with his brother Warnie about a medieval animal-land, Boxen* (based on India, an interest of Warnie's), but he said of Boxen in later life that its chief characteristic was that it excluded wonder. And it is wonder that infuses Narnia, the land where trees and animals talk and a mighty lion is always liable to irrupt when least expected.

NOTES

1 The early sources of Narnia are well documented by Walter Hooper, *Companion* (pp. 397ff) and *Past Watchful Dragons* (final UK version published Collins Fount, 1980).

2 In the world of fantasy role-playing games (where JRRT is a seminal influence), for example, Middle-earth completions have become a major industry, e.g. Iron Crown Enterprise's* (ICE) *Middle-earth Role Playing*, and *Middle-earth: The Wizards* collectable card game.

3 At least three books were published and withdrawn: *Return to Deathwater* by Curtis Norris, *The Sorceress and the Book of Spells* by Anne Schraff, and *Leap of the Lion* by Curtis Norris. The legal problems arose because of the narrow difference between a game and a multiple-choice adventure book. The series achieved a credible Narnian atmosphere and were up to ICE's usual high standards of research.

FOUR

J.R.R. Tolkien's Middle-earth

Much of JRRT's invention concerned the history, annals, languages, chronology, and geography of Middle-earth. He was concerned to make an inwardly consistent 'sub-creation'*. This was the very heart of his creative purpose. Middle-earth is his sub-created world that features in *The Silmarillion**, *The Hobbit**, and *The Lord of the Rings**, and his unfinished publications, including *The History of Middle-earth**. Middle-earth can refer to the whole world, but usually means only the land mass east of the great sea. The world of the early ages seems to be flat – JRRT envisaged a complex cosmology. The blessed realm of Aman, west of the Great Sea, could be reached by sea from the east, from Beleriand and other regions. This became increasingly difficult, because of the disobedience of some of the elves.

In the Second Age, after the destruction of Númenor, the shape of the world changed. Aman was removed from the physical geography of the world, though still a real place. Middle-earth is the planned habitation of humankind. Though elves had awoken here they were called on the great journey to Aman, to be with the Valar. Those who stayed in Middle-earth, or returned to it from Aman, enriched the life and language of humans, and lived in distinctive kingdoms. Eventually, most elves passed from Middle-earth, but left their mark genetically on humanity, most especially through the marriage of the elven-maiden Lúthien to the mortal Beren.

The history and Ages of Middle-earth

Before the change in the world, the Undying Lands of the West, including Valinor, were physically part of Middle-earth. The history of elves and humans incorporates events in Valinor. The history is divided into a number of Ages. JRRT also invented a beautiful cosmological myth, portraying events before the creation of the world.

Prior to the Ages Ilúvatar created the world, first in conception in Music and then in giving it actual being. Before the beginning of the First Age (taken as the rising of the sun) the Valar and later also many of the elves were established in the uttermost West. Fëanor made the great gems, the Silmarils, which provide the underlying motif for *The Silmarillion*. Morgoth darkened Middle-earth by destroying the Two Lamps and brought shadow to Valinor by extinguishing the Two Trees. He hid in the cold north of Middle-earth, north of Beleriand.

Beleriand in the First Age was the setting for the tales of Beren and Lúthien the elven-maiden, Túrin Turambar*, and the Fall of Gondolin. Eärendil the Mariner sailed to Valinor to intercede on behalf of the free peoples of Beleriand.

In the Second Age the star-shaped island of Númenor (Atlantis) was given to the Dunedain, the Men of the West, for their faithfulness in resisting Morgoth. Sauron, Morgoth's lieutenant, secretly forged the great Ring in Middle-earth. He succeeded in aiding the corruption of Númenor, resulting in its destruction. Valinor was no longer accessible, except by the Straight Road. There was a great and successful western alliance against Mordor.

In the Third Age the Ring remained lost for many centuries. Gondor became a great power. Hobbits migrated to the Shire. Later, the events of *The Hobbit* and *The Lord of the Rings* took place. The Fourth Age opened our present era of the domination of humankind, and the fading of the elves, where the Christian era has unfolded. The original geography of Middle-earth changed into its present shape, though some parts, such as turn-of-the-century Warwickshire and Worcestershire, still resemble that original world (in this case, the Shire). In unfinished stories of JRRT, Aelfwine voyaged to Tol Eressëa, and, in our own time, Alboin finds the lost road, travelling back in time to Númenor. According to JRRT's *Letters* (letter 211) we may now be in a Sixth or even Seventh Age.

The geography of Middle-earth

Two geo-catastrophic events affected the world of JRRT's sub-creation. The first was the ruin of Beleriand at the end of the First Age. The second was the even more dramatic drowning of Númenor in the Second Age, which resulted in a change in the world. It is only after the destruction of Númenor that the world is our familiar sphere. The Blessed Lands of the utter west were removed from the physical world. At different times in the history of JRRT's invented world there were significant land masses: Aman, Númenor, Beleriand (to the north of Middle-earth), and Middle-earth (as it existed at the time of the events recorded in *The Hobbit** and *The Lord of the Rings**).

Aman was a great western continent. It lay between the great sea of Belegaer, and the outer sea of Ekkaia, which was the boundary of the world. Parallel to the eastern coast of Aman ran the great mountain chain of the Pelóri. Valinor was to be found west of the Pelóri, and Eldamar between the mountains and the sea, near the pass of the Calacirya. North and south lay vast wastelands. The island of Tol Eressëa lay off the coast. To the east of the great sea of Belegaer lay Middle-earth.

In the First Age the northern region of Beleriand was significant, with settlements of elves, dwarves and humans. In later Ages all the land that was swallowed up by sea in the north of Middle-earth was described as Beleriand. All the area west of the Ered Luin, the Blue Mountains, was engulfed. This vast range of mountains provided a distinctive boundary for Beleriand to the east. In fact Beleriand was only part of this area in the First Age, with great areas to the north controlled by Morgoth, the source of struggle and many wars.

Beleriand was bounded to the north by the central highlands, to the east by Ered Luin, the Blue Mountains, to the west by the Great Sea of Belegaer (over which lay Valinor), and to the south by the Bay of Balar and by the largely impenetrable forest of Taur-im-Duinath. Strictly, its southern boundary was the River Gelion as it curved westward to the sea, but few elves or humans visited the coastal region between the estuaries of the rivers Sirion and Gelion.

The Blue Mountains, the Ered Luin, were one of the chief ranges of the world of the First Age, forming a natural boundary to Beleriand in the east. The mountains were the source of the tributaries of the River Gelion, flowing though Ossiriand, Land of Seven Rivers, 'filled with green woods wide and fair'. In the mountains only the dwarves lived. They carved out the cities of Nogrod and Belegost, and mined copper, iron and other ores.

After Beleriand's destruction, the more southerly regions became important. Also the star-shaped island of Númenor was raised in the middle of the great sea for a habitation for the Dunedain. These are the lands that are described in *The Silmarillion* and *Unfinished Tales*. The southern regions of Middle-earth are those regions which are familiar to the readers of *The Lord of the Rings*, and *The Hobbit*. Because of the growing importance of humankind, and gradual decline of the elves, regions generally express the political boundaries of mortals rather than elves. Physically, the north–south presence of the Misty Mountains and the River Anduin was significant. In the south the White Mountains of Gondor, and the mountain chains of Mordor imposed themselves. To the east, the Blue Mountains were notable. The most important eastern feature was the long coastline of the sea of Belegaer. Politically, the kingdoms of Gondor and Arnor were important, as well as the southern lands of the Haradrim.

The elven region of Eregion was important in the Second Age, with Grey Havens, Rivendell and Lórien retaining their significance into the Third Age. There were notable dwarf realms, including Khazad-dûm, abandoned by the time the Company of the Ring passed through the Misty Mountains.

The Shire was located in the old realm of Arnor. It was preserved from danger by its guardians, the Rangers of the North.

Elven-kingdoms

There were a number of significant elven-kingdoms over the Ages:

Gondolin. The subject of JRRT's earliest stories, this was a great city in the north of Beleriand whose name in elvish means 'The hidden rock'. It was built in a secret and protected realm by the elven-king Turgon, surrounded by the Encircling Mountains. For centuries it lay hidden from Morgoth who eventually sacked it with the help of Balrogs, orcs and dragons.

Nargothrond. Featured in *The Silmarillion*, this was a great underground fortress, consisting of many halls, beside the River Narog, and founded by Finrod Felagund, the elven-king. The name was also used to refer to the realm of the king, extending east and west of the river. Nargothrond was impregnable until Túrin persuaded the elves to build an access bridge over the river. Glaurung the dragon crossed this stone bridge to rout the elven caverns.

Doriath. A great elven-kingdom in Beleriand, associated with many events of the First Age. It was ruled by King Thingol and Queen Melian. Their beautiful daughter was Lúthien, called the Nightingale. To protect Doriath from the power of Morgoth, Melian wove a magic barrier around the mainly wooded kingdom. By demanding of Beren that he obtained a Silmaril in order to marry his daughter, Thingol enmeshed Doriath in the curse of Mandos.

Lórien. *The Lord of the Rings* describes Lórien, which was modelled upon Doriath. It was the realm of Celeborn and Galadriel between the rivers Celebrant and Anduin. It is also called LothLórien ('Lórien of the blossom'). Lórien was one of a few elvish areas left in Middle-earth in the Third Age. It best preserved the beauty and timelessness of Valinor. The chief city of Lórien was called Caras Galadon.

Rivendell. Founded in the Second Age by Elrond in the foothills of the Misty Mountains, in a hidden, deep-cloven valley. Rivendell lay between the rivers Hoarwell and Loudwater. Its elvish name was Imladris.

In *The Hobbit*, Rivendell is described as 'The Last Homely House East of the Sea', a place of refuge for any of the faithful, not just elves. Bilbo spent many years here translating the elvish tales of *The Silmarillion*.

The Hobbit tries to capture the special essence of Elrond's Rivendell:

His house was perfect, whether you liked food, or sleep, or work, or story-telling, or singing, or just sitting and thinking best, or a pleasant mixture of them all. Evil things did not come into that valley.

The mortal kingdoms

The Second and Third Ages are dominated by the aftermath of the destruction of Númenor. Particularly the North and South Kingdoms were established by the Númenoreans. In these ages the influence of mortals rather than elves predominates – the elves fade, and eventually pass out of Middle-earth.

Gondor. Founded in the Second Age by Elendil, the realm of Gondor plays a significant part in the events chronicled in *The Lord of the Rings.* At its founding it was the South Kingdom in Middle-earth.

Arnor. Only ruins remained in Frodo's day of the North Kingdom of Arnor. Elendil established it after escaping the destruction of Númenor. After the war of the Ring, the Kingdom was re-established.

The Shire. A region of Eriador, the area between the Ered Luin to the west and the Misty Mountains to the east, the home of hobbits, settled in the Third Age. Hobbits lived comfortably in its four Farthings. Its chief town was Michel Delving. Bilbo Baggins lived in Bag End, Hobbiton, where he was joined by Frodo when Bilbo adopted him after the adventures chronicled in *The Hobbit.* Frodo had grown up in Buckland. JRRT was attached to the West Midlands, and tried to convey the quality of life in turn-of-the-century Worcestershire and Warwickshire in his creation of the Shire.

FIVE

Arthur, Logres and the Empire

Arthur's magic is that he is a shape-shifter; but he does so subtly and slowly, changing his form to suit the needs of each new age.[1]

T he legends of King Arthur, his Knights of the Round Table and the Quest for the Grail, are rooted in history. Arthuriana is a myth founded on real events, though the original Arthur would have looked more like a guerrilla freedom-fighter than the splendidly attired Christian king of legend. He may have been a sixth-century Welsh chieftain, a late Roman general in Britain, or even both.

> Farther up country, in the out-of-the-way places, there would have been little courts ruled by real old British under-kings, talking something like Welsh, and practising a certain amount of the Druidical religion . . . One can imagine a man of the old British line, but a Christian and a fully-trained general with Roman technique, trying to pull this whole society together. There'd be jealousy from his own British family. And always that under-tow, that tug back to Druidism.[2]

Some have suggested Arthur was of Scottish origin: there is a site in the Eildon Hills that is said to be his grave, and a great rock said to be his seat dominates Edinburgh. There are many more places in Scotland and the North of England that are associated with him. Farther south, Cadbury Castle near Glastonbury in Somerset claims to be his burial place. Ancient tradition holds that Cadbury is Camelot itself, though some prefer Winchester (where there is a Round Table that nobody really takes seriously). The chronicler Geoffrey of Monmouth placed Camelot at Caerleon-on-Usk in Wales. And there are other candidates.

Britain is, in fact, full of places identified with Arthur by tradition and often by place-name. History tells us that he cannot have unified the nation to the extent that his name was honoured all over it. The real Arthur was most likely a West-Country local ruler, but wherever his base actually was, his power did not reach very far. Some have suggested another reason for his pervasive popularity was that he was a supernatural being. The truth is between the two. The historical Arthur's achievements as a local warrior would have made him a symbol of freedom for a much-conquered nation. Like Robin Hood, he became the possession of every locality's folklore. He became a symbol of freedom. All over Britain there are local hills, such as Alderley Edge in Cheshire, where Arthur is said to be sleeping an enchanted sleep with an army of his knights, ready to ride forth when the nation needs him most.

The elevation of local hero into national messiah came about partly because of the historians who celebrated him. Like the later medieval saints' lives, the purpose of a chronicler was often not so much painstaking research as the creation of edifying myth. Geoffrey of Monmouth, for example, writing around 1136, traces British history from the mythical Brutus son of Aeneas down to the solidly historical King Cadwalladr.

> For Geoffrey, his history was a pageant of striking personalities, moving forward to the greatest personality of them all, Arthur, son of Utherpendragon and Ygerna. With the passing of Arthur his interest gradually died away, and so, indeed, does that of the modern reader. Geoffrey's essential inspiration was a patriotic one.[3]

All who wrote of Arthur found the Arthur they wanted to find. By the medieval period they had made an epic myth* out of the scraps of historical fact and local folklore. Arthur was celebrated in Britain and in France. The French books of Arthurian tales were the source from which Thomas Malory drew for his *Morte d'Arthur*, and in 1485 Caxton printed Malory's great work, informing his readers that Arthur's table was still to be seen in Winchester and Gawain's skull at Dover Castle. Arthur had passed from shadowy legend into literature. In the stirring tragic set-pieces of Malory, a romance of the Middle Ages 'as they never were but as they should have been'[4] was superimposed on the historical known Britain. To writers of the time it became known as 'the Matter of Britain'. For many, it *was* Britain.

The development of the Matter is described in some detail by CW in his unfinished *The Figure of Arthur**, which, together with *The Arthuriad* (its completion by CSL) is still the best introduction to his Arthurian poems.[5] CW explicitly announced his intentions in *The Figure of Arthur* in a 'prefatory note':

> This book is a consideration of the tale of King Arthur in English literature. It does not pretend to investigate, or indeed to record, the original sources, the Celtic tales or the French romances, except in so far, as some mention of them is necessary to the main theme. That theme is the coming together of two myths, the myth of Arthur and the myth of the Grail; of their union; and of the development of that union not only in narrative complexity but in intellectual significance.[6]

CSL comments,

There is no question here of a modern artist approaching the old material as a quarry from which he can chip what he pleases, responsible only to his own modern art. It is more a 'dove-like brooding', a watching and waiting as if he watched a living thing . . . Nominally he is writing criticism or literary history, but in reality creation is going on. Perhaps if he had not been nominally writing criticism he could not have given us so deep an insight into the process whereby his own Arthuriad came into existence.[7]

CW's *Arthuriad* is complex and in places very difficult. But it is fine poetry, only very occasionally crippled by the complexity of its ideas. There are many lyrical passages and memorable lines, and CW, who was an accomplished literary critic, achieves a sinewy, energetic style that sounds better read aloud than read silently on the page – an appropriate quality in view of the fact that the central character is a bard.

The poems are in two volumes, *Taliessin through Logres* (1938) and *The Region of the Summer Stars* (1944). The best way of reading them is to follow the sequence recommended by CSL in chapter 1 of *Arthurian Torso**; an approach centred on the figure of Taliessin, the Welsh magician-poet who appears in *The Mabinogion* as Taliesin and was brought into the Arthurian story by Tennyson in his Arthurian poem *The Idylls of the King*.

CW, like many writers before him, placed the Arthurian myths into a spiritual landscape. His *Arthuriad* is constructed on the image of a female body, reclining across Europe. A map showing this superimposition was included on the end-papers of the early editions but was omitted in more recent reprints. The reason may well be that the figure, though lightly sketched, is naked; but it is a pity if that is the reason, for the map clarifies several difficult concepts in the poems. CW's visionary map is described in entries in the main section of this Handbook, but the general scheme will be briefly given here. The head is Britain, or Logres. Beyond is the sea-wood of Broceliande, and beyond that, if one can find the way, is Carbonek, the place where the Holy Grail is kept. But the Grail's true home is the holy island of Sarras, which lies beyond Carbonek, across the open seas.

Broceliande is an unformed place. Taliessin, on entering it, is full of fear. Only part of the wood leads on to Carbonek and heaven itself. Mistake the way, take the wrong road, and you will eventually circle the globe and arrive at the antipodean land that lies beyond the figure's feet.

To understand the antipodean realm it is necessary to look at the Empire, the state that the reclining figure represents. Logres (Britain) is its head, and Paris, famous for its learned colleges and educational nurturing, the breasts. The hands lie across Rome, where, CW shows, the hands of the pope perform the sacraments; and the navel is at Byzantium, the source and origin of the peoples of the Empire (though some have read the map differently and take Byzantium [logically enough] to be the genitals).

The Empire being portrayed in this way is the Byzantine Empire, the legacy of imperial Rome, drawing from Byzantium its spiritual power. The emperor rules an empire which he desires to be one of order and perfection. Logres, the head, is intended to be made the place where heaven and earth meet, and where Arthur, portrayed in the poems as the perfection of humanity, will reign.

The antipodes are where the lands of P'o-Lu are situated, the reverse in every way of the holy empire to which they are, in every sense, opposed. The emperor of the Antipodes has no head. He walks backwards. His feet are feet of clay. Even the perfection of the Roman/Byzantine Empire cannot escape the curse of the Fall; and that, just as it is the Matter of Britain, is the Matter of CW too.

The inhabitants of the Empire are introduced to us, if we follow CSL's reading plan for *The Arthuriad*, more or less as Taliessin encounters them (the main figures are discussed in their own articles in the main section of the present book). In the wood Broceliande lives Nimue, a character whose name appears in other versions of the myths but is remade by CW. She is the mistress of Broceliande, an image of Nature, who by responding to the 'Feeling Intellect',[8] brings all of Nature into being.

Her son and daughter are Merlin and Brisen, whom CW calls 'Time and Space'. In the wood that is itself a kind of absolute (always granted one takes the right road), the Absolute's emissaries set out on their task, which is, they tell Taliessin, to set up a kingdom in Logres comparable to the kingdom of Pelles, keeper of the Grail, at Carbonek.

Merlin gives Taliessin a mission, to go to Byzantium. To do so will be to collaborate in a kind of insurance against the possible failure of Merlin and Brisen. Merlin meets Arthur in Logres, which is suffering famine. Arthur defeats the last of the Roman conquerors in battle. The land is restored. Meanwhile Taliessin has reached Byzantium, where he has met with the emperor. If the emperor is intended to symbolize God, as seems the case, Byzantium, the city, is Order. Divine perfection is the heart of the city; the city reflects in every way that divine perfection; and Order becomes the regulating element and the glory of the Empire. It is in this light that CW's picture of the Empire as a human body finds its essential logic.

Armed with this revelation, Taliessin returns to Logres. We see another battle (Mount Badon), serving again as an image of the city, in which the disordered Saxons are defeated and the monarchy of Arthur established. In *The Crowning of Arthur* we see the achievement of union between

Broceliande and Byzantium, that union of heaven and earth for which the emperor longs and for which Logres, as the mind of the Empire, must be the location.

Thus *Taliessin through Logres* moves towards its conclusion, and with it the first part of CW's *Arthuriad*. But all is not well. Merlin prophetically sees the tragedies that lie ahead. Is the king made for the kingdom, or the kingdom for the king? The city is attained, but the unity is fragile.

Taliessin's mission, with which he returned from Byzantium, is clearly the imposition of the divine Order upon Logres, which as yet has not achieved it. The poems describing Logres after the coronation expound the theme of order in a variety of ways. But the Empire as well as the emperor has feet of clay. The fragile harmony is vulnerable from the outset, and it is ironic that Taliessin, himself unable to be loved by others (e.g. *Taliessin's Song of the Unicorn*), is the catalyst of love; yet it is failures of love that prove the undoing of the kingdom which it is his task to bring about. The two fatal catastrophes that strike at the heart of the new Order and put the achieving of the Grail in doubt are committed by Arthur, who without knowing it commits incest with Morgause; and Balin who kills his brother, also unknowingly, smiting the Dolorous Blow which is at the heart of the Matter of Britain.

The poetry of CW is nevertheless poetry of hope, and is the more real a hope because it acknowledges the Fall*. Taliessin and his (literally) soulmate Dindrane achieve a spiritual union, but it results in their physical separation as she takes the veil and he goes to Camelot. For the others, however, fallen human nature does not mean that Order is unachievable or that the Grail is forever out of reach. The purpose of Taliessin's mission is to create in Logres a kingdom of such sublime order that the Grail may be established there; that mission lost, CW expounds the forming of Taliessin's Company, which is a parallel to the church; the doctrine of Co-inherence* and of Exchange, which is a parallel to the work of the Holy Spirit in the church and the true fellowship of believers; and the quest* for the Grail, which takes its seekers out of Logres and three of them to Carbonek. The Grail can be achieved, even though humanity is fallen.

The price is the failure of the Round Table. The poem cycles end with the Grail returning to the holy place of Sarras, Logres returning to its disorder, and the Company gathering to celebrate Mass before going their separate ways. In many ways it could all be read as a picture of catastrophic failure. But P'o-Lu is not the victor. Instead, CW directs us to the mystical perception of Romantic Love* – ultimately a metaphor for Christ's love, and his eternal Exchange – and to the fact that though Logres has failed to be what Merlin and Taliessin dreamed it should and could be, the Grail exists, the central sacramental symbol, and that Sarras abides eternally, whatever damage the Fall inflicts on mere temporal structures.

'It is in one way a wholly modern work, but it has grown spontaneously out of Malory and if the king and the Grail and the beginning of Galahad still serve, and serve perfectly, to carry the twentieth-century poet's meaning, that is because he has penetrated more deeply than the old writers themselves into what they also, half-consciously, meant and found its significance unchangeable as long as there remains on earth any attempt to unite Christianity and civilisation.'[9]

NOTES

1 Richard Barber, *The Arthurian Legend: An Illustrated Anthology*, Boydell Press, 1979, p. 2.
2 C.S. Lewis, *That Hideous Strength*, Pan, abr. edn, 1955, pp. 18–19.
3 Geoffrey of Monmouth, trans. Lewis Thorpe, *The History of the Kings of Britain*, Folio Society, 1964. Thorpe's Introduction p. 9.
4 We borrow the phrase from the *New York Times* review of T.H. White's *The Once and Future King* (1958).
5 The two were published together as *Arthurian Torso* in 1948.
6 Quoted by CSL in *Arthurian Torso*, p. 93.
7 *Arthurian Torso*, p. 95.
8 *Arthurian Torso*, p. 102.
9 *Arthurian Torso*, pp. 199–200.

SIX

Theology and Fantasy in
the Inklings

The impulse of fantasy is fundamental to the writings of both CSL and JRRT, the core figures of the Inklings. It is also fundamental to CW. The imaginative work of these writers awakens a symbolic perception of reality. Their symbolic worlds, even though fictional, are in some sense solidly real. JRRT and CSL guide us in seeing this world with a thoroughly Christian understanding. This may well explain the continued popularity and thus cultural relevance of the fantasy fiction of CSL and JRRT – both avowedly anti-modernist.

Fantasy is a power and product of the imagination, as thought is a power and product of the intellect. As thought is the reason in action, fantasy is the imagination at work. Both imagination and fantasy are difficult to define. Colin Manlove's definition of Christian fantasy* is a good working one: 'By "Christian fantasy" I mean "a fiction dealing with the Christian supernatural, often in an imaginary world."' With both CSL and JRRT, their view of nature implied the reality of the supernatural world and its myriad connections with the natural world. Hence their Christian fantasy not only concerns the supernatural, but also illuminates the natural world, and brings us into contact with it. The same is true of CW.

JRRT saw the highpoint of fantasy as sub-creation*, and CSL viewed it as imaginative invention. JRRT had sub-creation as its defining feature, whereas CSL's interest was less structural; for him, fantasy was a prime vehicle for capturing the elusive quality of joy*. Both for CSL and JRRT, fantasy has a strong inventive and imaginative component. The two men were interested in carefully crafted literary fantasy.

Viewing the imagination

It was because of their common theory of imagination that CSL and JRRT naturally inclined to literary fantasy, rather than other modes of fiction, such as the realistic novel. CSL particularly saw the imagination as the 'organ of meaning' or reality rather than of conceptual truth. Both CSL and JRRT as writers valued looking at reality in a symbolic way. They believed we actually win truth by employing metaphor, including imaginative models.

There is, then, an understandable preoccupation in the fictional writings of CSL and JRRT with fantasy, a concern also shared by CW. This was an important basis of the remarkable friendship between CSL and JRRT. JRRT and CSL had childhoods strikingly dominated by their imaginations. Both started writing seriously during the First World War, in which CSL was wounded and JRRT lost two of his closest friends. JRRT was several years older than CSL, and had already taught in Leeds University before returning to Oxford to take up another chair and meeting CSL in 1926. The two met at an English faculty meeting and it was not long after that they discovered they shared similar worlds and their association began, often talking far into the night. Their association was the core around which their literary group, the Inklings, developed. CW came into the equation later in the 1930s, culminating in his wartime move to Oxford*.

The two friends had a great number of shared beliefs that derived from mutual tastes, and particularly from their common faith, which though orthodox, had an original cast, to say the least. These shared beliefs constitute the heart of a theology of fantasy.

Particularly they both shared a theology of romanticism, a movement that stressed the poetic imagination, instinct, emotion and the subjective over against what it saw as a cold rationalism. Like CW they worked in their fiction according to this theology which has great affinities with a nineteenth-century writer who was CSL's mentor, George MacDonald*. The term 'romantic theologian', CSL tells us, was invented by CW. What CSL says about CW in his introduction to *Essays Presented to Charles Williams** applies also to JRRT and himself.

'A romantic theologian', CSL points out, 'does not mean one who is romantic about theology but one who is theological about romance, one who considers the theological implications of those experiences which are called romantic. The belief that the most serious and ecstatic experiences either of human love or of imaginative literature have such theological implications and that they can be healthy and fruitful only if the implications are diligently thought out and severely lived, is the root principle of all his [CW's] work.'

Whereas a key preoccupation of CW was romantic love, CSL was 'theological' about romantic longing or joy, and JRRT reflected deeply on the theological implications of fairy tale and myth*, particularly the aspect of sub-creation. In his autobiography, *Surprised By Joy**, CSL reported some of his sensations – responses to natural beauty, and literary and artistic responses – in the belief that others would recognize similar experiences of their own.

JRRT was fascinated by several structural features of fairy tales and other stories that embodied myths. These features are all related to a sense of imaginative decorum, a sense that imagining can, in itself, be good or bad, as rules or norms apply strictly in fantasy, as they do in thought. Meaning* can only be created by skill or art, and play an essential part in human thought and language. As JRRT said, 'The incarnate mind, the tongue, and the tale are in our world coeval.' As OB has shown in his introduction to the second edition of *Poetic Diction**, the ideal in logical positivism and related types of modern linguistic philosophy is, strictly, absurd; it systematically eliminates meanings from the framing of truths, expecting thereby to guarantee their validity. In JRRT's view, endorsing Barfield's, the opposite is the case. The richer the meanings involved in the framing of truths, the more guarantee is there of their validity.

CW's 'romantic religion', though concerned with romantic love, took the form of what he characteristically called the 'way of the affirmation of images'. He developed a distinctive doctrine of the twofold way of the affirmation* and rejection of images. Here we say of any created person or thing in reference to the Creator: 'This also is Thou; neither is this Thou.' In his *The Descent of the Dove**, CW described the principle like this: 'The one Way was to affirm all things orderly until the universe throbbed with vitality; the other to reject all things until there was nothing anywhere but He. The Way of Affirmation was to develop great art and romantic love and marriage and philosophy and social justice; the Way of Rejection was to break out continually in the profound mystical documents of the soul, the records of the great psychological masters of Christendom. All was involved in Christendom . . .'

The validity of both aspects of the twofold way was connected in CW's thinking with another key doctrine of Christianity – Co-inherence*. This doctrine was captured for him, characteristically, in the beautiful image of the city*. This social image brings out, for CW, the dependence of each of us upon others' labours and gifts, and the necessity of bearing one another's burdens.

Of the friends, JRRT and CSL were particularly influenced by OB. He believed that humanity has moved away from a unitary consciousness into a division of subject and object. CSL came to believe that theoretical reasoning abstracts from real things, real emotions, real events. JRRT and CSL saw this desirable unity, for example, in the gospel story, where the quality of myth* is not lost in the historical facticity of the events. There is no separation of story and history. CSL wrote:

> There is . . . in the history of thought, as elsewhere, a pattern of death and rebirth. The old, richly imaginative thought which still survives in Plato

has to submit to the deathlike, but indispensable, process of logical analysis: nature and spirit, matter and mind, fact and myth, the literal and metaphorical, have to be more and more sharply separated, till at last a purely mathematical universe and a purely subjective mind confront one another across an unbridgeable chasm. But from this descent, also, if thought itself is to survive, there must be re-ascent and the Christian conception provides for this. Those who attain the glorious resurrection will see the dry bones clothed again with flesh, the fact and the myth remarried, the literal and the metaphorical rushing together (*Miracles*, chapter XVI).

Because of the importance they placed on the primary meaning-function of the imagination, both JRRT and CSL were particularly preoccupied with the imaginative fruit of pre-Christian paganism, particularly what might be called enlightened paganism. Most of JRRT's fiction is set in a pre-Christian world, as was his great model, the Anglo-Saxon *Beowulf*, according to his own interpretation of that poem. Similarly, CSL explored a pagan world in his novel, *Till We Have Faces**.

Nature and grace

In what CSL called the Old West* a framework of nature and grace was the pattern not only in theology and philosophy but throughout western culture, influencing artists and writers. CSL portrays the medieval and Renaissance world model in his book, *The Discarded Image**, a model dominated by nature and grace. Integral to the framework is a hierarchy to the created world, ranging from the inanimate, through vegetable and sensible life, to the rational. Humanity straddled the hierarchy present on earth; each was a 'little world' or microcosmos. Such a view of humanity was immensely liberating to the imagination. To the contrary, increasingly mechanistic views of reality reduced humans to a spatial segment of matter in motion, or to a dualism of mind and body. Expressing the view of humanity the microcosm, Gregory the Great wrote: 'Because man has existence in common with stones, life with trees, and understanding with angels, he is rightly called by the name of the world.' Similarly, and far later, John Calvin, in his commentary on Genesis, finds it quite natural to refer to a human being as a 'world in miniature'. Humanity is in the middle, between form and matter, God and nature. In a sense, persons in themselves are alternative worlds, potentially the creators of other worlds.

Natural theology JRRT, by confession, was a Roman Catholic. IVP's *The New Dictionary of Theology* defines natural theology as 'Truths about God that can be learned from created things (nature, man, world) by reason

alone'. JRRT's natural theology is unusual in that his stress is on the imagination, rather than on reason. In contrast, CSL's use of natural theology
applied to both the reason and the imagination. CSL was vigorous in
employing reason in defence of Christianity and of the objectivity of truth
and morality. For JRRT (and, to an extent, for CSL) imagination can show
genuine insight into God and reality independently of the specific revelation
of scripture. Whereas traditional Roman Catholic thought emphasizes the
rational and cognitive in natural theology, JRRT linked it with imaginative
meaning. The presence of story, like language, is evidence of the image of
God still remaining in fallen humankind.

Nature Both CSL and JRRT believed that worlds of the imagination are
properly based upon the humble and common things of life – what CSL
called 'the quiet fullness of ordinary nature'. JRRT and CSL defended fantasy
on this basis against the charge of escapism. In a sense, nature itself induces
fantasy. Again like CSL, JRRT believed that nature is better understood as
God's creation. When the storyteller is building up a convincing 'Secondary
World', essentially it is the imaginative equivalent of the reason's attempt
to capture reality in a single, unified theory. The natural world of God's
creating, however, imposes a fundamental limit to the human imagination.

Sub-creation and the world of elves

Central to human storytelling – its epitome – is the fairy story*, according
to JRRT. In the equation of story and grace, elves have a significant place.

In his invented mythology of Middle-earth, JRRT intended that his elves
were an extended metaphor of a key aspect of human nature. Elves, like
dwarves, hobbits, and the like, 'partially represent' human beings. The three
Ages recorded in JRRT's Middle-earth stories and annals are pre-Christian.
JRRT concludes: 'God is the Lord, of angels, and of man – and of Elves.' JRRT
saw the elven quality embodied and made real in the incarnation, death and
resurrection of Christ. In his *Letters* JRRT describes the mythology of
Middle-earth as being 'Elf-centred'. The embodiment or indeed incarnation
of an elven quality in human lives is part of JRRT's solution to the reconciliation of nature and grace.

Paganism

Exploring the pattern of nature and grace forces us to return to the matter
of paganism. JRRT's tales of Middle-earth are thoroughly set in a pagan
context. It is a pagan world, like the setting of his great model, *Beowulf*. In
holding a similar view of what may be called enlightened paganism, CSL
was heavily influenced by JRRT.

There are a number of parallels between the author of *Beowulf*, as understood by JRRT, and JRRT himself. JRRT is a Christian scholar looking back to an imagined Northern European past. Like the ancient author, also, JRRT created an illusion of history and a sense of depths of the past. Like the *Beowulf* poet, and characteristically, JRRT was concerned with the issue of evil*.

JRRT's world in general is replete with Christian heroes and yet it is a pagan world. Ultimately, grace successfully spiritualizes nature. JRRT's treatment of paganism has the same potency that he found in *Beowulf*. The potency is there also in CSL's own great exploration of pre-Christian paganism, *Till We Have Faces*. This novel strikingly reveals the imaginative and theological affinity between the two men.

The success of JRRT and CSL as contemporary Christian writers reveals that Christian faith can strike a deep chord in the world today, probably more so because of the latter's increasing shift to post-modernism*. In the same light, the writings of CW seem increasingly topical, even though he still awaits anything more than a minority readership.

Part Two

SEVEN

The Inklings A–Z

Abolition of Man, The (CSL, 1943)

Based upon a series of three Riddell Memorial Lectures for 1943 given at the request of University of Durham, Lewis expresses disquiet over values being presented in textbooks for students of English Literature in British sixth-forms (the upper years of high school). If values are objective, argued CSL, one person may be right and another wrong. Judging goodness or badness is not simply a matter of opinion. CSL argued indeed that there is a universal acknowledgment of good and bad over matters like theft, murder, rape and adultery, a sense of what CSL called the Tao. With the abandonment of this perennial human wisdom, identity values like freedom and dignity become meaningless; the human being is merely part of nature*. The book concludes with an Appendix featuring various illustrations of the Tao from representative cultures around the world, gleaned from the 13-volume *Encyclopaedia of Religion and Ethics*, edited by James Hastings (1908–26). CSL gave a fictional expression to his case in his science-fiction story, *That Hideous Strength**, which also features Edgestow, a university town partly modelled on Durham.

See also SCIENTISM

Ackroyd, Peter (b. 1949)

Ackroyd is a novelist and poet whose work has some themes in common with CW. For example *The House of Dr Dee* (1983) brilliantly combines the worlds of Elizabeth I and modern London. Like CW, Ackroyd is fascinated by the resonances of history, and the house in Ackroyd's novel has much in common with the house in *Descent Into Hell**; both involve modern people in the consequences and spiritual impact of events that happened centuries before; both create what might be called a 'spiritual map' of London; both present a believable, powerful supernatural and draw on extensive knowledge of arcane and occult lore; and both are crammed with the details of a well-stocked store of knowledge about Elizabethan England, about London, and about spiritual forces from the past that can bind or sometimes release those who become aware of them.

   While Ackroyd does not claim CW as an influence, and does not claim to write as a Christian, he is a profitable author to explore for readers interested in CW's central concerns.

Adult education

It was not until 1944 that children in England were legally bound to attend school beyond the age of 14. Though continuation classes existed to extend education to the age of 18, many adults possessed only a rudimentary education. Organizations such as the Workers Educational Association (founded in 1903) played an important part in providing equality of opportunity and the chance to develop intellectual interests. London County Council established a number of evening classes for the same purpose. Under the Council's auspices CW lectured frequently to middle-aged and elderly audiences at the City Literary Institute, the Holloway Literary Institute and other similar places. These well-attended institutions, though they did not prepare students for recognized qualifications, organized lectures on a wide range of topics, charging only a small fee.

CW gave evening lectures at the City Literary Institute for many years. A.C. Ward, a fellow lecturer, encouraged him to write *A Myth of Shakespeare* (1929) for a Shakespeare festival. CW taught a course of lectures at the Institute in 1931 that later became *The English Poetic Mind* (1932), and another that became *Reason and Beauty in the Poetic Mind* (1933). CW enjoyed his work at the Institute and hoped to resume after the war. Having himself been prevented by circumstances from taking the conventional university degree course at which he would certainly have excelled, he was highly committed to students who, like him, had studied in their spare time or in difficult circumstances.

From this modest beginning he was later to become an extremely popular and influential lecturer at Oxford University. His fellow Inkling 'Hugo' Dyson* was also involved with adult education.

Advent of Arthur, The

See ARTHURIAN POEMS

Adventures of Tom Bombadil, The (JRRT, 1961)

A collection of light verses from *The Red Book of Westmarch*, supposedly written by Bilbo Baggins, Sam Gamgee, and other hobbits, and rendered into English from Westron by JRRT.

Aeneid, The Story of the (CW, 1936)

This is an example, according to Alice M. Hadfield, of CW's 'gift for presenting a beautifully clear outline of a difficult literary work'. Virgil (70–19 BC) created in the *Aeneid* a patriotic epic, a great love story, and authentification of Latin antiquity.

CSL made his own translation of the *Aeneid*, never published, from which he read on occasions to the Inklings.
See also VIRGIL

Affection
See FOUR LOVES, THE

Affirmation, way of; affirmative way

A major theme in CW's writings. (See also *THE DESCENT OF THE DOVE*.) It represents a positive corollary to the better-known mystical way, the way of rejection, as seen in the ascetic life. Richardson in *The Place of the Lion*, for example, represents the way of the rejection of images. The affirmative way is sometimes called the 'sacramental' way, where objects are invested with profound significance because seen in the light of eternal truth. A classic study of this is Henri de Caussade's *The Sacrament of the Present Moment* (1741), written when Quietism was in effect advocating the way of rejection alone. Richard Foster, introducing Kitty Muggeridge's translation (1966), reflects, 'Teaching students, answering correspondence, playing with my boys, repairing broken window panes . . . paying bills, washing dishes. How could these events take on sacramental significance?' The way of the affirmation of images shows how. An influence on de Caussade was Francis de Sales, whom CSL much admired.

In an article, 'The Church Looks Forward' (*St Martin's Review*, 1940), CW provides theological backing for his belief that for Christians, God is to be found, under the tutoring of the Holy Spirit, as much in the physical, known present as in the supernaturally spiritual, unknown future, and that the physical world of images is to be embraced ('under authority') rather than purged from one's spiritual life. The climax of the article relates the discussion to his key concern, the way of affirmation. He begins by pointing out that the church 'does not, even in her fullest existence, look forward' – its focus is the here and now, its future bound up with the activities of the Holy Spirit in teaching us more of Christ; but that teaching is known in the here and now and the church cannot 'under present conditions' realize the 'continuity of glory'. Thus its looking forward is a matter of faith and hope. But these are not at all abstractions.

Similarly the church's separation from the world does not preclude an intense relation to the world in terms of physical, natural existence. But for the Christian that physical experience is illuminated with a new 'kind of experience', which, under authority, it must pursue. For CW this means a twofold path: the nature of things in God, and the nature of God. They are not mutually exclusive: 'the most remote hermit generally has to attend occasionally to his own meal . . . The most overworked doctor has to say the Lord's prayer with its clauses concerning God in Himself.' CW develops this to justify Christian concern for material things, for good government, fidelity and love in marriage, and – in a very effective passage – honesty in Christians, especially in missionary and contemplative activities. His injunction never to 'lie on the Lord's behalf' by, for example, pretending that arguments are conclusive when in fact they are weak, is a valuable principle for Christians even today.

He argues strongly against a split between the intellectual and physical. If the church's honesty can be recovered, he suggests, then without denying the order that has developed in the church, its 'charismatic and prophetic ministry' might be recovered too; a ministry the New Testament takes for granted, with significant references to safety from 'casual "deadly things"' and perhaps from disease too, unless deliberately welcomed in 'the cause and name of charity'.

CW acknowledges that this is a distant prospect, and suggests it will not happen until we have learned to 'welcome those distresses on behalf of others'. But what the church must do here and now is to recapture the life of faith, for then the Holy Spirit will 'do what He will'.

Within this here and now of the everyday physical world, says CW, Christians must recover the concept of substitution*, for it is on the substitution of Christ for us that the doctrine of the Christian church depends. We are enabled to do this by the atonement and empowered to do it by the Holy Spirit. 'In the old legend Adam and Eve were, originally, one being. It is a profound symbol. Justice, charity, union; these are the three degrees of the Way of the Affirmation of Images, and all of us are to the images affirmed.'

This key concept in CW's writing is present in his early writing on marriage, where sex is seen as an affirmation that the immediate and physical is a legitimate part of spiritual experience. He also introduces the thought that the way of affirmation is paralleled by the way of rejection: 'This also is Thou; neither is this Thou'. Affirmation was therefore for CW a twofold path. Glen Cavaliero has pointed out that in the Arthurian poems Bors is 'the type of the affirmative way and himself the chief of the images' – the images being seen in the 'grand Rejection (Galahad) born of the grand Affirmation (Lancelot)' (CW, *Poet of Theology*, 1983).

Both ways are to be held in tension, whereas commonly the way of affirmation tends to be seen as the secular way and the way of rejection the religious one. But because any image in a created world bears the impress of its maker, images are to be affirmed; and because an image can distract one from its creator, there is a place for the rejection of images in the Christian life also.

See also CHAPTER 6; *DESCENT OF THE DOVE, THE*

All Hallows' Eve (CW, 1945)

CW's last novel was completed in 1944 and published less than a month before his death in 1945. It incorporates fragmentary material from the unfinished *The Noises that Weren't There* (1943).

There is a marked technical skill in handling the structure of the novel by comparison with his first novel of almost two decades earlier. The action and the thought are driven by events, rather than as (for example in *Shadows of Ecstasy**) the novel being a container into which CW fits a multitude of ideas as best he can. The reader is allowed to respond to what is happening, rather than being constantly prompted how to respond. There is some acute characterization, and CW's descriptions of places are evocative: his descriptions of wartime London seen through the eyes of a dead character are especially convincing.

For *All Hallows' Eve* is remarkable in that the first character whose thoughts and ideas we meet is dead. Lester Furnival, a young woman alone on Westminster Bridge, looks out over a deserted, twilit London. A plane has crashed into the Embankment, near her home. Her husband appears, demanding incredulously how she had escaped from the crash; then he fades from her sight. She realizes that she has been killed in the crash. The relationship between husband and wife tells us an enormous amount about Lester in a very few pages. Another woman, her friend Evelyn Mercer, approaches, killed too in the crash. Where Lester is competent and pragmatic, Evelyn is desolate, unwilling to stop talking, bemoaning how little she has done in life; Lester, wishing that her husband of six months were with her in this dead world, agrees, and looking at the companion she does have, Evelyn, exclaims in frustration, 'Oh my God' – an appeal that will have repercussions. Despite her irritation, she takes Evelyn under her wing as they go off into their new life.

A month later Richard Furnival visits an artist friend, Jonathan Drayton. Jonathan is 'practically engaged' to Betty Wallingford, an acquaintance of Lester and Evelyn. He is an offical war artist, and shows Richard his latest work, and also a painting of a spiritual leader, Father Simon ('Simon the Clerk') preaching. Richard comments on the remarkable presence of light in the first and absence of light in the latter, as the painting's commissioner, Betty's mother Lady Wallingford, arrives with her daughter. She condemns the painting as making Simon look like a malevolent insect preaching to insects, and sweeps out declaring that the engagement will not now take place. Richard, intrigued, decides to hear Simon for himself in Holborn. On the way, he glimpses the ghost of his wife.

Later, Simon visits Jonathan to inspect the picture and declares himself very pleased, and tells Jonathan that he must paint more portraits of him; he hints at a great work to be done, and makes vague messianic allusions. In an extended passage, CW compares Christ, the Jewish lord, and Simon, the Jew whose Jewish forebears had bequeathed him 'the Jewish, the final word of power'. Simon has a grand plan: 'a fame beyond any poet's and a domination beyond any king's'. In that plan Jonathan has a useful role as artist; 'but Betty was for another purpose'; just as Simon is to be a parallel of Christ, of whom he is a distorted inversion, so Betty is to play the role of Mary.

Betty's peculiar background is next explained. She is adopted, and knows nothing of her real parents. Sometimes Lady Wallingford takes her to a cottage in Yorkshire where she is treated as a slave and given only popular music and newspapers for entertainment. Her only friends – though rather cruel friends – Lester and Evelyn, are dead. Grieving over this one night she is summoned by Lady Wallingford, who tells her that 'Our Father' needs her. There follows a strange, disturbing session in which Simon appears to be exerting immense psychological control over an unresisting Betty. Free of her body, she walks out into a bright London morning, ranging over space and time; this is Simon's 'purpose', that she should glean information of use to him. Her concentration on the task is diluted by her worry over Lester and Evelyn, and Simon is later somewhat disturbed by the strong attachment of love that Betty has for Jonathan. The purpose of the dream walk is achieved however, for Betty, now in the future, is able to read the newspaper and obtain the information Simon seeks; that his plan to master the world will progress well.

At one point she calls out for Jonathan, and the two dead girls come looking for her; Lester out of desire to help, Evelyn to resume the taunting relationship she had with Betty in life. She flees back to Simon's house, and Lester, still anxious to help, follows her in.

Simon skilfully draws his characters together, all designated to serve him: Betty, the obedient downtrodden servant; Lester, who might be of use to him; Lady Wallingford, the disciple (and, we learn, the mother of Simon's child – Betty); Jonathan, the servant artist (though he is reluctant to take the task on).

At Holborn, Richard sees more of Simon's disciples, people who have been healed of fatal illness or saved in other ways, gathered in an artificial atmosphere of religious tranquillity. CW here expounds Simon's inverted doctrine of exchange; Betty, the emissary *into* the afterlife, Lester (through Richard), the emissary *from* it. But there is true exchange to balance it: the love between Richard and Lester is a counterbalance to the strong attraction Richard is beginning to feel for Simon and his message. The theme of exchange continues in the relationship between Lester and Betty, to whom she appears: she wants to help Betty, but first Betty must forgive her for her past treatment of her.

This is entirely CW's theme: the grand plan of Simon is, by uttering the great name of the Tetragrammaton, to exert power between the worlds of living and dead (hence the novel's title: the events take place on Hallowe'en, when the two worlds are accessible). The uttering of the Tetragrammaton, or the anti-Tetragrammaton (the Name reversed), was a ritual of which CW would have been aware from his membership of the Order of the Golden Dawn*, in which it was much discussed.

In the novel the power of the Tetragrammaton is a corrupting process mirroring the healing that is going on between Lester and Betty, and the bridge of love between Lester and Richard. Betty is to be despatched by that inverted utterance into the dead world, but there must be an exchange, someone must be brought back, and Lester is Simon's choice. (The exchange fails, for it is the weak-willed, easily manipulated Evelyn who is brought back.) Lester is made of stronger stuff. In a dramatic scene she comes between Simon and Betty to deflect Simon's curse that would send Betty's spirit into death. CW develops the biblical parallel with crucifixion in a resonant passage that nevertheless takes its images of salvation from the simplest human kindnesses (just as in *Descent Into Hell*, damnation comes in the end from the most elementary cheating). Against the curse, the inverted Tetragrammaton, CW places the utterance of Lester's name by Betty, a name which is a symbol for the divine name (in this novel, many utterances are taken to mean far more than their utterers realized). Lester, too, utters Richard's name, and is comforted.

Each character in the novel is headed towards redemption or loss. Evelyn, for example, joins Simon's side and is rewarded by being given a new magical body: a poor exchange, for the body is a dwarved, rudimentary one. It is, says Simon, for Lester and Evelyn. Characteristically, Evelyn reacts with anger, Lester sees it as a chance to help, to 'take and give pardon and courage'. By the use of this poor broken body, Lester is able to meet with Richard at Jonathan's flat and by exchange of pardon the imperfections of their short-lived marriage are resolved.

Having failed to kill Betty by cursing her Simon tries to do it with a voodoo doll, using scraps of Betty's hair supplied by Lady Wallingford. In another inversion (of Lester's interposition), Lady Wallingford, holding the doll for Simon to stab, is herself wounded, thus suffering on behalf of Betty.

The novel ends at Simon's house. Lester and Richard, Jonathan and Betty and Evelyn force entry in the middle of a ritual. As Evelyn is drawn to enter a magic circle Betty attempts to save her, but Evelyn spurns her. Rain pours through the roof, washing away the voodoo doll and the dwarf body. Lester, again disembodied, is now free to leave Richard, who is now able to come to terms with his loss. Lady Wallingford, manipulator and oppressor, suffers a stroke and becomes dependent on Betty whom she once abused. Evelyn is doomed to wander in the city, having turned away from joy. Simon's followers find that their illnesses have come back and their healer is now impotent to save them – he is, in fact, destroyed by his own creation, two zombie-like beings he has created to serve him (as they are really clones of himself, nurtured over many years and enshrining 'the most secret corridors of his heart', he is really involuntarily destroying himself by his own hand). His healing gifts pass to Betty, but like so many of the exchanges in this novel, they are in her hands transformed into servants of good.

Allegory

An extended metaphor, or sustained personification. In literature, a figurative narrative or description which conveys a hidden meaning, often moral. Key examples in English literature are John Bunyan's *The Pilgrim's Progress* and Edmund Spenser's *The Faerie Queene*. JRRT's short story, *Leaf by Niggle* is an allegory.

When JRRT's *The Lord of the Rings* first appeared some interpreted the One Ring as meaning the atomic bomb. Apart from the fact that the Ring was conceived before the bomb existed or was known about as a possibility, such an interpretation is wrong in treating the work as an allegory. JRRT pointed out that such an interpretation confused meaning with applicability. In his Foreword, he writes: 'I much prefer history, true or feigned, with its varied applicability to the thought and experience of readers. I think that many confuse "applicability" with "allegory"; but the one resides in the freedom of the reader, and the other in the purposed domination of the author.'

JRRT, like CSL and CW, valued myth* above allegory. He was critical of CSL's fondness for allegory, in the Narnian Chronicles* for example. OB early on expressed a preference for myth. He wrote, in an Appendix to *Poetic Diction** :

> Allegory [is] a more or less conscious hypostatization of ideas, followed by a synthesis of them, and myth the true child of Meaning, begotten on imagination*.

Barfield speaks of Greek philosophers contaminating their original myths with allegory. A modern poet creates a new myth, or makes a true use of an old one, according to Barfield, if he or she succeeds in directly embodying concrete experience, rather than his or her idea of that experience. If the poet only deals with ideas he or she has only invented an allegory, or has made allegorical use of a myth.

Barfield's distinction between allegory and myth rings true of Tolkien's perception, leading to his dislike of allegory, and his concern, for example, about CSL's fondness for allegory.

CSL's liking for allegory was part of his eclecticism. He was at home in the

vast range of the pre-modern imagination, from the ancient Greeks through the entire medieval and Renaissance periods. JRRT's interests were much more narrowly focused around the period of Anglo-Saxon literature.
See also FANTASY; ASLAN; *THE ALLEGORY OF LOVE*

Allegory of Love, The (CSL, 1936)

Subtitled 'A Study in Medieval Tradition', this book by CSL is among the outstanding works of literary criticism of the last century. CSL traced the concept of romantic love from the beginnings of allegory* through Chaucer and Spenser. In the process he depicted the long struggle between its earlier manifestation, the romance of adultery, and its later incarnation, the romance of married love between the sexes. The Middle Ages provide the key and the background to both CSL's thought and fiction.

CW developed a theology of romantic love (*see* CHAPTER 6). The common interest in romantic love on the part of CSL and CW was an important element in their friendship. JRRT, too, explored the theme in his fiction, in the love of Beren and Lúthien, and Aragorn and Arwen, and other instances. In the biblical tradition shared by CSL, JRRT, and CW, romantic love is distinctively explored in the histories of Isaac and Rebekah, Jacob and Rachel, David and Bathsheba, the lovers in the Song of Songs, and elsewhere.

The Allegory of Love demonstrates CSL's concern to help the reader enter as fully as possible into an author's intentions. He concentrates on textual criticism, which he valued above other types of critical activity, as a later comment makes clear: 'Find out what the author actually wrote and what the hard words meant and what the allusions were to, and you have done far more for me than a hundred new interpretations or assessments could ever do'. CSL was committed to the *author*ity of the author. It also expresses his characteristic interest in the Christianization of paganism (in this case, romantic love) an interest deeply shared by JRRT.

Harry Blamires points out that CSL 'revived the genre of historical criticism by his work on Medieval and Renaissance literature in *The Allegory of Love* (1936) and *English Literature in the Sixteenth Century* (1954)'. His revival of this genre is perhaps even more significant than these works themselves. Notably, while CSL's conclusions in the books are by no means always accepted, the books as historical scholarship are universally admired.

Allingham, Margery (1904–66)

A crime writer whose many thrillers were (in Torqemada's phrase) 'distinguished novels', Allingham's career began when she left school at 15 and started to publish short stories in a variety of magazines. She introduced her aristocratic detective Albert Campion for the first time in her novel *The Crime at Black Dudley* (1929). Campion has much in common with Dorothy

L. Sayers'* detective Lord Peter Wimsey; both are somewhat estranged from the noble families they belong to, though Campion's background is far more sketchily drawn. Both detectives mature from novel to novel, Campion more successfully and with a more convincing love story and marriage. Both are erudite and have a languid, witty style, though Campion's relationships with his 'social inferiors' are much more attractively drawn – Campion's manservant Lugg is a redoubtable sparring-partner; Wimsey's Bunter is a devoted servant with a fund of useful specialist knowledge whose function is merely to exemplify his master's intellectual and detective brilliance. Both writers place their descriptions of crime into a strong moral framework that operates within the structures of Christian absolutes.

Allingham continued to write novels during the war and published several after it, though the later novels often lack the almost mythic quality that she brought to her descriptions of pre-war England, especially London and the Essex countryside. But in *The Tiger in the Smoke* (1952) she achieved an elegiac lament for the losses wrought by war, and an intriguing detective puzzle set in a moral framework of considerable power. The central image of damnation as a staircase (expounded to the villain in a chapter 'On the Staircase' which has points in common with a similar conversation between Wimsey and the self-confessed murderer Tallboy in Sayers' *Murder Must Advertise*, 1932), is very reminiscent of the image of the rope in CW's *Descent Into Hell*. She was a friend of CSL and Joy Lewis*, and her books were on the Lewises' bookshelves at the Kilns.

Allingham's last novel was *Cargo of Eagles*, completed by her husband Philip Youngman Carter and published in 1968. He also wrote two further Albert Campion novels.

Alpha thinking

OB invented this term to describe thinking associated with science. This is thinking about objects in a reduced way – considering them only as they might exist independently of human consciousness (*Saving the Appearances*, 1957, pp. 24–25). Science is the most systematic and developed form of alpha thinking: scientific methodology is based upon it. This kind of thinking reaches its extreme in twentieth-century positivism, and is at its most naive in common-sense realism. In extremity it is a form of idolatry*.

Looked at historically (as OB does in *Saving the Appearances*) alpha thinking excludes participation*, another key concept of OB's. This is done methodologically, in order to make natural phenomena more predictable and measurable. OB, following Coleridge*, believed that our perceptions of objects are in fact representations, intimately linked with our participating minds and consciousness, and indeed our organic unity as human beings. *See also* BETA THINKING

Angels

As orthodox Christians, CSL, CW and JRRT believed in the literal existence of angels. They appear historically, for example, in the Gospels, at the annunciation of Christ and after the resurrection, and in the Book of Acts. In parts of *The Discarded Image** CSL summarizes medieval beliefs about angels.

Angels feature particularly in JRRT's fiction. For imaginative force and freshness, he, like CSL, avoids the term, 'angel'. CSL, in his *The Cosmic Trilogy* (for which he acknowledged that the Book of Ezekiel was an important source for angels) employs the terms, 'Oyarsa' and 'eldila', while JRRT writes of the Valar and Maiar. The latter wished to capture the imaginative vitality of the Old Norse or Olympian gods, yet to portray beings acceptable to someone who believes in 'The Blessed Trinity'. The Valar and Maiar represent the activity of God (Ilúvatar).

The Valar and Maiar are partly modelled on biblical angels. The biblical angels are witnesses of creation, whereas the Valar participate in making the world (even though they are distinct creations of God themselves). The nearest biblical equivalent to the Valar is the personification of Wisdom in Proverbs 8.

Like biblical angels (e.g. Abraham's visitors) the Maiar can take on human (or human-like) form, as with Gandalf, Melian, Sauron in Númenor, and Tom Bombadil. The intermarriage of Melian and the elvish King Thingol echoes the marriages of 'sons of God' and daughters of men in early Genesis. The Valar also take on appearances at will (as Ulmo, for example, appears to Tuor).

As in the Bible, there are fallen angels: Sauron, Morgoth or Melkor (equivalent to Lucifer), and the Balrogs. There seems no equivalent of ordinary demons. The orcs do not seem to be capable of moral choice (being bred into evil by Morgoth, originally from captured elves). Also like biblical angels, the Valar can be militant, as at the end of the First Age, when Morgoth and his forces are overcome by their intervention.

Unlike in the Bible, the Valar in JRRT are more like intermediaries between God (Ilúvatar) and the beings of Middle-earth. They also have a demiurgic role in creation, like God in Plato's myth of *Timaeus*. In JRRT, angels have a subtle and pervasive role in providence, working in and behind events. One of the functions of Gandalf the Maia is that of interpreting providential events.

Elves, who symbolically represent an aspect of humankind, have some angelic qualities. Their elvish quality enters human life and history through example and intermarriage (such as the marriage of Beren and the elf-maiden Lúthien).

It is interesting that CSL does not have an intermediary role for angelic beings. God directly and personally communicates (as in Aslan, the creator-lion of Narnia) as well as using messengers and angelic interpreters. His most important imaginative use of angels is in his science-fiction trilogy, where he draws upon a medieval imaginative picture of reality, admirably documented elsewhere in his *The Discarded Image*.

CSL's most well-known depiction of angels is in his *The Screwtape Letters**, which concerns the machinations of fallen angels, or demons, in trying to ensure the damnation of a young man, who is entrusted to the bungling demon, Wormwood.

CW's *The Place of the Lion** has some parallels with angelic theology in that the 'platonic principles' come to inhabit the human world yet live outside the dimension of the perceived and understood, though the parallel is often tenuous. It is strong in two areas, however: the principles are ultimately servants of humanity, just as biblically, believers will 'judge angels' (1 Corinthians 6:3); and they have a consoling function and also one of personal protection. CW implicitly confirms the point made by CSL, that the appearance of angels always excited fear and dismay. In *War in Heaven** the character Prester John, the supernatural protector of the Graal, has some angelical characteristics but these are soon swallowed up in his final appearance as Christ in the Mass that ends the book. But there are few close parallels to conventional angels (as, for example, CSL expounds them in *Preface to Paradise Lost*) in CW's fiction: in situations where one might expect them – consoling the newly dead, for example, in *All Hallows' Eve** and *Descent Into Hell** – they are conspicuous by their absence. The two supernatural servants of Simon the Clerk in CW's *All Hallows' Eve* might be seen as an inversion of angelic visitations – formed by Simon to do his will, privy to his thoughts and plans, executing his wishes. They are also the agents of his destruction.

Famous forerunners of CSL, JRRT and CW on angels include John Milton (*Paradise Lost*), William Blake (many works) and Dante (*The Divine Comedy*). They also include the unjustly neglected John Macgowan, and his *Dialogues of Devils*.

Anthroposophy

A modern 'spiritual science' founded by Rudolf Steiner (1861–1925) and followed and promoted by OB. It contains eastern and western philosophical elements. Both Steiner and OB consider this gnostic movement compatible with Christianity, even though it is far from orthodox. OB felt deep affinities with the thinking of Samuel Taylor Coleridge*, who also had an allegiance to Christian faith. Because of the generally orthodox Christian climate of the Inklings it is worth exploring the claim of anthroposophy to be compatible with Christian belief. On 13 July 1914, Rudolf Steiner gave a public lecture on 'Anthroposophy and Christianity' in Norrköping, a lecture subsequently translated and published in English by the Anthroposophic Press. In this he sets out his claim that anthroposophy provides an interpretation of Christianity that is based on scientific principles and particularly appropriate for today. Steiner claimed that spiritual science (that is, anthroposophy) does not wish to usurp the position of Christianity. Rather, it wanted to be an instrument for making Christianity understood by people today in a deeper and more heartfelt way. Anthroposophists recognize that the being they call Christ is to be acknowledged as the centre of life on earth. His claim was no less than that 'the Christian religion is the ultimate religion for the earth's whole future'.

In the same lecture, Steiner drew elaborate contrasts with ancient gnosticism and the pre-Christian religions. Though he recognized their significant contribution to humanity's spiritual evolution, they were one-sided as they only came to fruition in the Christian faith. The key difference between the old gnosticism and the new spiritual science is that all people are able to acquire a new consciousness, not merely an elite:

A truly religious person can grasp that religion is only enriched and deepened by scientific knowledge. Spiritual science doesn't want to have anything to do with founding a new religion or to give rise to prophets or founders of sects. Mankind has matured; the time for prophets and founding religions is over.

Rudolf Steiner advocated a new perception of Christianity which is really also a new perception of reality itself. He drew an analogy with Copernicus, whose ideas altered the very way we look at nature, rather than reshaped its order. 'Nature stayed as it was, but people learned to think about nature in a way that accorded with the new view of the world.' Like natural science, Steiner argued, Christianity is rooted in reality; it is 'mystical fact'. He then said, 'Christianity is not a mere doctrine to be interpreted this way or that; it has entered the world as a fact that can only be understood spiritually.' OB believed that this central point of Steiner's anticipated the discovery CSL made at his conversion to Christianity, where JRRT persuaded him that the Gospel narratives have all the qualities of a good story, yet also actually happened in history; in CSL's terms, 'myth became fact'. Yet although there does at first sight seem to be a strong parallel here between Steiner and CSL, it is only based on the ambiguity of the term 'fact', a notoriously difficult term. For both CSL and JRRT, the factual nature of the Gospel narratives was understood in terms of normal historical documents, whereas Steiner allowed himself to be free and easy in his interpretation of the four Gospels according to the esoteric 'spiritual' and 'scientific' discipline of anthroposophical meditation. Continuing the parallel with Copernicus, Steiner argued that just as the natural world did not change because of Copernicus' insights, 'nor does the truth of Christianity change when spiritual science is used as a tool for understanding it more completely than was possible in times gone by'.

The 'times gone by' included the period of pre-Christian paganism. Certain of these pagans, with their gnostic mystery religions, were able to be initiated into a knowledge of 'body-free soul life'. They were able mystically to experience the arrival of Christ. The 'Christ-event' they anticipated is the 'pivotal event in man's evolutionary history'. Prior to the advent of Christianity, esoteric gnostic initiations were 'the only way to leave the world of the senses and gain entry into the world of the spirit'. This is why, according to Steiner, figures such as Plato* or Heraclitus were called 'Christians' by the church fathers.

The arrival of Christianity made a dramatic difference to the human approach to spiritual reality. Now 'every soul can undertake for itself to succeed in entering the spiritual world'. Using scientific, disciplined methods, any soul by self-education can ascend to the spiritual world. Christianity has made this possible; prior to its advent the authoritative guidance of teachers was necessary. Before Christ's human presence in the world, he could only be found in the spiritual world by esoteric, gnostic knowledge. Now, however, he 'can be found since the Christ-event by every human soul willing to make the effort'.

Part of Rudolf Steiner's new perception of Christianity is his reinterpretation both of the facts and meaning of Christ's life in a way alien to the orthodox Christian understanding of JRRT, CSL and CW, but palatable to OB. At Jesus' baptism, according to Steiner, the human person Jesus was possessed by a 'Being' not there before, who stayed with him for the next three years up to the human Jesus' death and resurrection. Steiner denies the incarnation of Christ at the moment of conception in Mary's womb, replacing it with a gnostic idea of an embodiment of a higher spiritual being in the human Jesus at his baptism, symbolically uniting 'with earthly humanity'. Ironically, a great deal of the New Testament writings are taken up with counteracting gnostic teaching similar to Steiner's.

Related to his reinterpretation of Christianity is Steiner's belief in reincarnation:

> Mankind changes as each individual goes from life to life in succeeding epochs. Our souls incarnated in times before Christ united with the earth, and they will continue to be reborn into further earth-lives in which Christ is joined with the earth . . . Christ lives in each human soul.

Because Christ lives in each soul, he believed, spiritual science can speak to everyone in speaking about Christ.

OB drew inspiration from anthroposophism and Rudolf Steiner for his many writings, and his adherence to this view formed the basis for the 'great war' between CSL and OB. OB's influence on CSL and JRRT was mainly through his early work, *Poetic Diction**, and concerned the nature of poetic language and a theory of an ancient semantic unity, which require no commitment to anthroposophical interpretations of Christianity. Even though OB influenced CSL through the 'great war' of ideas in the 1920s, this helped to prepare CSL for accepting orthodox Christianity, rather than any anthroposophist ideas. Significant differences remained between CSL and OB until the end of his life. Once he left Oxford, OB was rarely able to attend Inklings meetings, so he was not a constant influence on the group, except through the important legacy of his ideas in *Poetic Diction*. However, CSL continued to be familiar with his developing ideas and incorporated a number of them in his writings.

Rudolf Steiner's ideas can be seen as part of a contemporary quest for a new consciousness which tries to transcend the rational-scientific model of reality imposed by the Enlightenment, despite his claim to be following a 'scientific method'. In his important study, *The Magical World of the Inklings*, Gareth Knight attempts a somewhat New Age interpretation of their thought and writings, playing down the enduring significance of Christian orthodoxy in CSL, JRRT and CW. He is particularly helpful however on OB.

FURTHER READING

Rudolf Steiner, *Anthroposophy and Christianity* (English translation, 1985).

Arthurian myth

The legend of Arthur dominates the poetry of CW, who, in *Taliessin through Logres* and *The Region of the Summer Stars*, produced the first major retelling of the Matter of Britain and the story of the Grail since Tennyson. Like Tennyson, CW portrays Arthur as ideal man, who has created, in his kingdom of Logres, a point of perfect union between earth and heaven. Logres is the head and brain of the female figure underlying Arthurian cosmology.

Standard figures from the old Arthurian legends such as Malory's appear in CW with new, mystical roles and significance. Thus Nimue of Broceliande has two children, Merlin and Brisen, whom she charges with the task of creating unified perfection by creating the kingdom of the Grail, the holy city of Carbonek, which will achieve a fusion of body, mind and soul. Arthur and his kingdom of Logres are the key to this task, and Taliessin, a pagan poet, their companion. Taliessin's part in the mission of Merlin and Brisen is that of bringing Logres out of chaos and into order, a necessary condition of the coming of the Grail to Logres; to be the means by which Britain/

Logres will be brought to mirror the 'ordered passion' of Byzantium, where 'the streets repeat the sound of the throne'.

His mission succeeds to a limited extent, mirrored in Taliessin's household, which is ordered by 'the law of Exchange'; mutual labour in the kingdom, corporate devotion in the church, mutual satisfaction of each other's needs; and the sacrificial bearing of each other's burdens (a major theme in *Descent Into Hell**) 'according to the grace of the Spirit'; and all lived out against the backdrop of the supreme Exchange, Christ's death on the cross and the mutuality of the triune Godhead.

But the Grail never comes to Logres. Two acts in particular prevent it, and neither is deliberate. Arthur, without realizing it, sleeps with his sister, Morgause; Balin unknowingly kills his brother and smites the Dolorous Blow. Yet all is not lost. Though the Round Table is broken up, and only three of Taliessin's Company reach Carbonek, that which is redeemable in Logres is redeemed through Exchange. The Grail returns to Sarras, its true home, Logres returns to chaos, and for the last time the Companions meet to celebrate Mass and the completion of the task, which has been achieved inasmuch as achieving it was ever possible. The words of dismissal, *Ite, missa est*, bring to an end the task, and the role of Taliessin. (There are many echoes here of the final Mass in *War in Heaven**.)

There are two useful aids in getting to grips with the world of CW's Arthurian poems. The first is the handbook *Arthurian Torso**, co-written by CSL who, as a close friend of CW, read the poems as they developed, and knew them intimately. The second is reading the poems aloud. The flow of the verse and the power of incantation they possess are remarkable, and they gain in clarity when spoken.

Arthurian poems

CW's earliest Arthurian poems are a cycle known as *The Advent of Galahad*, written mainly between 1929 and 1931. They remained unpublished for many years after CW's death and were not taken into account in CSL's *Arthurian Torso**, although he knew of their existence. The collection existed in a typescript book compiled in 1940 as a result of a request from Margaret Douglas to CW asking if he had any unpublished material. It included several poems that had already been published in *Heroes and Kings** (1930/1), *Three Plays** (1931), Gollancz's *New English Poems: A Miscellany of Contemporary Verse* (1931) edited by Lascelles Abercrombie, and *Time and Tide*, March 1941.

In 1991 the poems were published together for the first time in David Llewellyn Dodds (ed.), *Arthurian Poets: Charles Williams* (Boydell Press, 1991), with an extensive introduction charting the origins and development of the poems; a number of other unpublished poems are included.

CW's first generally published collection of Arthurian poems is *Taliessin through Logres* (1938), which he described as 'an attempted and unfinished cycle'. It was followed in 1944 by *The Region of the Summer Stars*. Both books remained little known except to admirers for many years, a reprint in 1969 appearing after the books had been out of print for some years. T.S. Eliot*, who admired CW greatly, wrote : 'I should not advise a new reader to start with his poetry. Out of his early, and rather conventional style, he developed an original, more modern idiom. But his later and best poems are not easy reading. He could and did write clearly and simply: but in these poems he expects a good deal of the reader . . . His long poem "Taliessin in Logres" is absorbing after we have got the hang of what he is after' (*Listener*, 19 December 1946).

Arthurian Torso, ed. CSL (1948)

After the death of CW in 1945, CSL addressed the problem of the incomplete Arthurian material by publishing in one volume the unfinished prose work 'The Figure of Arthur'* and *The Arthuriad*. The title therefore is a pun, referring both to the unfinished state of CW's contribution and to the map of the body that underlies CW's Arthurian cosmology (*see* CHAPTER 5). He described his own contribution, intended to complement the poems and the prose work, as adding to CW's history of the Arthurian legend 'an account of the last poet who has contributed to it – namely, CW himself'. The book does not contain the Arthurian poems, not included in the two main collections, that were left unpublished on CW's death; these, together with earlier poems gathered under the title *The Advent of Galahad*, were first published in David Llewellyn Dodds, *Arthurian Poets: Charles Williams*.

CSL treats the two collections as a corpus: 'there is no certain evidence how the book would have gone on'. He begins by collating the two sequences into a single sequence, establishing a narrative continuity. He suggested that this was the most helpful order in which to read them (though Alice Hadfield later made a strong case for retaining the two distinct sequences).

He next considers 'The establishment of Arthur', beginning with a discussion of Taliessin's lineage and his growing awareness of Byzantium and quest to find it. He clarifies the nature of Broceliande, explaining it as the 'unlimited, the formless origin of forms' – Carbonek is beyond, but only beyond a certain part of it. CSL guides his readers through the early poems, laying out the main landscape and themes of the poems in a particularly helpful way, pointing out for example where CW is inventing, as when Britain is made a Byzantine province; and he explains the precise content CW is putting into traditional concepts: there is a useful discussion of Byzantium and Order. He takes the opportunity to comment on the map of the body which, though provided in the first edition of *Taliessin through*

Logres, was not explained. He completes his commentary on the poems up to the end of the first cycle, the precarious resting-place of 'The Crowning of Arthur'.

In the third chapter CSL comments on the poems between the crowning of Arthur and Palomides' Quest. Two important concepts are introduced: CW's doctrine of love, and his doctrine of exchange*, or substitution*. Palomides comes out of Islam, and CSL shows how strong is CW's criticism, based chiefly on Islam's rejection of the incarnation. Palomides' quest for Iseult and his journey to Britain is characterized as 'a Beatrician experience gone wrong', and a vision that transmutes into the search for the Questing Beast, romantic love turned into frustrated jealousy.

CSL's analysis continues in chapter 4, 'The Beginning of Separations', starting with the story of Lamorack and Morgause, Arthur's half-sister with whom he has unwittingly committed incest, and is pregnant with Mordred, Arthur's doom. This episode, like the slaying of Balan by Balin, 'shares ... the dishonour of having frustrated the whole design of Logres and foiled the work of the Grail'. CSL applies the legends to the Christian doctrine of the fall of humanity. He shows that the great events that will destroy the Grail-quest have repercussions in the everyday life of the kingdom and the Empire; and out of that disorder, the Companions of the Household of Taliessin emerge. CSL is frank about the difficulty of some of these poems, acknowledging that he has not yet 'mastered' all their meanings. The implications of the fractured task continue to reverberate in every aspect of the poems, not least in the portrayal of Guinevere. The poems in this section culminate in Taliessin's finalizing of his vocation and the developing, imminent catastrophe that will strike the Round Table.

In the fifth section, 'The Grail and the Morte', CSL begins by identifying 'The Son of Lancelot' as the turning-point of the whole cycle. Lancelot, deceived by magic, has slept with Elayne, daughter of Pelles, because she looks to him like Guinevere. It happens in Carbonek, which means that Lancelot has travelled through Broceliande, but has clearly missed that 'certain part' that leads to Sarras. He becomes a werewolf, and takes on the aspect of P'o-Lu – 'he grew Backward all summer'.

The die firmly cast now for the failure of Taliessin's task, CSL explains how the various disruptive and chaotic strands in the poems – Palomides, Lancelot, and others – are both the cause and the antidote of catastrophe. He makes clear CW's orthodoxy – 'God and his service must fill the whole of life' – but shows how 'the distance from the Antipodes is no greater, in Grace, than from, say, Camelot'.

Galahad, in the end, achieves the Grail; Merlin 'fades away into the forest dim'; Palomides makes a good end. But it is Galahad who enters the holy castle, heals the wounded king, and achieves the Grail. CSL's commentary on these poems is as much CSL as CW. His account of the doom of Logres and the emergence of Co-inherence* as 'the one grand secret', as the apparently disbanded Company continues in 'little groups or pairs of those who still follow the Way of Exchange', has much in common with CSL's other writings.

In the last chapter, CSL presents his own apologia for the poems, demonstrating that their obscurity is a valid obscurity that justifies the effort expended in reading and understanding them. But really he has justified them in the preceding chapters, by (a) showing that these colourful and sometimes dazzlingly strange poems are in fact expressions of biblical orthodoxy; (b) demonstrating that the central 'message' of the cycle is that even in collapse of empires, there will always survive a remnant; and (c) identifying the implicit theological discourse of the poems on matters such as incarnation and love.

Aslan

CSL's invented world of Narnia* contains many talking lions, the kings of beasts, but Aslan is not only this, but also the creator and ultimate sovereign of the land. His father is the Emperor-over-sea, dwelling beyond the Eastern Ocean, past Aslan's Country and the World's End. Aslan (Turkish for 'lion') is intended to be a symbol of Christ, Christ not as he appeared and will appear in our world (as a real man), but as he appears in Narnia (as a 'real' Narnian talking lion). The symbol of the lion (a traditional image of authority) perhaps owes something to CSL's friend CW's novel *The Place of the Lion**.
See also CHAPTERS 3 AND 6

Auden, W.H. (1907–73)

A major figure in Anglo-American poetry, and a literary critic, W.H. Auden was born in Britain and later became a US citizen. Like JRRT, his family took him to Birmingham as an infant. He went up to Oxford in 1925, the year JRRT moved there from Leeds to become Professor of Anglo-Saxon. His tutor was Nevill Coghill*. As an undergraduate, Auden developed a particular liking for Old English literature. Like JRRT, he had a deep interest in Norse mythology. Like CSL, he was a late convert to Christianity: he acknowledged the influence of CW's *The Descent of the Dove* in his conversion. He had met CW in connection with the *Oxford Book of Light Verse* (CW recommended Auden as editor); Auden met him only once more. He wrote of their meeting, 'For the first time in my life [I] felt myself in the presence of personal sanctity.'

Auden referred to the effect that JRRT had on him during his inaugural lecture, delivered as Professor of Poetry before the University of Oxford on 11 June 1956:

> I remember [a lecture] I attended, delivered by Professor Tolkien. I do not remember a single word he said but at a certain point he recited, and magnificently, a long passage of Beowulf. I was spellbound. This poetry, I knew was going to be my dish. I became willing, therefore, to work at Anglo-Saxon because, unless I did, I should never be able to read this poetry. I learned enough to read it, however sloppily, and Anglo-Saxon and Middle English poetry have been one of my strongest, most lasting influences.

JRRT was greatly encouraged by Auden's enthusiasm for *The Lord of the Rings*. He wrote on the quest* hero in JRRT's work, and corresponded and discussed with him about the meaning of his work (*see* THE LETTERS OF JRRT).

His reviews counteracted some of the negative criticism of the trilogy. In Humphrey Carpenter's biography of Auden there is reproduced a photograph of him absorbed in reading *The Hobbit**, taken in the 1940s. In 1965 Auden intended to collaborate with the writer Peter Salus on a short book on JRRT in the Christian Perspectives series. He failed however to gain JRRT's approval for such a project and, so, unfortunately, it was dropped.

FURTHER READING

W.H. Auden, *Secondary Worlds* (Faber, 1968)
Humphrey Carpenter, *W.H. Auden: A Biography* (Allen and Unwin, 1981)
Neil D. Isaacs and Rose A. Zimbardo (eds), *Tolkien and the Critics* (University of Notre Dame Press, 1968)

Bacon, A Myth of (CW, c.1930)

See MYTH OF [FRANCIS] BACON, A (c.1930)

Baker, Leo Kingsley (1898–1986)

A contemporary and friend of CSL, Leo Baker was a fighter pilot with the RFC (RAF) during the First World War. He was awarded the Distinguished Flying Cross after being severely wounded in August 1918. The following year he returned to Oxford as an undergraduate, and introduced OB* to CSL. Leo Baker was a frequent visitor to the CSL–Mrs Moore household, as recorded in CSL's *All My Road Before Me*.

After graduation he became an actor, a profession he eventually had to give up because of his war wounds. He and his wife set up a weaving business in Chipping Campden. During the Second World War he taught in a Rudolf Steiner* School in Gloucester. After this he became Drama Advisor for the Regional Authority in various senior roles. The Bodleian Library, Oxford, houses CSL's letters to him.

Barfield, Owen (1898–1997)

A core member of the Inklings, OB was a child of 'more or less agnostic' parents, one a London solicitor, the other a suffragette. They had been brought up Congregationalists, but abandoned any church participation. They retained a deep respect for Christianity, and for the person of Jesus Christ. OB was born in Muswell Hill, London, in 1898, and lived there until he was six or seven. He had two sisters and a brother. His mother was musical, and also taught him to read. Just before he was eight he went to preparatory school in nearby Highgate. Then he proceeded to upper school in Highgate until he was 17. At school he was keen on gymnastics. In the spring of 1917 he was called up to the army; he was then 18.

He served with the Royal Engineers, and joined the Signal Service. In the wireless department he studied the theory of electricity. He had already learned Morse code from his elder brother. While he was still training the armistice was signed, so he had no combat experience at all, though he was sent to Belgium. There he had very little to do, as pigeons were still used for communications. He had already won a scholarship to Oxford*. He did not get up to Oxford until October 1919. He studied at Wadham College, reading English, and attempted some of his own writing. At Oxford he formed a lifelong friendship with CSL*, and also later became an anthroposophist*, an advocate of the religious school of thought developed by Rudolf Steiner.

While an undergraduate OB experienced what has aptly been described as an 'intellectual epiphany' (*New York Times* Obituary, 19 December 1997) while studying the Romantic poets. As with JRRT, his main intellectual stimulus came from language. OB recalled in 1966: 'What impressed me particularly was the power with which not so much whole poems as particular combinations of words worked on my mind. It seemed like there was some magic in it; and a magic which not only gave me pleasure but also reacted on and expanded the meanings of the individual words concerned' (*New York Times* Obituary). Language, he believed, had the power to transform human consciousness and to embody historic changes in this consciousness.

He married Maud Douie soon after graduation, in 1923. Like him, she danced, and he met her at the English Folk Dance Society. She was looking for a male dancer for a concert party around Cornish Villages. She was 13 years older than him. (She died in 1983, almost making her century.) His wife came into a little money, and for several years he was a freelance writer,

B

doing various odd jobs to supplement his income. He started writing poetry while at high school.

After graduation he began a B.Litt., the thesis of which became his book *Poetic Diction** (1928). In 1925 he published a children's book, *The Silver Trumpet**, which later was a success in the JRRT household. In 1926 his study, *History in English Words**, appeared. *Poetic Diction* deeply influenced CSL and JRRT, and thus the central preoccupations of the Inklings. It was in the Autumn term of 1919 that OB met CSL, when they were both undergraduates. A college friend, Leo Baker*, introduced him to CSL, and he had tea in his rooms. They would walk together or ask each other to lunch, but did not really see a lot of each other until after graduation, when the 'great war' started between them.

OB and his wife lived for a time near Oxford in the Buckinghamshire village of Long Crendon, making it easy for he and CSL to see each other. Also they carried on an extensive correspondence (through which much of the battle was fought). It was between graduation and his move back to London that OB saw most of CSL.

In 1929 he settled in London, to train in his father's firm of solicitors. He attended Inklings meetings a dozen or more times. He would visit Oxford once a term, and this sometimes coincided with an Inklings meeting. He always saw himself as a fringe member. About 1930 he had finished his 'metaphysical argument' with CSL, the 'great war'. This roughly coincided with the process of CSL's conversion to Christianity. After the 'war' he had jokingly said to CSL that while CSL had taught him to think, he had taught CSL what to think. CSL undoubtedly forced him to think systematically and accurately, passing on hard-won skills he had acquired from his tutorage under W.T. Kirkpatrick*. He in his turn helped CSL to think imaginatively more; to combine his imagination with his formidable intellect. This was a 'slow business' however, according to OB.

Maud Barfield, his wife, was an Anglican, and somewhat antipathetic to Steiner and anthroposophism. She gradually modified her resistance, and he in turn became an Anglican in 1950, but was embarrassed by CSL's 'fundamentalism'. Christianity for him meant the 'working of the Logos in human destiny and human life'. Like Rudolf Steiner, he became convinced that the incarnation, life and death of Christ was at the centre of the 'evolution of consciousness'*. Also like Steiner, he believed in reincarnation. He had encountered the writings of Steiner, and anthroposophism, as early as 1922. OB was influenced by Steiner, the Romantic poets and writers, (particularly Coleridge*), and also the poet and philosopher Novalis. He appreciated George MacDonald*, who was also indebted to Novalis. OB had no children of his own, but he and Maud adopted two children, and fostered a third. The daughter, Lucy (to whom *The Lion, the Witch and the Wardrobe* is dedicated) had multiple schlerosis.

During his early years as a solicitor – 1929 to 1934 – he contributed essays, poems and reviews, mostly in anthroposophical journals. There was then a quiet period until a collection of essays, *Romanticism Comes of Age*, was published in 1944. At the Little Theatre, Sheffield, his poetic drama *Orpheus** was performed in 1948. An autobiographical novel appeared in 1950, entitled *This Ever Diverse Pair**, under the pseudonym G.A.L. Burgeon. OB continued to write essays. A major statement of his philosophy, as significant as *Poetic Diction*, came out in 1957, called *Saving the Appearances: A Study in Idolatry**, concerned with the implications of a scientific perception of reality upon ordinary human consciousness.

Two years later OB retired from his legal profession and his writing output significantly increased, including *Worlds Apart* (1963), *Unancestral Voice* (1965), *Speaker's Meaning* (1967), *What Coleridge Thought* (1971), *The Rediscovery of Meaning* (1977), *History, Guilt and Habit** (1979) and *Owen Barfield on C.S. Lewis* (1990). In 1994 *A Barfield Sampler* was published. His reputation steadily grew in the American academic world, and he gave a number of lectures there. He was for many years CSL's literary executor, soon joined by Walter Hooper. When he originally started advising CSL legally, he saved him from a major catastrophe over his income tax, an episode captured in a chapter in *This Ever Diverse Pair* (1950).

CSL's debt to OB was enormous. He paid tribute to him in *Surprised by Joy** and earlier in *An Allegory of Love** ('the wisest and best of my unofficial teachers'). JRRT too was shaken to his roots by OB's insights in *Poetic Diction*. More recently OB has been appreciated as a leading twentieth-century thinker by figures as diverse as Saul Bellow, Theodore Roszak, G.B. Tennyson and Norman O. Brown. He outlived CSL by 34 years and JRRT by 24, dying peacefully on 14 December 1997, in Forest Row, East Sussex.

FURTHER READING

Lionel Adey, *C.S. Lewis's 'Great War' with Owen Barfield* (1978)
Owen Barfield (Edited by G.B. Tennyson)
Owen Barfield on C.S. Lewis (1989)

Bennett, J.A.W. (1911–81)

A New Zealander, Inkling, and colleague of CSL's at Magdalen College, Oxford, from 1947. In 1964 he took on CSL's post as Professor of Medieval and Renaissance Literature at Cambridge. His inaugural lecture was devoted to the subject of CSL, entitled 'The Humane Medievalist' (1965).

B

'Beowulf: The Monsters and the Critics' (JRRT, 1936)

Like JRRT's essay, 'On Fairy Stories'*, this lecture provides an important key to his work both as a scholar and a writer of fiction. *Beowulf* is one of the earliest works of English literature, and one of the greatest. In his lecture, the professor expresses dissatisfaction with existing Beowulf criticism. In fact, it had not been criticism proper, he complains, as it had not been directed to an understanding of the poem as a poem, as a unified work of art. Rather, it had been seen as a quarry for historical data about its period. In particular, the two monsters which dominate it – Grendel and the dragon* – had not been sufficiently considered as the centre and focus of the poem. JRRT argues that what he called the 'structure and conduct' of the poem arose from this central theme of monsters.

JRRT's approach to literature here resembles that of his friend, CSL, who argued for an intrinsic rather than extrinsic concern with works of poetry and fiction, notably in his book, *The Personal Heresy** (1939), co-written with E.M.W. Tillyard, who took a somewhat contrary position. In a literary study of *Beowulf*, JRRT argues, we must deal with a native English poem that is using in a fresh way ancient and mostly traditional material. The important question is not the poet's sources, but what he did with them.

What JRRT then goes on to say is strikingly true of his own stories: 'The significance of myth is not easily to be pinned on paper by analytical reasoning. It is at its best when it is presented by a poet who feels rather than makes explicit what his theme portends; who presents it incarnate in the world of history and geography, as our [*Beowulf*] poet has done.'

JRRT points out the danger and difficulty of accounting for the mythical mode of imagination* in a work like *Beowulf*. 'Its defender is thus at a disadvantage: unless he is careful, and speaks in parables, he will kill what he is studying by vivisection, and he will be left with a formal or mechanical allegory, and, what is more, probably one that will not work. For myth is alive at once and in all its parts, and dies before it can be dissected. It is possible, I think, to be moved by the power of myth and yet to misunderstand the sensation, to ascribe it wholly to something else that is also present: to metrical art, style, or verbal skill.' Myth is extra-literary, as was argued by CSL in *An Experiment in Criticism* 25 years later.

The question of the power of evil*, the question of Job, is central. *Beowulf* 'moves in a northern heroic age imagined by a Christian, and therefore has a noble and gentle quality, though conceived to be a pagan.' In *Beowulf* there is a fusion of the Christian and the ancient north, the old and the new.

The *Beowulf* poet indicates the good that may be found in the pagan imagination, a theme powerfully explored by CSL in *Till We Have Faces**. In holding such a view, CSL was heavily influenced by JRRT (*see* MYTHOPOEIA).

JRRT's conclusion is that 'In *Beowulf* we have, then, an historical poem about the pagan past, or an attempt at one . . . It is a poem by a learned man writing of old times, who looking back on the heroism and sorrow feels in them something permanent and something symbolical. So far from being a confused semi-pagan – historically unlikely for a man of this sort in the period – he brought probably first to his task a knowledge of Christian poetry'.

There are a number of parallels between the author of *Beowulf*, as understood by JRRT, and JRRT himself. JRRT is a Christian scholar looking back to an imagined Northern European past. The *Beowulf* author was a Christian looking to the imaginative resources of a pagan past. Both made use of dragons and other potent symbols, symbols which unified their work. Both are concerned more with symbolism than allegory. As with the *Beowulf* author, what is important is not so much the sources but what JRRT did with them. Like the ancient author, also, JRRT at his most successful created an illusion of history and a sense of depths of the past.

Beren and Lúthien the Elf-maiden, The Tale of (JRRT)

This is one of the greatest stories of *The Silmarillion**, like *The Lord of the Rings**, a heroic romance, though on a smaller scale. JRRT himself, in a long letter (letter 131), reveals that it is 'the chief of the stories of the Silmarillion, and the one most fully treated'. There are both poetic and prose versions, though none of the poetic versions is complete. The story has great beauty in itself, but much of the unfinished poetry is outstanding, found in *The Lays of Beleriand*. The story had a personal meaning for JRRT, also, as Beren and Lúthien were pet names for himself and his wife, Edith. The conception of the story was tied up with an incident where the two of them had wandered in a small wood in Roos, north of the Humber estuary. There, among hemlock, she danced and sang to him. Beren, in the story, encounters Lúthien dancing among hemlock in the woods of Neldoreth. For both Beren and JRRT it was a time of memories of danger: JRRT was on leave from the battles of the First World War. When Edith died in 1971 he included 'Lúthien' on her gravestone.

The tale of Beren and Lúthien belongs to the history of Beleriand, during the First Age of Middle-earth*. Lúthien was an elven princess, the daughter of King Thingol, ruler of Doriath, and Queen Melian, and thus immortal. Beren was a mortal man, the son of the heroic Barahir.

Many of JRRT's characteristic themes emerge in this story, including healing* and sacrifice, evil*, death and immortality, and romantic love*. The motif of the Silmarils is a unifying thread of the stories of the First Age, part of the greater motif of light and darkness. Another unifying feature is the shadow of Morgoth, and his lieutenant Sauron. Through the marriage of

Beren and Lúthien, the elvish quality was preserved in mortals in future generations – even into the Fourth Age when they became ascendant, and the elves waned.

In the tales of sorrow and of ruin of that period, when Morgoth and Sauron achieved such wickedness, the story of Beren and Lúthien brought hope and consolation both to elves and to those humans who were faithful against the darkness.

The writer of *The Silmarillion* observes of Lúthien, who had beauty of both spirit and form: 'In her choice the Two Kindreds have been joined; and she is the forerunner of many in whom the Eldar see yet, though all the world is changed, the likeness of Lúthien the beloved, whom they have lost.'

JRRT, in the same letter mentioned above, points to its theme of apparent foolishness. He comments:

> Here we meet . . . the first example of the motive (to become dominant in Hobbits) that the great policies of world history, 'the wheels of the world', are often turned not by the Lords and Governors, even gods, but by the seemingly unknown and weak – owing to the secret life in creation, and the part unknowable to all wisdom but One, that resides in the intrusions of the Children of God into the Drama. It is Beren the outlawed mortal who succeeds (with the help of Lúthien, a mere maiden even if an elf of royalty) where all the armies and warriors have failed (letter 131).

Beta thinking

This was OB's invented term for the kind of thinking we do when we consciously consider our collective representations. These are representations of any kind of fact, such as physical objects, other people, or even God. This kind of thinking is artificial, rather than 'natural', in the sense that we construct such thoughts – they are artifacts, and we know they are artifacts. In beta thinking, we are thinking about thinking. 'Natural' thinking would be 'unreflective' thinking. 'Alpha thinking'* is also distinct from beta thinking, in that the former chooses to ignore the necessary relation between our collective representations and our minds, which can lead to idolatry*.

A common mistake, influenced by beta thinking, is to suppose that very much of what is represented lies with ourselves, because of the dependence of such representations upon our minds.

Betjeman, Sir John (1906–84)

CSL was Betjeman's tutor in English language and literature, a period in which antipathy grew between the two, expressed at times in the latter's poetry. CSL was impatient over Betjeman's reluctance to work, while the poet blamed CSL for his leaving Oxford without a degree. Many years later the two were reconciled and became friends. Sir John was chosen as Poet Laureate in 1972.

Biographies by Charles Williams

Considered by T.S. Eliot as books that tell us very little about the author, the biographies do in fact belong firmly in the CW corpus. Alice Hadfield has pointed out that several of them fall within the Elizabethan period, which was an especially congenial field of study for him. All are marked by his ability to identify movements and ideas, while presenting authentic and vivid portraits of individuals. The biographies are: *Bacon* (1933), 'Lord Macaulay' in *Six Short Biographies*, ed. R.C. and N. Goffin (1933), *James I* (1934), *Henry VII** (1935), *Rochester** (1935), *Queen Elizabeth** (1936), *Stories of Great Names* (1937), 'Queen Victoria' * in *More Short Biographies*, eds R.C. and N. Goffin (1938), *Flecker of Dean Close** (1946). *Bacon, James I, Henry VII* and *Rochester* were commissioned by Arthur Barker, and *Elizabeth* by Duckworth. The biographies were popular with the public and some (e.g. *James I* and *Rochester*, the latter having given him considerable difficulty in writing) were highly praised by critics.

Bird and Baby

See EAGLE AND CHILD, THE

Birmingham

A major city in England which, along with the West Midlands, JRRT regarded as home. When his father, Arthur Tolkien, died in 1896, the family settled at Sarehole Mill, then outside the city boundary. JRRT attended King Edward's School, then located near the city centre. JRRT was part of a schoolboy club which would meet at the tea room in Barrow's Stores in Corporation Street.

Black Bastard, The (CW)

See SHADOWS OF ECSTASY (1933), of which this was a late-1920s draft version.

Body, Index of the

See CHAPTER 5

Book of Lost Tales, The, 1 and 2 (JRRT, 1983, 1984)

These make up the first two volumes of *The History of Middle-earth**, a collection of early or unfinished pieces edited by JRRT's son, Christopher Tolkien*. Explanatory commentaries are added.

The Book of Lost Tales represents JRRT's first major imaginative work.

He began it during the First World War, and abandoned it several years afterwards.

The first volume contains narratives relating to Valinor, the Undying Lands to the uttermost west of Middle-earth. The second is made up of stories set in Beleriand in the First Age. *The Book of Lost Tales* is the first form of the 'Quenta Silmarillion', the Silmarillion proper which only consitutes part of the published book, *The Silmarillion**.

A striking feature of *The Book of Lost Tales* is JRRT's attempt to put *The Silmarillion* into an accessible narrative framework. It concerns Aelfwine (or Eriol) who, by chance, sails to Tol Eressëa, an elvish island close by the coast of Valinor. There, in a Warwickshire-like setting, he discovers the Cottage of Lost Play. Here is narrated to him the tales of the creation of the world, Morgoth's destruction of the light of the Two Trees of Valinor, and other stories of *The Silmarillion*. There are significant differences of detail from the final form of the stories, but they are clearly recognizable. In *The Book of Lost Tales* are the only full narratives of the Necklace of the Dwarves and the Fall of Gondolin. The second volume contains the history of Aelfwine, a narrative picked up in 'The Lost Road'*.

Boxen

An imaginary kingdom created by CSL as a young child, in collaboration with his brother, W.H. (Warnie) Lewis*. The stories have been collected and edited by Walter Hooper into a book of the same name (1985). In his autobiography, *Surprised by Joy**, CSL describes the origin of Boxen. The first stories were written, and illustrated, 'to combine my two chief literary pleasures – "dressed animals" and "knights-in-armour". As a result, I wrote about chivalrous mice and rabbits who rode out in complete mail to kill not giants but cats.' In creating an environment for the tales, a medieval Animal-Land was born. In order to include Warnie in its creation and shaping, features of the modern world like trains and steamships had to be included. Thus a history had to be created, and so on.

Buchan, John (1875–1940)

The novelist John Buchan, first Baron Tweedsmuir, was a contemporary of CW and was like him widely read in the occult, as can be seen for example in his novels *Witchwood* (1927) and his short story 'The Wind in the Portico' (*The Runagates Club*, 1928). In his character Medina in *The Three Hostages* (1924) Buchan creates a character very like those in CW's novels: knowledgeable in the occult and arcane, willing to use his knowledge in order to gain power, and ultimately destroyed by the reality of the corporeal world (losing a battle of wits in the Scottish glens between himself and the bluff, practical soldier Richard Hannay – though the choice of escape and redemption remains to the very end) and the spiritual force of simple goodness represented by a woman (in his final confrontation with Hannay's wife Mary). In *Greenmantle* (1916), the concept of an Islamic messianic deliverer is the core of the plot and, as in CW's *Arthuriana*, the worlds of Christendom and Islam are the landscape of the novel.

Buchan's *Prester John* (1910) features a legendary character of the same name as the character in CW's *War in Heaven**, but a different tradition is involved and the context is South African.

Byzantium

Occupying part of the site of modern Istanbul, Byzantium was a major port and trade centre of antiquity, fought over in many wars. The emperor Constantine (the first Christian emperor) rebuilt the ancient city and made it his new capital in AD330, naming it Constantinople after himself. It was the capital city of the Byzantine empire – the eastern part of the Roman empire – and after the fall of the western empire in the fifth century AD it became the chief city of the Roman empire until it was conquered by the Turks in 1453. Over the centuries Byzantine culture developed as a blend of Roman, Christian and Greek culture. In the ninth century there was a revival of Byzantine culture, resulting in great prosperity, increased trade, world influence, and a rebirth of learning coupled with a return to classical styles.

By the eleventh century the Byzantine empire was under continuous threat from the Turks, and the Schism of 1054 had brought separation between the papacy and the Orthodox Church. The West's first crusade of 1096–99 against the Turks helped Byzantium, but by changing the balance of power in the region, the crusades weakened the city in the long term. In 1204 the crusaders took advantage of a weakened Byzantium to set up a Latin empire of Constantinople. In the fourteenth century the Ottoman Turks conquered what was left of Byzantine Asia Minor, eventually taking Constantinople in 1453. It had a population of 1 million and at that time was the greatest city of medieval Christendom.

CW uses Byzantium and its emperor as a metaphor for the perfect Christian city/state. In the Arthurian poems, the empire is defined by its antitheses, Islam* and the antipodean empire of P'o-Lu. It is to Byzantium that Taliessin is sent in *Taliessin through Logres*, returning with the mission to establish in Arthur's Logres* the model of Christian order he found there. He makes use of the fiction that Britain is a province of the Byzantine empire (helped by the historical fact that the Byzantine empire took over the old western, Roman empire and later embraced old Latin cultural and intellectual models). The historical struggles between Islam and Byzantium become, in CW's cycle of poems, metaphors for the spiritual conflicts of the cosmos of the poems.

An interesting footnote to CW's use of the image of Byzantium is that through his membership of the Order of the Golden Dawn* he knew W.B. Yeats – in whose poetry Byzantium was a potent image indeed, representing the undying world of art. A quotation from Yeats is printed at the beginning of CW's *The Silver Stair**.

See also CHAPTER 5; ARTHURIAN MYTH; *ARTHURIAN TORSO*

Campbell, Roy (1902–57)

A South African poet who briefly encountered the Inklings in October 1944. JRRT noticed him, a little like Strider, in the Eagle and Child* pub, and he was invited to an Inklings. Though CSL was uneasy about his pro-Franco ideals (CSL regarded communism and fascism as equal evils), it must be noted that Campbell served the anti-fascist cause in the war years.

Canterbury Festivals

In the English church, the prohibition against acting in churches which had survived from the time of Oliver Cromwell was lifted when George Bell, Dean of Canterbury and later Bishop of Chichester and President of the Religious Drama Society, launched the Canterbury Festivals in 1928. Productions included plays by John Masefield, T.S. Eliot* (*Murder in the Cathedral*, 1935), CW* (*Thomas Cranmer of Canterbury*, 1936) and Dorothy L. Sayers* (*The Zeal of Thy House*, 1937). It was partly as a result of the latter that the BBC commissioned Sayers to write the radio plays *Man Born to Be King* (first transmitted 1941–2), which controversially broke precedent by use of naturalistic dialogue and a determined rejection of stained-glass characterization. CW first came to Bell's attention when he was editing the bishop's biography of Randall Davidson, Archbishop of Canterbury (1935), though the suggestion that CW should write the play to follow T.S. Eliot's came from E. Martin Browne. Browne, a leader of the Religious Drama Society, first encountered CW when the latter was lecturing on Milton and was deeply impressed.

Cecil, Lord David (1902–86)

David Cecil taught English literature and modern history as a fellow at Wadham College, Oxford*, before becoming a fellow of English at New College. In 1948 he took on the new Goldsmith's Chair of English Literature. He was a member of the Inklings and author of many books, including *Poets* *and Storytellers* (1949), *Visionary and Dreamer: Two Poetic Painters – Samuel Palmer and Edward Burne-Jones* (1969) and *A Portrait of Jane Austen* (1978).

FURTHER READING

Hannah Cranborne (ed), *David Cecil: A Portrait by His Friends* (Stanbridge, England: Dovecote Press, 1991)

David Cecil, *The Cecils of Hatfield House* (Constable, 1973).

'Celia'

See JONES, PHYLLIS

Chesterton, Gilbert Keith (1874–1936)

A celebrated convert to Christianity who particularly influenced CSL's thinking. He wrote, like CSL, in ebullient defence of Christian faith and fantasy. An essayist, critic, novelist and poet, his best-known writings include *The Everlasting Man, Orthodoxy*, the Father Brown stories, *The Man Who Was Thursday, The Napoleon of Notting Hill*, and biographies of Robert Browning and others. Typical of his astuteness as a critic is his comment on George MacDonald* in his *The Victorian Age in Literature*: 'a Scot of genius as genuine as Carlyle's; he could write fairy-tales that made all experience a fairy-tale. He could give the real sense that every one had the end of an elfin thread that must at last lead them into Paradise. It was a sort of optimist Calvinism.'

Christendom

The concept of Christendom as a spiritual map of the visible church runs through the work of CW, who wanted to call *The Descent of the Dove** 'A Short History of Christendom'.

Christian fantasy

Colin Manlove defines Christian fantasy as 'a fiction dealing with the Christian supernatural, often in an imaginary world'. We would widen this definition slightly, for the supernaturalism may not be obvious at first. It is likely to be evidenced in a sense of the other, otherness, arresting strangeness and wonder.

What is striking is that for nearly 2,000 years, when Christianity was dominant in western thinking and imagination*, there is so little Christian fantasy in literature, so little exploration of heaven, the afterlife and the supernatural. In the Bible itself there are elements similar to fantasy, as in it is an integrated picture of both the seen and the unseen world. There are visions of heaven and God, talking snakes and asses, and dragons. Colin Manlove picks out what he sees as the key works of Christian fantasy, many by British authors.

These include the thirteenth-century French *La Queste del Saint Graal*; Dante's great narrative poem *The Divine Comedy* in the fourteenth century; the poignant Middle-English poem, *Pearl*, much loved by JRRT; Spenser's *The Faerie Queene*, Book 1; Marlowe's *Dr Faustus*; some of the work of the seventeenth-century metaphysical poets such as John Donne and Henry Vaughan; John Milton's epic poem, *Paradise Lost*; Bunyan's seminal allegory, *The Pilgrim's Progress*; and fantasies of George MacDonald, CSL and CW. With our wider definition we would add to this mainstream the Old-English poem, *Beowulf*, which so inspired JRRT; and the work of JRRT himself.

Colin Manlove points out a sharp change in twentieth-century Christian fantasy, with the decline of a supporting belief in the Christian supernatural in the culture at large. Christian fantasy has put a greater stress on inventiveness, and has a strongly apologetic role, that is, presenting the case for a Christian vision of reality.

With the lack of a general support for Christian belief in society at large, Colin Manlove suggests, the impulse behind Christian fantasy has dispersed. There are now alternative transcendent fantasies, some gnostic and most in science fiction, and some both gnostic and science fiction.

This observation of Manlove's is astute. CSL constantly argued with his gnostic friend, OB, one of the Inklings, on the deepest of philosophical subjects. OB followed Rudolf Steiner, who tried to make a synthesis of Christianity and gnostic thought. CSL, like his friend JRRT, explored pre-Christian paganism, seeing how far its imaginative insights pointed to the truth of Christianity.

CW explored the black spirituality of the occult in his thoroughly Christian novels. CSL made a dramatic impact on science-fiction writing with his trilogy beginning with *Out of the Silent Planet*, as he sought to redeem the genre. JRRT avidly read science fiction, and science-fiction authors were discussed by the Inklings.

Colin Manlove isolates three straightforwardly Christian fantasists in this century – CW, T.F. Powys (who wrote *Mr Weston's Good Wine*), and CSL. Our broader definition would include JRRT.

According to Colin Manlove, there exists a more dispersed, less Christian fantasy. It is widespread and carried by the same impulse; and some of it is avowedly agnostic. The gnostic includes the late science-fiction writings of Philip K. Dick and, notably, David Lindsay, whose *Voyage to Arcturus* had a dramatic impact on the imagination of CSL, for example, suggesting the idea of the floating islands which appear in his Perelandra. Manlove points out that there are some works of Christian science fiction, such as James Blish's *A Case of Conscience* (1958) and the science-fiction classic, Walter M. Miller Jr's *A Canticle for Leibowitz* (1960).

Professor Tom Shippey pointed out an important phenomenon. In a paper he gave at a conference on JRRT in Finland, he pointed out links between several apparently disparate writers just after the Second World War. The writers were linked in struggling with the appalling reality of evil in the modern world, a theme which forced them to create new forms and abandon the received canons of what constitutes a proper novel and fiction. The writers and their books are: William Golding's *The Lord of the Flies* (1954); JRRT's *The Lord of the Rings* (1954–55); CSL's *That Hideous Strength* (the final part of his science-fiction trilogy); George Orwell's *Animal Farm* (1945) and *Nineteen Eighty-Four* (1949); and T.H. White's *The Once and Future King* (published 1958 but written long before). Tom Shippey points out that 'they are all non-realistic works, whether one regards them as science fiction, fantasy, fable or parable (all descriptions which have been applied)'.

Christian Reflections (CSL, 1967)

Published after CSL's death, this collection of essays represents the breadth of his popular theology. One essay, 'Christianity and Literature'*, had previously appeared in *Rehabilitations and Other Essays**.

Christian Symbolism, ed. Michal Williams (1919)

A book compiled by CW's wife and to which he contributed some passages on emblem and symbol.

'Christianity and Literature' (CSL, 1939)

An essay which first appeared in *Rehabilitations and Other Essays**. It represents CSL's early thinking on the subject. For his fully developed views on the place of literature in human life, see his book, *An Experiment in Criticism** (1961).

Christian meanings in the fiction of JRRT

According to Paul Kocher, JRRT was inspired and guided on his way by the mythology of Denmark, Germany, Norway, and especially Iceland (*see* MYTH). The Norse pantheon of gods was headed by Odin. This is particularly clear as embodied in the Icelandic Elder Edda and Younger Edda, and the Icelandic sagas. As a Christian, JRRT rejected much of the Norse world outlook, but admired its imaginative power. Those elements that he could transform into Christian meaning, he kept. He attempted to portray a biblical vision of providence. This was a central theme of his fiction. Equally central was a passionate portrayal of free will, which also rejected fate.

JRRT sets *The Silmarillion** in a pre-Christian age (like the author of *Beowulf*, so it cannot express the full hope of Christianity, only prefigure it). According to Kocher, its theme is 'Morgoth's implanting of the seeds of evil in the hearts of Elves and Men, which will bear evil fruit until the last days'. In this outworking of the theme of evil*, Sauron plays a crucial role in the first three Ages of the world of Middle-earth*.

An important element in the embodiment of Christian meaning in JRRT's fiction comes from his theory of sub-creation*. *The Silmarillion, The Lord of the Rings**, and even *The Hobbit** are attempts at sub-creation, and as such try to 'survey the depths of space and time'. JRRT is particularly concerned with time, and Christian apocalyptic. That is, his theme is to reveal the essential meaning behind human history. Pre-eminently like the biblical book of Revelation, he is concerned to bring hope and consolation in dark and difficult days.

To appreciate the freshness and depth of Christian meaning in JRRT's work, he can be compared with John Milton, the author of the epic poem, *Paradise Lost*. It could be argued that the legacy of Milton's work is with us still, in science fiction and fantasy. There are important parallels between JRRT's fiction and Milton's great work – both are a study of evil, and a defence of God's ways to humanity. To JRRT, Morgoth, and his servant Sauron, are of central importance, as Satan is in *Paradise Lost*. The very title of JRRT's popular trilogy refers to Sauron, the dark lord of the Rings. As also in Milton's work, the theme of fall from grace (disgrace) and into sin or chosen wickedness predominates.

JRRT's thinking about an inevitable structure to the language of story is most clearly found in his essay, 'On Fairy Stories'*. Here he finds the attributes of escape, recovery and consolation. Consolation, particularly, is loaded with Christian meaning, focused on the *evangelium*. This structure of story is vindicated by the greatest story of all, told in the biblical Gospels. This has the story qualities of escape, recovery and consolation, yet is, astoundingly, true in the real world, in actual human history.

The inspiration for JRRT's fiction came from such Christian works of medieval English literature as *Beowulf* and *Christ*. One sentence in the latter, in particular, inspired the tale of Eärendil the mariner. The line was *Eala Earendel engla beorhtast ofer middengeard monnum sended*. Commenting on this sentence in a letter to Clyde S. Kilby, JRRT declared: 'These are Cynewulf's words from which ultimately sprang the whole of my mythology.' JRRT gave a literal translation of the line to Kilby: 'Here Eärendel, brightest of angels, sent from God to men.'

In a letter to W.H. Auden* (in 1965), JRRT commented on *The Lord of the Rings* in relation to Christian theology:

> I don't feel under any obligation to make my story fit with formalized Christian theology, though I actually intended it to be consonant with Christian thought and belief.

See also CHAPTER 6

FURTHER READING

Clyde S. Kilby, *Tolkien and The Silmarillion* (1976)
Paul H. Kocher, *A Reader's Guide to The Silmarillion* (1980)

Chronological snobbery

CSL believed that one of the strongest myths of our day is that of progress. Change is considered to have a value in itself. We are increasingly cut off from our past (and hence a proper perspective on the strengths and weaknesses of our own age). He expressed this concern with the myth of progress in his inaugural lecture at Cambridge University, 'De Descriptione Temporum'*. From his friend OB he gained the term 'chronological snobbery' to characterize this attitude. He explains this snobbery in *Surprised By Joy*:

> Owen Barfield . . . made short work of what I have called my 'chronological snobbery,' the uncritical acceptance of the intellectual climate common to our age and the assumption that whatever has gone out of date is on that account discredited. You must find out why it went out of date; was it ever refuted (and if so by whom, where and how conclusively) or did it merely die away as fashions do? If the latter, this tells us nothing about its truth or falsehood. From seeing this one passes to the realization that our age is also 'a period', and certainly has, like all periods, its own characteristic illusions. They are likeliest to lurk in those wide-spread assumptions which are so ingrained in the age that no one dares to attack or feels it necessary to defend them.

There are several instances where OB's idea is played out in CSL's *That Hideous Strength**. Arch modernist Wither of the NICE displays this snobbery when he pronounces about Merlin, the 'Great Atlantean':

> Certainly, one must not be – ah – narrow-minded. One can suppose that the Masters of that age were not quite so sharply divided from the common people as we are. All sorts of emotional and even instinctive, elements were perhaps still tolerated in the Great Atlantean which we have had to discard.

See also OLD WEST; *HISTORY, GUILT AND HABIT*

City

A major image in CW, being a physical demonstration of the Co-inherence. It is the culmination of *He Came down from Heaven** and *The Figure of Beatrice**; is prominent in most of his non-fiction writings; provides one of the chief images of the Arthurian poems*; was chosen as the title theme by Anne Ridler for her 1958 CW anthology *The Image of the City and Other Essays* (section 3 is called 'The City' and contains nine essays); and is significant in his literary criticism (e.g. 'The Image of the City in English Verse' [1940]). In *Taliessin through Logres**, for example, Bors contrasts the order of his household under Elayne's authority with the beginnings of disorder in London, and his forebodings are part of the beginnings of disintegration of the kingdom.

Besides his profound use of the city as image and symbol, CW also portrayed the city in his novels, creating a most striking portrait of the city seen through a pair of unusually spiritually perceptive eyes, very like William Blake's perceptions. There is the striking picture of London as seen by the dead in *All Hallows' Eve** and *Descent Into Hell**; a Chesterton-like picture of the city at war in *Shadows of Ecstasy**; the visionary vista of London dominated by principles and powers in *The Place of the Lion**; and much more.

He was a Londoner with a cockney accent (CSL) who devoted much of his time to the city, lecturing in the evening for the City Council and working in central London, only later in life moving out to Oxford.

City of London Literary Institute

See ADULT EDUCATION

Coghill, Nevill (1899–1980)

Professor of English Literature at Oxford* from 1957 to 1966, and a member of the Inklings. After serving in the First World War, he read English at Exeter College, Oxford, and in 1924 was elected a Fellow there. He was a friend of CSL's from undergraduate days, and like him hailed from Ireland. His Christianity influenced CSL as a young man. As an undergraduate attending the Essay Club at Exeter College, he heard JRRT read aloud 'The Fall of Gondolin'*, from *The Silmarillion**. He was also a member of the Kolbitar* reading club. Coghill was admired for his theatrical productions, and for his translation of Chaucer's *Canterbury Tales* into modern English couplets.

Co-inherence

For CW, a concept very close to those of substitution and Exchange. All life depends on mutual giving and receiving, ultimately derived from the Trinity and most powerfully displayed on the cross. This idea runs through all his writing; for example, in *The Greater Trumps**; and is explained in detail in an Appendix to *The Descent of the Dove**.

CW portrays the experience of being 'in love' as a kind of naive apprehension of Co-inherence, a heightened awareness of the interdependence and interconnectedness of all. In 1938 CW proposed the formation of an Order, a proposal set out in the Appendix to *The Descent of the Dove*, which is dedicated to 'The Companions of the Co-inherence'. The seven Statements of the Order declared Co-inherence to be a natural and supernatural matter, by nature Christian; cited such precepts as 'Am I my brother's keeper?' and 'Bear ye one another's burdens'; and invoked the atonement as 'the root of all'. The Companions in *Taliessin through Logres** are a picture of the Order.

Coleridge, Samuel Taylor (1772–1834)

An important figure in the Romantic movement, he was poet, critic and philosopher, much influenced by German Romanticism and philosophy. Coleridge had a profound influence upon OB, who wrote an important study. Like many of the Inklings, and George MacDonald*, Coleridge explored a Christian Romanticism.
See also CHAPTER 6

FURTHER READING

Owen Barfield, *What Coleridge Thought* (London: Oxford University Press, 1972).

Collects Composed for a Marriage (CW, 1938)

Included in Anne Ridler, *The Image of the City* (1958), these Collects blend the language of the Anglican Prayer Book with CW's own heightened vocabulary, and incorporate his characteristic concerns: 'Increase among us the knowledge of the exchanges of Thy love, and from the common agony of our lives redeem us to the universal joy of Thy only city'.

Collective representation

A term of OB's to describe 'the world we accept as real' (*Saving the Appearances*, p. 20), that is, the phenomena we all share and which have been represented through our active thinking. Like Coleridge* and Immanuel Kant, OB believed that our minds are active in the knowing process. In opposition to Kant, however, he believed that the imagination* has a central role in real knowledge of the world. OB's term deliberately plays with Jung's concept of the 'collective unconscious', in that our active knowledge of the phenomenal world is a sort of 'collective consciousness'.

Companions of the Co-inherence (CW)

See CO-INHERENCE

Consciousness, human

See EVOLUTION OF HUMAN CONSCIOUSNESS

Constantinople

See BYZANTIUM

Corpse, The (1926)

See WAR IN HEAVEN (1930)

Correspondences

A recurring theme in CW, this is a dominant theme in philosophy, theology and literature – for example, it appears in the concept of Platonic absolutes. It is important in *The Place of the Lion** and *The Greater Trumps**; the Index of the Body in the Arthurian poems* and elsewhere is also a development of the theme. The desire to find parallels between the natural and supernatural worlds, the physical and the spiritual, has preoccupied many writers including the seventeenth-century English Puritans such as John Flavel and the later Evangelicals such as William Cowper. For Wordsworth, correct apprehension of correspondences was a barometer of spiritual health (for example in the Alpine sequences of Book VI of *The Prelude*, 1805). The theme of correspondences has interested some contemporary writers includ-ing Norman MacCaig, *Tree of Strings* (1977). Among philosophers who have expounded the theme of correspondences is Emmanuel Swedenborg (1688–1772), for whom the physical world was merely a symbol of the spiritual. Swedenborg influenced William Blake, whom CW had read in his entirety and whom he quotes in chapter 7 of *The Forgiveness of Sins**.

A characteristic of CW's fiction is that a related kind of correspondence frequently appears – between a thing and its inversion. Thus the doppel-ganger* that stalks Pauline in *Descent Into Hell** corresponds to the Succubus in the same novel, which appears to enable Wentworth to possess Adela, albeit in appearance only. In *Shadows of Ecstasy** and *All Hallows' Eve**, Nigel Considine and Simon the Clerk respectively are explicitly portrayed as inversions of Christ. In *All Hallows' Eve*, CW – as he sometimes does – takes the inversion a stage deeper, when Lady Wallingford, assisting Simon with the voodoo doll that is his second attempt to kill Betty, accidentally stabs herself, thus taking on herself some of the pain destined for Betty; this is an inverted parallel to the act of Lester Furnival who earlier, in Simon's first attempt upon Betty, has taken upon herself the force of Simon's curse. To complete this system of inversions, the presiding image in both is, of course, the cross.*

Cross in CW, the

The defining point of human history is discussed specifically by CW and implicitly in his novels, by frequent crucifixion allusions and imagery (for example, in *Descent Into Hell**, Wentworth refers to Battle Hill as 'the place of a skull', and in the chapter 'Junction of Travellers', the Suicide finds his release through the charity of Pauline and Margaret Anstruther. The cross, an event fixed in history, is effective throughout all history: as CW expresses it in a beautiful sentence: 'The silence groaned . . . The groan was at once dereliction of power and creation of power. In it, far off, beyond vision in the depths of all the worlds, a god, unamenable to death, awhile endured and died.' (There is perhaps something of the same image in the Wood Between the Worlds in CSL's *The Magician's Nephew**, 1955, where Aslan is in effect present at every point in history.) In *All Hallows' Eve**, when Lester Furnival takes on herself the pain of the curse directed at Betty, CW uses strong imagery of the cross: 'She was leaning back on something, some frame which from her buttocks to her head supported her; indeed she could have believed, but she was not sure, that her arms, flung out on each side held on to a part of the frame, as along a beam of wood . . . She pressed herself against that sole support.'

CW's main short exposition of the cross is in an article contributed to the symposium, *What the Cross Means to Me* (1943), which addresses a matter of perennial concern to him; the fact that God maintains a creation that is suffering infinite pain, and chooses not to end it. It is at the cross, he suggests, that God becomes 'tolerable as well as credible', for he becomes helpless and submits to what is in fact the best that human justice can do: 'They chose the least imperfect good that they could see. And their choice crucified the Good.' God submitted to the pain that the world bears. He whose birth had caused the massacre of the innocents is the Innocent who dies on the cross. Justice is taking place in this unjust execution, and in submitting to it God has proved himself honourable. We no longer need to pretend to be naturally optimistic. Our rejoicing is in the context of a suffering that God has chosen to share. The paradox runs through the essay: 'The supreme error of earthly justice was the supreme assertion of the possibility of justice.'

In the 'sorrow and obscenity' of the cross, says CW, the physical body that was his means of union with matter was 'exposed to the complete contradiction of itself'. But it was the creator submitting to it. The resurrection, like the crucifixion, is an act of divine will, and Easter begins with Jesus' words, 'It is finished.' What was added to the incarnation by the cross was the divine substitution, the heart of God's justice. Through that sacrifice he made the ruined creation whole, not by healing it but by enabling it to grow. But the cross was a cost. 'Supernaturally He renewed our proper nature. By so doing, it is true, He redoubled, at least within the Church, our guilt and our distress.'

So CW concludes with the necessity of faith. We must bless the creation, we must 'repose in His blessing of Himself', just as in the Eucharist our ability to bless comes from him: 'Only Beatitude can properly bless, as only Love can love.' The cross restores relations with God. So a mutual exchange is made possible: pardon, says CW, is only half pardon unless desired. Yes, by his will God maintains us in our state of sin; but by his will he also enables us to know it, and to know what he offers.

The cross itself is then a necessity. It enables our experience of good to be alongside our experience of evil, though the experience of good is 'united with that other authority of the God who endured His own. It is the Christian religion that makes the Christian religion possible. Existence itself is Christian; Christianity itself is Christian. The two are one because He is, in every sense, life, and life is He.'

An extended treatment is found in *He Came down from Heaven**.

Crowley, Aleister (1875–1947)

Born Edward Alexander Crowley, Crowley became interested in the occult while at Cambridge. He was a member of the Order of the Golden Dawn* until expelled for extreme practices. He was proud of his self-imposed title 'The Great Beast' and liked to be called 'the wickedest man alive'. After leaving the Order of the Golden Dawn he founded his own order and attracted great notoriety with rumours of child sacrifice and other ceremonies. Those associated with him often met strange deaths, and his wife and child died tragically. Crowley was probably the inspiration for Montague James' story 'Casting the Runes' and for the character Simon the Clerk in *All Hallows' Eve**.

d'Ardenne, Simonne

A philologist who was a student of JRRT's in the 1930s, studying for an Oxford B.Litt. She was a Belgium graduate who eventually taught at the University of Liege. She and JRRT collaborated on several projects, including her edition of *The Life and Passion of St Juliene*. The advent of the Second World War interrupted their association, and they did little work together after the war though their friendship continued.

See also PHILOLOGY, JRRT AND

Dante Alighieri (1265–1321)

Dante, born of a wealthy Florentine family, first saw Beatrice Portiani, whom he was to love all his life, when he was nine. She was married very young to a Florentine nobleman and Dante himself married, but he never lost the ardent platonic love he felt for her even after she had died. He tells the story in *La Vita Nova* (The New Life), c.1292.

He left Florence in 1301 and never returned. In c.1307 he began the *Divina Commedia* (*Divine Comedy*), recording travels through Hell and Purgatory to Paradise, where his guide is Beatrice. He wrote other minor works but it is his two masterpieces that appealed to the Inklings, notably to CW, who wrote one of his finest books, *The Figure of Beatrice**, in 1943 and a pamphlet *Religion and Love in Dante** in 1941. Dorothy L. Sayers* was inspired to translate Dante after reading CW and corresponding and meeting with him. There are many references to Dante in the writings of CSL, for he was within CSL's area of literary expertise.

See also ROMANTIC LOVE

'Dark Tower' and Other Stories, The (CSL, 1977)

A collection of two unfinished narratives of CSL, and three short stories, two of which appeared in *The Magazine of Fantasy and Science Fiction*. One fragment, 'The Dark Tower', was apparently written after *Out of the Silent Planet** and before *Perelandra**, and is about time rather than space travel. It owes much to David Lindsay's* *A Voyage to Arcturus*. CSL abandoned it as unsatisfactory. The other fragment, 'After Ten Years', was unfinished because of illness and age, and perhaps his grief over the death of Joy Davidman Lewis*. It is a historical novel which shows the promise of his great novel, *Till We Have Faces**.

Davidman, Helen Joy

See LEWIS, HELEN JOY DAVIDMAN

'De Descriptione Temporum' (CSL, 1954)

This was CSL's inaugural lecture as Professor in the newly formed Chair of Medieval and Renaissance English Literature at the University of Cambridge. The lecture reveals his sympathies with an earlier age, even though he was ever concerned to communicate as a writer to a modern reader. CSL argued that he was a relic of Old Western Man, a museum piece, if you like; that even if one disagreed with his ideas, one must take account of them as being from a rare (and therefore valuable) specimen of an older world (*see* OLD WEST). There is a great divide between that world and our modern one, where the machine has been absorbed into our inner lives as an archetype. Just as new and better machines replace older ones, so too (believes the modern) do superior ideas, beliefs and values (*see* CHRONOLOGICAL SNOBBERY). The modern world is post-pagan and post-Christian, Lewis believed, and carries an agenda which might well abolish humanity (*see* ABOLITION OF MAN, THE).

See also HISTORY, GUILT AND HABIT

Death

Death is an important theme in George MacDonald*, CW and CSL. But it is particularly important to the writings of JRRT. JRRT commented, in his essay on fairy stories, that 'Death is the theme that most inspired George MacDonald'. Like MacDonald, none of the Inklings presumed to be presenting esoteric knowledge about death and the afterlife, but remained within the orbit of orthodox Judeo-Christian teachings, with the exception of OB. OB adhered to the gnostic doctrines of Rudolf Steiner and anthroposophism*, which claimed special enlightenment.

Death is a theme that greatly inspired JRRT, and is central to his mythology of Middle-earth*. Centrally, JRRT saw 'mortality' as a special gift of God to human beings. The immortal elves have certain aspects of human beings, as well as the freedoms and powers humans desire. JRRT's invention of a mortality–immortality contrast opens up all kinds of imaginative possibilities, for example, sacrifice in the elf-maiden Lúthien's momentous choice of mortality for the sake of Beren. Escape from death, and healing, is a constant theme in JRRT's tales of Middle-earth.

Outside his Middle-earth tales JRRT explores themes of afterlife and purgatory in his allegorical story, *Leaf by Niggle**. CSL memorably explores the afterlife in his *The Great Divorce** and *The Last Battle**. His *The Problem of Pain** has chapters on heaven and hell. In CSL's *The Last Battle* the children who are the protagonists in Narnia are already dead as a result of a train crash.

CW's perspective on time and eternity makes it natural for him to have characters interrelating from the long-dead past and the present. He portrays after-death experience in *All Hallows' Eve** (which begins with its main character dead), and *Descent Into Hell** (in which a suicide finds that death has not brought him oblivion). The former is immediately linked with Dante by its first chapter-title, 'The New Life' and pursues similar themes of redemption, explicitly invoked in *Descent Into Hell* by an allusion to the atonement. Death was, for CW, the 'great physical ratification' of the breach between body and soul, by which chastity (courtesy towards God) and courtesy (chastity towards humans) were lost in both body and soul (*The Forgiveness of Sins**). CW seems to be exploring the possibility of redemption after death, though his exact theology of this is difficult to define, and certainly in *All Hallows' Eve* the dead Lester Furnival is on her way somewhere else; she is very much present and tied to the physical world, and it is only when reconciliation with her husband is achieved, and her works of grace towards others completed, that she seems free to move on. Perhaps her situation is intended to be seen as purgatorial; the qualities of the dead in CW's fiction tend to be qualities they possessed in life, and the same is true of their flaws.

CW is also concerned with perceptions of death as an enemy to be conquered; either, for example, in the activities of Nigel Considine in *Shadows of Ecstasy**, where his conquest is a distorted version of the triumph of Christ over death; or in the account of Margaret Anstruther in *Descent Into Hell*, for whom approaching death is conquered by joy, so that it entirely loses its sting. In *The Figure of Beatrice**, even the death of a beloved is seen as a necessary step in spiritual growth, for though the vision is withdrawn when Beatrice dies, the vision is not thereby invalidated – and in *The Divine Comedy*, Dante's guide through Paradise is Beatrice, now able to be the object of romantic love in a truly platonic sense.

CW's own death is remembered in CSL's moving words in *Essays Presented to Charles Williams**: 'No event has so corroborated my faith in the next world as Charles Williams did simply by dying. When the idea of death and the idea of Charles Williams thus met in my mind, it was the idea of death that was changed.' CSL's introduction to this symposium becomes a moving meditation on death, prompted by the loss of CW in 1945.

Descent Into Hell (CW, 1937)

CW's sixth novel was declined by Gollancz and published by Faber. It is an explicitly developed exposition of substitution* and exchange* worked out in the parallel stories of one individual's salvation and another's damnation.

Like *All Hallows' Eve**, much of the action takes place in a half-world of the supernatural set against the familiar London landscape; in this case a housing estate, Battle Hill, built on the site of ancient conflicts. There the poet Peter Stanhope is reading the script of his new play to a group of local people. It is a masque (which immediately recalls the Great Dance*) based on local history. It is appreciated by Pauline Anstruther; Catherine Parry and Adele Hunt compete to be director. Another in the group, Myrtle Fox, represents uncomprehending prosaic common sense, a failure to grasp the immense and dangerous power of good. In this novel, good heals some characters and breaks others. The difference depends on individual choice. Such reflections remind Pauline of her recurrent nightmare; a doppelganger*, or replica of herself, following her constantly.

Battle Hill itself is described as an arena for the passage of souls; it is historically so, and most specifically so when an anonymous labourer chose to hang himself there while the estate was being built. He desired annihilation, but his existence continues after death. CW describes him lost in a grey after-reality ('Gomorrah'), absent from Co-inherence*; the consequence of choice. He wanders off, away from Battle Hill.

Lawrence Wentworth, a historian, now lives in the house from which the Suicide jumped. He has a tendency to cheat by forcing historical facts to fit his opinions. He is engaged in a running argument with Aston Moffat, another historian, over a minute historical detail; he argues more for the sake of his own prestige than for objective truth. His 'descent into hell' is a matter of small, apparently inevitable choices. Like Pauline he has a recurring dream: he is descending a rope into darkness, though it is a rope with knots – there is a choice; one could ascend.

He is attracted to Adela Hunt, who is already in love with Hugh Prescott. They consult Wentworth over a detail of the costumes for the masque. Later Adele and Hugh ignore an invitation to Wentworth's home and go to London instead; Pauline is the only guest who turns up. She asks him about doppelgangers; he, distracted by jealousy, dismisses them as superstition. Later he defies his own exhaustion as he attempts to spy on the returning lovers.

Pauline's grandmother Margaret Anstruther tells her about their ancestor John Struther, burnt at the stake under Mary Tudor – salvation, like love, can be a terrible thing. They are joined by Lily Sammile, whose name indicates her role as one of the evil protagonists. Later still Stanhope and Myrtle Fox arrive. Margaret's awareness of her approaching death and the interconnectedness of all emphasizes CW's theme of love and salvation as terrible glories. For her, likewise experiencing the doppelganger confronta- tion, love transforms even the fact of self encountered.

Margaret's imminent death is the focus for a vision of the cosmos as struggling towards eminences of light, summits to which humanity is des- tined to rise in apotheosis. It is Margaret's vision in the novel, but clearly also CW's as author; it embraces Pauline and offers an explanation for the doppelganger haunting (Pauline is fearful of addressing her true self); but it accurately locates the Suicide, Wentworth, and Sammile in their theological relationship to divine love.

For Wentworth is inexorably bent on hell; in the bitterly paradoxical chapter 'Return to Eden' he and the Suicide are both shown to have made choices, though their situations differ. For Wentworth, the path to damnation is one of slow, deliberate steps, the descent down the knotted rope. His desire for Adela makes him bitter when Aston Moffat is knighted – an 'opportunity for joy' which he spurns. His other great passion, his historical work, will later provide the final, damning choice. Already the distinction between fact and fantasy is blurring, most of all in his longing for Adela which is satisfied in the form of a succubus. This pseudo-Adela offers a synthetic, fantasy, selfish love which Wentworth finds headily superior to the giving, sacrificial love that is being lived out in the lives of the 'good' characters. In the description of Wentworth's state of mind, linked to the twilight world of Battle Hill and the lonely unpeopled world of the Suicide, CW explores some of the themes of the city*, the map and the body that will later figure in the Arthurian poems*. But for Wentworth, who rejects even the Suicide, there is no turning towards salvation.

Another major theme of CW's writing is introduced explicitly now: the doctrine of substituted love, the way of exchange; Stanhope offers to take upon himself Pauline's fear of the doppelganger – an exchange he explicitly associates with Christ. It is part of Pauline's redemption to accept this offer, for this too she finds dreadfully humiliating. The city that is built on Exchange is contrasted tellingly with the lonely garden of Eden towards which Wentworth, his human relationships foundering, is bound.

Pauline accepts Stanhope's offer, and her fear is transformed. On her way home, in place of the doppelganger, she encounters a series of enjoyable small happenings. At home, she reads the story of her ancestor's martyrdom and reflects that perhaps she too can now take her share of bearing others' burdens. In the context of these new discoveries she is able to resist the allure of Lily Sammile, who arrives with the offer of happiness – significantly, it is to be a secret happiness denied to others. In the next chapter the Suicide finds peace through the ministrations of Margaret and Pauline (*see* THE CROSS), and CW makes it clear that it is Christ's death that saves him; just as it delivers Pauline's ancestor, as she takes on herself his 350-year-old fear.

Wentworth's mental state is deteriorating, the result in part in his acceptance of the succubus as a false Adela. He arrives at the dress rehearsal and is asked if the uniforms are correct, and he says they are, though he is aware that they are wrong in a small detail. By such tiny details, step by step, Wentworth has proceeded to his damnation. Conversely, when she recognizes that the masque is being performed at the place where her ancestor was burned, Pauline makes the final acceptance of joy that secures her salvation.

Margaret dies. Hugh and Adela witness with Lily Sammile a scene of disturbance in the graveyard, a reference to events at the time of the crucifixion. Adela, fleeing for help to Wentworth, meets the succubus and plunges into wild despair. She persuades Pauline to go with her to Lily for help. Pauline knows no help can come from Lily, and responds to Lily's incoherent ministrations with laughter; Lily collapses, her makeshift dwelling falling with her.

The novel ends with Pauline leaving to work in London and saying goodbye to Hugh. At the station she sees Wentworth, bound for London to a dinner honouring Moffat. She invites him to travel with her; he refuses, possibly his last conscious choice against joy and Co-inherence. The last pages are a brilliantly imagined conclusion to the descent, as Wentworth finally gets to the end, lets go, and sees the rope disappear. His last conscious thought is, 'I've been cheated' – a reference to the argument of *He Came down from Heaven**, that the continued potential for sin and damnation demands justification only possible in terms of the cross. 'He might even then have laid hold on the thing that was abroad in the world and been saved.' But he had ignored those who would have helped him. His world falls away, familiar objects have no meaning any more, even the rope is no longer there by which he might have escaped. As his surroundings fade into incoherence, he is drawn 'inward and down through the bottomless circles of the void'.

There are strong enough links with Margery Allingham's* *The Tiger in the Smoke* (1952), and its central concepts of the staircase of descent, the science of luck and the impact of choices on eternal destiny, to suggest that Allingham may well have been familiar with *Descent Into Hell*.

Descent of the Dove, The (CW, 1939)

The book, commissioned by Longmans, is dedicated to the 'Companions of the Co-inherence', the order that CW established in the same year. It was completed under the shadow of inevitable war and of romantic love; Phyllis Jones* returned from Java that summer and CW desperately wished he could be free of his long love for her. One of the book's many admirers was W.H. Auden*: it was the first theological book he had studied, and he acknowledged its influence.

Subtitled 'A Short History of the Holy Spirit in the Church', it covers from AD 30 (the ascension) to 1939 (the outbreak of European war). He divides history up into concepts, his chapters being: 1. The Definition of Christendom; 2. The Reconciliation with Time; 3. The Compensations of Success; 4. The War of the Frontiers; 5. The Imposition of Belief; 6. Consummation and Schism; 7. The Renewal of Contrition; 8. The Quality of Disbelief; 9. The Return of the Manhood.

In his introduction he explains his choice of frontispiece (a painting by Ludovic Brea) as expressing his main concerns: the presidency of the Holy Spirit over the 'holy and glorious' flesh; humanity as all travelling on one or other of the two ways (of affirmation and rejection); 'but the painting . . . is of the co-inherence of the whole redeemed City'. He emphasizes that the history is a theological history; Dante will appear more than will Descartes. And he quotes the phrase he quotes often in his work: 'This also is Thou; neither is this Thou' which he regards as the summary of the history of the Christian church. The book discusses themes that have appeared in *Descent Into Hell**, *He Came down from Heaven** and *Taliessin through Logres*.

The dedication is very apt, for the co-inherence of God and humanity, and of humans with humans, is what the book is about. The Trinity is an Exchange within Co-inherence*, and without a trinitarian view of God it is impossible to think of a God of love who is transcendent. Translated into human terms, this means that Christian doctrine is doomed to be corrupted if it is kept to one person. 'The value of dogma . . . is the opportunity it gives for the single mind to enter the Communion of Saints.' It is in this context that he places the importance that he does on the concept of Christendom.

The book (which is written in a particularly lucid, creative fashion: CW's heightened language is here almost always easy to translate and is always used for a purpose) discusses the two ways, of affirmation* and rejection, within the overall ambit of the Co-inherence. He uses Dante's *The Divine Comedy* and the mystical text *The Cloud of Unknowing* as examples, and as elsewhere, argues strongly against the way of rejection being identified as the proper way for religious people. Here, as so often in CW, the exposition and defence of the way of affirmation is one of the major contributions that CW makes to theology.

'Theology' is defined at the beginning of the book:

> The beginning of Christendom is, strictly, at a point out of time. A metaphysical trigonometry finds it among the spiritual Secrets, at the meeting of two heavenward lines, one drawn from Bethany along the Ascent of Messias, the other from Jerusalem against the Descent of the Paraclete [= Holy Spirit]. That measurement, the measurement of eternity in operation, of the bright cloud and rushing wind, is theology.

For CW the Eucharist is about Co-inherence and substitution, for it is a symbol of the cross* on which the greatest exchange of all took place. (One is reminded of some lines from William Blake: 'So throughout eternity/I forgive you, you forgive me/Thus the dear Redeemer said/This the wine and this the bread).' The themes of the descent of the Paraclete and the return of Christ/Messias (often looked-for but certain to happen one day) create the book's dynamic, in which events and people are recorded according to how they relate to the central themes, rather than as events in a calendar.

The book, which is generally considered CW's masterpiece, at least among his non-fiction writings, was very well received by the critics.

Discarded Image: An Introduction to Medieval and Renaissance Literature, The (CSL, 1964)

The Discarded Image arose out of a series of lectures CSL gave many years earlier on the medieval world image which provided a background to literature up to the seventeenth century. The lectures did the same sort of thing that

Basil Willey's books did for the background to seventeenth, eighteenth and nineteenth-century literature.

CSL concluded that a world model is not meant to represent reality itself literally (though obviously people have identified such models with reality). If it did literally represent reality, some element from the real world could be substituted for the model; the model did not really matter. CSL employed the medieval world model in his science-fiction trilogy and *The Chronicles of Narnia**. CSL thereby helps his reader to feel the imaginative power of this model. CSL argues that our world model will eventually change, like others before it. This change in mentality will shape questions asked of nature*, and thus what is considered evidence in support of a world model. (*See also* EVOLUTION OF HUMAN CONSCIOUSNESS.)

Each age inevitably has its own 'taste in universes'. Thinking of chronological snobbery*, CSL observed:

> We can no longer dismiss the change in Models as a simple progress from error to truth. No Model is a catalogue of ultimate realities, and none is a mere fantasy. Each is a serious attempt to get in all the phenomena known at a given period, and each succeeds in getting in a great many. But also, no less surely, each reflects the prevalent psychology of an age almost as much as it reflects the state of that age's knowledge.

This view has many affinities with OB (*see HISTORY, GUILT AND HABIT; SAVING THE APPEARANCES*).
See also LITERARY CRITIC, CSL AS A

Divine Comedy, The

See DANTE

Divorce (CW, 1920)

CW's third volume of poetry, published by Humphrey Milford; the title refers to the death of his father. The poems celebrate, among other things, his father, the beginnings of a concept of Co-inherence*, friendship, the persistence of friendship beyond death, and the image of the city*. There are hints of the stresses that the CW's marriage was already experiencing.

Doppelganger

In CW's *Descent Into Hell**, Pauline Anstruther is experiencing terror because she is being stalked by a duplicate of herself – a doppelganger. The doppelganger is a well-known figure in European folklore, appearing in the work of such writers as Theodore Sturm (*Ein Doppelgänger*, 1887) and Heinrich Heine, who wrote an untitled poem that is known as 'Der Doppelgänger'. In

Descent Into Hell, CW introduces the idea with a quotation from Shelley that Pauline had learned at school and hated: 'The Magus Zoroaster, my dead child, /Met his own image walking in the garden.' She has seen such apparitions throughout her life, and more often of late.

Peter Stanhope offers to bear the fear and pain of her dread, which is the initiating act of her salvation. Once she has accepted the offer fear turns to delight in other things, and Pauline makes her first steps in the way of charity.

The doppelganger theme is mirrored in the succubus with which Lawrence Wentworth gratifies his desire for Adela Hunt, whose glimpse of the succubus in Wentworth's home precipitates her breakdown at the end of the novel.

Downe House School

See MYTH OF [FRANCIS] BACON, A

Dragons

Bred by Morgoth, these evil beings brought terror to Beleriand and else-where, as chronicled in *The Silmarillion**. In *The Hobbit**, Bilbo encounters the winged dragon, Smaug, in Erebor.

In his essay, 'Beowulf: The Monsters and the Critics', JRRT paints a vivid picture of the symbolism of the dragon as an enemy more evil than any human foe. The *Beowulf* poem is something new, 'a measure and interpretation' of all Norse legends of dragons. He explains: 'Something more significant than a standard hero, a man faced with a foe more evil than any human enemy of house or realm, is before us, and yet incarnate in time, walking in heroic history, and treading the named lands of the North.'

In the human beings of Middle-earth*, such as elves, hobbits and humans, there can also be a dragon-like quality. It could be presented as a psychological state, the 'dragon-complex' (to invent a name for it). The quality is that of possession, or possessiveness. A dragon like Smaug embodies possessiveness vividly in his great, but useless, hoard. But possessiveness applies to knowledge, power over others, and many other areas. Fallen creatures like Fëanor, Morgoth, and Sauron are characterized by the dragon-complex, the lust to possess. The Silmarils (and later, for the Dark Lord, the Ring) symbolize this lust.

As a foil to this complex are creatures who have no desire to possess, or who are lost in their joy in creating. They include Ilúvatar himself, father of all, Aulë the Valar, Sam (over whom the Ring has little power), and Tom Bombadil.

JRRT could be criticized for attributing such evil to dragons which, like orcs, were bred for wickedness, and hence had no moral choice. Human beings are wrong to be dragon-like, bestial, but a dragon is a dragon. However, as symbolic embodiments of nameless evil they have great imaginative power.

In the Narnian* chronicle, *The Voyage of the 'Dawn Treader'**, an old and dying dragon is discovered by Eustace Scrubb on Dragon Island. (It later turns out to be one of the lost Narnian Lords – Octesian – for whom the party of voyagers is searching, transformed into the hideous shape.) Upon his death, the unpleasant Eustace himself becomes a dragon, and only Aslan* is able to restore him to his boy nature.

See also HERO; EVIL

Dundas-Grant, Commander James (1896–1985)

After being wounded by poison gas in the First World War, 'DG', as he was later dubbed, became an underwriter at Lloyds of London, and enlisted in the Royal Naval Volunteer Reserve. He was recalled to military service at the outbreak of the Second World War. In 1944 he was appointed commander of the Oxford University Naval Division, taking up residence in Magdalen College, where he met CSL. CSL looked to him like a gentleman farmer in his scarecrow clothes. He was invited to a Thursday Inklings, and later to the Tuesday gatherings at the Eagle and Child*. 'DG' recalls the Thursdays:

> It was thus that I came to meet his great friend Tolkien: tall, sweptback grey hair, restless. He read to us parts of his manuscript for *Lord of the Rings*, asking for criticism. Colin Hardie was there and sometimes our doctor friend Havard, known as Humphrey. His brother, too, was usually in attendance. It was at these sessions that I found out how much one learned just sitting and listening (*C.S. Lewis at the Breakfast Table*, ed. James T. Como, 1980, pp. 230–31).

He also vividly remembered the Tuesdays in the pub:

> We sat in a small back room with a fine coal fire in winter. Back and forth the conversation would flow. Latin tags flying around. Homer quoted in the original to make a point. And Tolkien, jumping, up and down, declaiming in Anglo-Saxon (p. 231).

Dymer (CSL, 1926; new edition, 1950)

An anti-totalitarian poem that has some similarities with *Spirits in Bondage**, and written while CSL was still an unbeliever in Christianity. It is included in *Narrative Poems**. The hero, Dymer, escapes from a perfect but inhuman city into the soothing countryside. Various adventures overtake him. In contrast to Dymer's idealism, a revolutionary group rebels against the Perfect City in anarchy, claiming Dymer's name. Fresh in CSL's mind when he wrote were the bloody events of the Russian Revolution and of his native Ulster. He regarded popular political causes at that time as 'daemonic'.

Dyson, H.V.D. 'Hugo' (1896–1975)

A member of the Inklings, Dyson was seriously wounded at Passchendaele before reading English at Exeter College, Oxford*. He was scarred both physically and mentally by war, as CSL observed: 'a burly man, both in mind and body, with the stamp of war on him' (letter to Warnie Lewis, 22 November 1931). As an undergraduate, Dyson heard JRRT read 'The Fall of Gondolin' (part of *The Silmarillion**) to the Essay Club at Exeter College. On a night in 1931, he helped JRRT to persuade CSL of the truth of Christianity. He initially lectured in English at Reading University, near enough to Oxford to keep in touch with fellow Inklings. There he pioneered a Combined Humanities course in 1930. He also encouraged the development of a School of Fine Arts, and was considered a distinctive and outstanding lecturer. Like CW, he gave lectures to the Workers' Educational Association (*see* ADULT EDUCATION). He poured more of himself into teaching than into his writing – he was involved in very few publications. He was, in 1945, elected Fellow and tutor in English literature at Merton College. He retired in 1963.

Dyson was cool about JRRT's constant reading of *The Lord of the Rings* to the Inklings. He appears in fictional form in JRRT's unfinished 'The Notion Club Papers'*, as Arry Loudham. His theatrical nature contributed an important dimension to the Inklings, and he was very important to CSL in providing emotional support.

Eagle and Child, The

A public house in St Giles, Oxford*, which was one of the favourite haunts of the Inklings, particularly for Tuesday (later Monday) meetings. The literary meetings tended to meet on Thursdays in CSL's rooms at Magdalen College, and occasionally in JRRT's at Merton College. In his *Memoirs of C.S. Lewis* (kept in the Marion E. Wade Collection), Warnie Lewis* records that the Tuesday meetings gained 'a certain notoriety' by being referred to in chapter 8 of Edmund Crispin's crime story, *Swan Song*. The detective don Gervase Fen and others are perched 'before a blazing fire in the small front parlour of the Bird & Baby... "There goes C.S. Lewis," said Fen suddenly. "It must be Tuesday."'

Eärendil, The Voyage of (JRRT)

JRRT considered this as one of four key stories of *The Silmarillion**, standing independently of the history and annals of the First Age. In his *Letters* (letter

131), JRRT wrote of Eärendil that 'He is important as the person who brings the Silmarillion to its end, and as providing in his offspring the main links to and persons in the tales of later Ages.' Unfortunately, the tale, or tales, of Eärendil cannot be reconstructed from JRRT's unfinished work in as great detail as the tales of Beren and Lúthien, and Túrin Turambar.

Eliot, T.S. (1888–1965)

Thomas Stearns Eliot was a leading poet, literary and social critic, publisher and dramatist of the century. In 1922 he founded *The Criterion*, a quarterly review. In 1925 he joined the publishing house Faber and Gwyer (later called Faber and Faber). In 1927 he joined the Anglican Church. CSL disliked Eliot's earlier, modernist poetry for its lack of stock responses. He also criticized evaluative criticism associated with Cambridge critics like I.A. Richards, and saw Eliot's criticism as displaying similar tendencies. However, later in life the men became acquainted through membership of a 'Commission to Revise the Psalter' in 1959. In 1961, CSL submitted the manuscript of his *A Grief Observed** to Faber and Faber for publication.

T.S. Eliot was an admirer of CW, whom he met at literary parties organized by society hostess Lady Ottoline Morrell. Eliot endorsed CW's work in an obituary article 'The Significance of Charles Williams' (*The Listener*, 1946). Glen Cavaliero suggests that a poem from CW's *Divorce** may have been in Eliot's mind when he wrote section II of *Little Gidding*. CW in turn deeply admired Eliot, assuring him that future generations would regard him as a great poet. They became friends, visiting the theatre together and enjoying long discussions. When CW began to write for Faber and Faber (Eliot's publishing house), it was Eliot who encouraged him to go on with his Arthurian poems even though Faber was also hoping to persuade him to write more prose. Of the novels, Eliot wrote, 'What CW has to give is . . . the work of imagination, based upon real *experience* of the supernatural world, of a supernatural world which is just as natural to the author as our everyday world. And he makes our everyday world very much more exciting, because of the supernatural which he always finds active in it.' Of Eliot, CW said, 'The English poets have not waited for Eliot to tell us about the Waste Land, nor English theology to learn from him' – perhaps, suggests Alice M. Hadfield, 'he found the meaning spread rather thin in Eliot's highly effective verse'. He also took issue with Eliot critically, defending Milton against a school of criticism in which Eliot was prominent. Eliot wrote in 1936, '[Milton] may still be considered as having done damage to the English language from which it has not wholly recovered' (he changed his views in a paper published in 1947). CW wrote in his 'Introduction' to the 1940 World's Classics edition of Milton: 'We have been fortunate enough,' he began provocatively, 'to live at a time when the reputation of John Milton has been seriously attacked.' He named Eliot as an example, who responded by reviewing the edition appreciatively.

While Eliot, as a leading Christian poet himself, could be expected to admire CW's poetry and other writing, it was an imaginative understanding of what CW could contribute in unexpected spheres that led him to commission *Witchcraft**. His confidence was justified, for the book that resulted takes its place not with CW's 'supernatural thrillers' but with his theological writings.

See also PREFACE TO PARADISE LOST, A

Elizabeth I, Queen (CW)

See QUEEN ELIZABETH

English Literature in the Sixteenth Century (Excluding Drama) (CSL, 1954)

Published as volume 3 of *The Oxford History of English Literature* (later, the numbering changed). The book is based upon embryonic lectures given at Cambridge University in 1944. CSL's introduction is of great interest to theologians, philosophers, and historians of ideas, as well as literary students. Some critics, such as Helen Gardner, were unhappy about CSL's dismissal of the humanism of the period.

As well as providing a thorough history of the period, the book is notable for its introduction, 'New Learning and New Ignorance', which adds to the themes laid out in *The Discarded Image** and his inaugural lecture to the Chair of Medieval and Renaissance Literature at Cambridge, *De Descriptione Temporum**.

See also LITERARY CRITIC, CSL AS A

English Poetic Mind, The (CW, 1932)

Based on lectures given by CW at the City Literary Institute, it was published by the Oxford University Press despite his lack of formal academic credentials. CW approaches poetry as an object in its own right, making a distinction between the poem and what the poem is about. Yet great poetry is related to its subject and it puts us into relationship with it; a delight in the subject is allied to delight in the words used. 'Our capacities . . . for some sort of general experience of the world are awakened by the greater masters: [Macbeth and Samson] both express our sense of a faculty for taking in as many experiences as a whole, for knowing and enjoying them, for knowing and enjoying them in the exquisite sensuous delight of words. Anybody who can cause us to do that is a great poet.'

He considers Wordsworth, the poet most conscious of his own development as a poet; Shakespeare, and the development of a relationship with an audience; and Milton, aware of his genius in a way that Shakespeare was not. ('We have neither an account, as with Wordsworth, of the growth of his genius, nor, as with Shakespeare, a mass of poetry covering all his working life . . . [We are concerned]only with what his poetry did, and the witness it bore in itself to the place where 'twas nourished.' He finishes by contemplating the future of poetry.

The ideas in this book were further developed in *Reason and Beauty in the Poetic Mind*.

Escape, escapism

See 'ON FAIRY STORIES'

Essays Presented to Charles Williams (ed. CSL, 1947)

This posthumous tribute brings together essays by CW's friends. The Preface by CSL is more than a preface; it is one of the most eloquent and moving assessments of CW that we possess (*see* DEATH). Dorothy L. Sayers* contributes '. . . And Telling You a Story', an account of her discovery of Dante* through CW's *The Figure of Beatrice**. The next chapter is JRRT's seminal paper 'On Fairy Stories'*, first delivered at St Andrews in 1938. Equally important is CSL's 'On Stories', and OB follows it with his paper on 'Poetic Diction and Legal Fiction'. Gervase Mathew*, the Roman Catholic priest, lecturer and Inkling, wrote on 'Marriage and Amour Courtoise in Late Fourteenth-Century England', and Warnie Lewis contributed a piece on 'The Galleys of France'. In his Preface CSL remarks, 'The variety displayed by this little group is far too small to represent the width of Charles Williams's friendships.'

CSL's Preface is also an important source of information about his friendship with CW, and about CW as an Inkling. In it he describes CW as a 'romantic theologian'; that is, someone who considers the theological implications of romanticism. All contributors are CW's fellow Inklings, except Dorothy L. Sayers, a friend of CW and CSL.

CSL writes, in his Preface, that the collection represents many typical talks in the Inklings. He points out,

> The first three essays are all on literature, and even on one aspect of literature, the narrative art. That is natural enough. His *All Hallows' Eve* and my own *Perelandra* (as well as Professor Tolkien's unfinished sequel to *The Hobbit*) had all been read aloud, each chapter as it was written. They owe a good deal to the hard-hitting criticism of the circle. The problems of narrative as such – seldom heard of in modern critical writings – were constantly before our minds. The last two essays are historical. Father Mathew's bears on an aspect of the Middle Ages which always seemed to Charles Williams of deep significance and which had, indeed, been the

common interest that first brought him and me together. The final essay carries us to seventeenth-century France. My brother's lifelong interest in the reign of Louis XIV was a bond between CW and him which no one had foreseen when they first met. Those two, and Mr. H.V.D. Dyson of Merton, could often be heard in a corner talking about Versailles, *intendants*, and the *maison du roy*, in a fashion with which the rest of us could not compete. Between the literary and the historical essays stands Mr. Barfield's work, which is literary and historical at once.

See CHAPTER 1

Every, George

A member of the Society of the Sacred Mission, Kelham, Brother George Every was an occasional contributor to the periodical *Theology* in which, in March 1939, he wrote an article that appeared to equate culture and good taste with Christianity. CSL answered Every in *Theology* 12 months later, arguing that culture had a part in bringing people to Christ but could of itself save nobody. In March/April 1948, Every published the text of a lecture to the Chelmsford Diocesan Worship and Drama Association on CW: *I The Accuser* and *II The City and the Substitution*. The title of the first part is taken from an image in CW's *Grab and Grace** (1941), the second part expounds the familiar doctrine of exchange* in CW. Both the 1948 articles are useful in their examination of CW's minor writings.

Evil

This is a major theme particularly preoccupying JRRT, CSL and CW.

The Lord of the Rings*, according to Tom Shippey, attempts to reconcile two views of evil, the Manichaeist (associated with Boethius) and the Judeo-Christian (represented by Augustine). One is an objective view of evil, and the other subjective. The Augustinian view can be called subjective in the sense that evil is a negation, not being in itself. For Augustine, all God's creation was pronounced by him to be good.

JRRT, believes Professor Shippey, tries to take account of both sides, each of which is true to our experience. He sees this happening with the symbol of the Ring borne by Frodo. It is an objective reality, the power of which is to be resisted. It also however appeals subjectively to a person's weakness. For instance, the ring appeals to possessiveness in Bilbo, fear in Frodo, patriotism in Boromir, and pity in Gandalf.

In achieving a realistic tension between subjective and objective evil, JRRT's fertile imagination creates many embodiments of evil – balrogs, dragons, orcs, the fallen Valar, Morgoth, and his servant, the Maia Sauron, the ringwraiths, spiders such as Shelob or Ungoliant, werewolves and trolls.

Set against evil in JRRT's world are many elements, but rarely physical force (as in the overthrow of Morgoth at the end of the First Age, the destruction of Númenor, or Gandalf's fight with the Balrog). One important element is healing*. Another is art, in many forms of creativity, such as song. Another is the renunciation of possession. A further element is sacrifice. Underlying them all is faith in providence, hope in the ultimate happy ending even if a person does not live to see it.

Because of his theology of Middle-earth, JRRT is able to portray evil as utterly real, without falling into a dualism of good and evil. The many occasions of tragedy within his tales (pre-eminently in the story of Túrin) emphasizes the reality of evil in the world, evil originated by the fall of Melkor (Morgoth). Evil is only possible to creatures capable of creativity and free will. The orcs, to the contrary, are programmed to inflict evil, tools rather than agents of Morgoth and Sauron.

Much of JRRT's invented mythology concerns creativity and art, the foundation of language and culture. The making of the world by the demiurgic Valar, the fashioning of the Silmarils, and the forging of the Rings, shape all events. For JRRT, a study of evil necessarily has to do with the use and misuse of creativity and free will. Both salvation and damnation involve moral choices. Thus evil is indivisible: its implications are applicable to the real world, as well as to JRRT's invented, secondary world (itself one example of creativity).

CSL wholeheartedly endorses JRRT's view of the moral responsibility involved in human freedom. CSL's exploration of evil spans his fiction and non-fictional writings. His post-war science-fiction story, *That Hideous Strength** (1945) has a striking affinity with JRRT's *The Lord of the Rings* (1954–55). They were both composed in the war years and try to come to terms with an almost unthinkable evil. *That Hideous Strength* gives fictional expression to ethical themes explored in *The Abolition of Man**, grappling with a subjectivism and scientism* characteristic, CSL believed, of a post-Christian world, and at the heart of evil, in view of the demons they unleash. He explores the problem of suffering with great power in *The Problem of Pain**. He movingly portrays the redemption of suffering in *Till We Have Faces**.

CW shared many of the other Inklings' concerns with evil. In his work evil is often shown as an offence against order: thus in the Arthurian poems the kingdom begins to be weakened, and the structures of the city and the state are threatened. Sin breaks the Co-inherence*, it is greed in what should be an exchange of love. Often evil is pictured as an inversion of something that has already been shown to us as an image of the good, or which is good in itself; several evil characters in the novels (Nigel Considine, Lily Sammile, etc.) are counterfeits, mimicking the acts of charity and grace (as for example

Lily's offer of help and private healing). In *The Descent of the Dove** evil is structural; heaven is a place of mutuality, hell a place of selfishness.

His *Witchcraft** defines witchcraft as the way of the perversion of images, a direct contrary to his most explicit definition of the Christian life – the holding in balance of the way of affirmation and the way of rejection. In *The Forgiveness of Sins* he sees sin as demanding reconciliation: the Fall was an inversion, 'after which, in the process of knowing good and evil, all virtues were bound, both in their physical and spiritual categories, to be understood rather by their positive denials than by their positive affirmations: even sometimes by their vicious opposites rather than by themselves'.

For CW sin was a structural aberration, witchcraft a psychological perversion, evil an erosion of the Co-inherence and the life of the city under authority – because it opposed that authority. And just as, in *Descent Into Hell**, Wentworth's damnation came by tiny sins rather than by huge outrage, so the aberration of hell needs only minor flaws to show itself: 'Hell is always inaccurate,' wrote CW in his introduction to Milton*. Considine dominated a hemisphere, Simon the Clerk wanted the world, Sir Giles Tumulty (in *Many Dimensions**) wanted Time itself. Lawrence Wentworth 'only' approved an inaccurate shoulder-knot. It was enough. The smallest aberration will always be enough to threaten the life of the Co-inherence and the city, will always be enough to demand atonement.

FURTHER READING

Tom Shippey, 'J.R.R. Tolkien as a Post-War Writer', in *Scholarship and Fantasy* (*Anglicana Turkuensia No. 12*)
Paul H. Kocher, *A Reader's Guide to 'The Silmarillion'* (1980)
C.N. Manlove, *Modern Fantasy: Five Studies* (1975)
T.A. Shippey, *The Road to* Middle-earth (1982)

Evolution of human consciousness

OB believed that, corresponding to stellar and biological evolution, there has been an evolution of consciousness. Evolution has been guided by a telos, design or purpose, and not by chance or chaos. The emergence of the human mind is at the very centre of evolution. In holding to such a view, OB admired the teaching of Pierre Teilhard de Chardin.

The evolution of consciousness is reflected precisely in changes in language and perception, from a primitive unity of consciousness to a future acheivement of a greater human consciousness. In this the subject–object dichotomy is overcome in a harmonious human participation with nature.
See also ORIGINAL PARTICIPATION; PARTICIPATION

Exchange; Way of Exchange

See CO-INHERENCE

Experiment in Criticism, An (CSL, 1961)

Though literary criticism, this book should be read by all who take reading seriously. CSL argues that literature exists for the enjoyment of readers and books therefore should be judged by the kind of reading that they evoke. Good reading has something in common with love, moral action, and the growth of knowledge. Like all these it involves a surrender, in this case by the reader to the work being read. CSL's attitude is to ask the reader, 'What is literature?'

CSL tries to present the evidence of his own lifetime's reading, and adds: 'I regret that the brutes cannot write books . . . In reading great literature I become a thousand men and yet remain myself. Like the night sky in the Greek poem, I see with a myriad eyes, but it is still I who see. Here, as in worship, in love, in moral action, and in knowing, I transcend myself; and am never more myself than when I do.'

See also LITERARY CRITIC, CSL AS A

Fairies

Beings from myth and folklore represented as elves in JRRT's fiction.
See also 'ON FAIRY STORIES'

Fairy story

See 'ON FAIRY STORIES'

Fall, the

The theology of an ancient fall of humankind permeates the thought and writings of both JRRT and CSL.

JRRT isolates the theme of fall as one of the central concerns of his mythology of Middle-earth*. His theology of the Fall is taken from the Bible (*see* CHRISTIAN MEANINGS IN THE FICTION OF JRRT), but he shapes it according to his artistic purposes.

There is no direct equivalent of the biblical Fall of humanity and some angels* as (1) JRRT is writing fiction; and (2) there are races other than humans. Fallenness is experienced in both aspects of the human, however, the elvish and the mannish. Elves are not fallen as a race, and only rarely turn to wickedness individually, so they have no original sin. The position of humans is different. JRRT introduces the idea of Re-formation to cover the good human beings in his tales of Middle-earth. These are distinguished from Black Númenoreans (Númenor has its own, second fall), and other wicked people, such as the Haradrim. JRRT explains:

Men have 'fallen' – any legends put in the form of supposed ancient history of this actual world of ours must accept that – but the peoples of the West, the good side are Re-formed. That is they are the descendants of Men that tried to repent and fled Westward from the domination of the Prime Dark Lord, and his false worship, and by contrast with the Elves renewed (and enlarged) their knowledge of the truth and the nature of the World.

In this way JRRT pictures a pagan, pre-Christian, naturally monotheistic group of people. To them has been revealed part of God's purposes, inklings of what is to come in the gospel story, a revelation to which they have faithfully responded according to their light. CSL makes a similar exploration of what might be called enlightened paganism, on a smaller scale, in his historical novel, *Till We Have Faces** (*see* CHAPTER 6).

The Fall in the garden of Eden does not come into JRRT's tales – it happens off-stage, as it were. JRRT regarded the events of Eden as part of actual human history, accounting for the darkness of the world. In his fantasy, he explored the fall theme primarily in the fall of Morgoth (Melkor) before the making of the world, and in the disobedience of the Númenoreans in breaking the Ban of the Valar against setting foot on the shores of the Undying Lands.

These moral falls, which, like the fall of Lucifer and the fall of Adam, are related, account for the separation of elves and humans. More dramatically, they account for the destruction of Beleriand and Númenor, and the change in the shape of the world, making it normally impossible to reach the Uttermost West, the lost Eden. On an individual scale, the story of Túrin explores the effects of evil* on a good man who has a tragic flaw. Other explorations include the fall of Saruman and the more tragic Denethor, and the corrosive effect of the One Ring on Gollum, and to a lesser extent, on Bilbo and Frodo. There is denial of fall, too, in the faithful of Númenor like Elendil, and those that refuse possession of the Ring like Gandalf and Galadriel.

In speaking of human beings in relation to fall and to sin, JRRT argued that we are still moral, free-willed beings, to whom is revealed something of God's purposes.

Like JRRT, CSL held the doctrine of the Fall at the very centre of his theology. He saw it as one of the beliefs that unite all Christians, past, present and future. He believed that, though the fall of humankind may be unique in the universe, yet its redemption spreads outwards and enobles all creatures (*Miracles*, ch. 14). The centrality of the Fall is reflected in many writings. In his fiction he particularly explored the doctrine in his science-fiction trilogy. This earth is called the Silent Planet, because it is cut off from

the blessedness of the rest of the cosmos by humankind's moral fall. In *Perelandra**, CSL takes up themes from John Milton's epic poem, *Paradise Lost*. *The Screwtape Letters** concern non-human intelligences (*see* ANGELS) who had undergone their own moral fall in the depths of the past and are committed to perpetuating their wickedness by meddling in and deliberately destroying immortal human souls. There is no doubt that CSL saw in the Fall a central explanation for what he saw as the abnormality of the human condition. He explores this theme theologically in his *The Problem of Pain**. CSL was a staunch defender of human freedom, holding that each of us is a morally responsible being.
See also EVIL

Fantasy
See CHRISTIAN FANTASY; CHAPTER 6

Farmer Giles of Ham (JRRT, 1949)
This is a light-hearted short story. One night a rather deaf and short-sighted giant wandered by mistake near Farmer Giles' farm, trampling his fields and animals. The nervous farmer let fly with a blunderbuss, stuffed with wire, stones, and other bits. The giant, not hearing the bang, supposed himself stung, and quickly left that place with its apparently unpleasant horseflies. Farmer Giles was now the village hero. Even the King of the Little Kingdom heard of his deed and sent him the gift of a long sword.

The Farmer enjoyed his reputation until a dragon* heard of the rich kingdom from the giant, and the tale tells how Giles tames him.

This humorous story, though on the surface very different from the tales of Middle-earth*, is characteristic of JRRT in its themes. The story's inspiration is linguistic: it provides a spoof explanation for the name of an actual village east of Oxford* called Worminghall, near Thame. A parson in the story is a grammarian (the equivalent of a philologist), making him shrewd and wise (*see* PHILOLOGY, JRRT AND). The Little Kingdom has similarities with the Shire, particularly the sheltered and homely life of Ham. Farmer Giles is like a complacent Hobbit, with unexpected qualities. The humour – with its mock scholarship – is similar to that in the collection of hobbit verses, *The Adventures of Tom Bombadil**.

Farrer, Austin (1904–68)
A distinguished theologian, clergyman and friend of CSL. He was chaplain and Fellow of Trinity College, and warden of Keble College, Oxford*. His writings are marked by an imaginative originality, as in his study of the biblical Book of Revelation, *The Glass of Vision*, the Bampton Lectures for

1948. Like CSL, he emphasized the importance of images in capturing truth. He had a deep interest in natural theology*.

FURTHER READING

P. Curtis, *A Hawk Among Sparrows: A Biography of Austin Farrer* (1985).
A. Farrer, *The Glass of Vision* (Dacre Press, 1948)
A. Farrer, *Rebirth of Images* (Dacre Press, 1949)

Father Christmas Letters, The (JRRT, 1976)

This is a collection of letters, edited by Baillie Tolkien (wife of Christopher Tolkien*), that JRRT wrote to his children in the 1920s and 1930s. They were written as from Father Christmas. The book contains many illustrations that JRRT made to accompany the letters.

Fellowship of the Ring, The (JRRT, 1954)

The first volume of *The Lord of the Rings**, comprising Books One and Two. It tells of Gandalf's discovery that the magical Ring possessed by Frodo the hobbit, is in fact the One Ring, controlling all the other Rings of Powers. It records the formation of the Company of the Ring to support the Ring-bearer, and their perilous journey on the way to destroy the Ring.

Book One tells of Bilbo's farewell party, as he leaves for retirement in Rivendell; Gandalf's account of the history of the Ring to Frodo long after; Frodo's sad departure from Hobbiton with Sam and Pippin; encounters with Sauron's Black Riders; their arrival at Buckland; the journey through the Old Forest, and visit to the house of Tom Bombadil; the capture of Frodo by a barrow-wight; their stay at Bree, where Aragorn joins them; and the attacks by Black Riders, where Frodo is badly wounded.

Book Two narrates Frodo's healing* in Rivendell. It tells of the great Council of Elrond, in which it is decided to form the Company of the Ring, and to take what seems a foolish course of bearing the Ring to Mordor. It recounts the dangerous journey south, and through Moria, where Gandalf is lost fighting the Balrog. It describes the passage of the Company through Lórien, and their meeting Galadriel. Leaving Lórien, the Company travels south once again, on the river Anduin, until they reach the Falls of Rauros. Here Boromir tries to seize the Ring from Frodo, the Company is divided, as Sam and Frodo set out alone for Mordor, and the remainder are scattered by a sudden orc attack.

'Figure of Arthur, The' (CW)

The incomplete fragment that forms the first part of *Arthurian Torso**.
See also GRAIL, THE (HOLY); CHAPTER 5

Figure of Beatrice, The (CW, 1943)

This book represents the most extended treatment of romantic love that CW wrote, having written the shorter studies *Religion and Love in Dante** and a chapter in *He Came down from Heaven**. It is a book that considers Dante* not as a man from antiquity but as a contemporary with whom modern men and women can identify and whose experiences and thoughts are relevant to modern life. 'We have looked everywhere for enlightenment on Dante, except in our lives and our love-affairs.' His first love for Beatrice was for him a religious experience as well as a romantic one; and because Williams recognized that the experience was one universal to human beings, he considered that Dante's masterpieces have much to say to modern readers, in terms far beyond literary criticism.

The book has three themes, described by CW as:

(1) The general way of the Affirmation of Image as a method of process towards the in-Godding of man, (2) the way of romantic love as a particular mode of the same process, (3) the involution of this love with other images, particularly (a) that of the community – that is, of the city, a devotion to which is also a way of the soul, (b) that of poetry and human learning. The general maxim of the whole way of Dante is *attention*; 'look', 'look well'.

He begins by associating the figure of Beatrice in Dante with the beginning of the way of affirmation*, an 'astonishment of the mind' prompted by a particular image, in this case, a girl: and it must exist in itself, says CW, it must derive from something greater than itself, and it must represent in itself that greatness from which it derives. Thus Beatrice for Dante represents an image of God and his attributes, an image which is not invalidated when the glory is withdrawn (as when Beatrice dies). In fact it must be withdrawn if the way is to be properly pursued.

Recognizing that the vision can come more than once, CW acknowledges (as well he might) that though this is intellectually welcome, practically the appearance of a second romantic vision can cause problems, especially if the visionary is married. His solution is a platonic one, though most will fall short of the ideal he proposes: 'to create in marriage a mutual adoration towards the second image'. His densely argued commentary on *The New Life* centres on the 'Beatrician moment', in which 'Imagination in action becomes faith, the quality by which the truths within the image are actualized within us. But the temptation . . . is to live only for the recurrence of the moment.'

He sees the *Inferno* as perverted way of affirmation, a funnel down to 'the last cold and self-devouring Hell'. In the section on hell CW recalls his arguments in *He Came down from Heaven*; what is at stake at the cross is justice. We did not ask to be tempted. 'We do not want, in that sense, to sin.'

But romantic love 'at once sensitively exposes our guilt, and makes it both tolerable and intolerable.'

Purgatory, then, is a passage to justice, where grace and punishment combine, and paradise is 'an image of the whole act of knowing which is the great Romantic Way'. The journey upon which Beatrice takes him is a journey of affirmation of images, for here as everywhere else CW recognizes the eternal significance and sacramental quality of each image and object; but it is in the essence of heaven and hell that choices are implicit. The way of affirmation goes hand in hand with the way of rejection.

The book ends in mutuality, in reciprocation, in exchange; and CW appeals to his readers to apply the lessons of Dante to their own lives. How do we work out the way of affirmation and the way of rejection? For the former, he says, quoting Dante, has scarcely begun to be looked at.

Flecker of Dean Close (CW, 1946)

CW's biography of W.H. Flecker (1859–1941), headmaster of Dean Close School, Cheltenham (1886–1924) and vicar of St Peter's, Staines (1927–41) was published by the Canterbury Press. Flecker was an evangelical, and Dean Close School – of which he was first headmaster – an evangelical foundation. One of Flecker's pupils was Stephen (later Bishop) Neill, who contributed a warm appreciation to the biography. The biography contains rather more quotations from Flecker and others, and rather less of CW, than his other biographies; doubtless because he was working directly from Flecker's family papers at the request of his widow; significantly, he gave the preface over to the appreciation from Stephen Neill. He draws extensively on his own experience when setting the scene (mentioning for example his father's political opinions), but it remains an oddity among the biographies, most interesting when its author's interest is caught by some minor characteristic of his subject, as when he speculates on Flecker's potential as a critic when he quotes his opinion on a topic (such as the dating of Shakespeare's plays) with which he obviously agrees.

See also BIOGRAPHIES BY CHARLES WILLIAMS

The Forgiveness of Sins

See HE CAME DOWN FROM HEAVEN

Four Loves, The (CSL, 1960)

The four loves distinguished by CSL are affection, friendship, eros and charity (divine love). Affection is the humblest and most widespread of the four loves. It is not a particularly appreciative love. It is the medium of the operation of the other loves.

Friendship is the least instinctive, biological and necessary of our loves. CSL points out that the ancients put the highest value upon this love, as in the friendship between David and Jonathan. Friendship, as the least biological of the loves, refutes sexual or homosexual explanations for its existence. Friendship was deeply important to CSL throughout his life, as this Handbook demonstrates. Friendship, reckoned CSL, made good people better and bad people worse.

Eros is the kind of love that lovers are within or 'in' – the state of being in love. CSL's friend CW explored eros, and in his thought, fiction and poetry, developed a theology of romantic love. This deeply influenced CSL, and eros is an important theme in *That Hideous Strength** (in the marriage of Jane and Mark Studdock) and in *Till We Have Faces** (in Psyche's love for the god of the mountain, the Westwind). It was to have been a theme of CSL's unfinished novel, *After Ten Years*.

Charity, or divine love, the fourth love, transcends all earthly loves in being a gift-love. All human loves are by nature (even unfallen nature) need-loves. Our human loves are potential rivals to the love of God, and can only take their proper place if our first allegiance is to him. It is the divine likeness in all our human loves (affection, friendship, and eros) that is their heavenly, and thus permanent, element. Our own loves, like our moral choices, judge us.

CSL has been criticized for possibly overdistinguishing these loves as they exist in Greek thought. The New Testament employs existing Greek terms but transforms the concepts, making less of a distinction between natural and spiritual loves than CSL makes. The basic tenor of CSL's thought, however, is opposed to a gnostic view of life and love – that is, a view which downplays the importance of our bodies and the physical world to what makes us human. Salvation, for CSL, involves our full humanity, body and all.

See also ALLEGORY OF LOVE, THE; AFFIRMATION, WAY OF

Fox, Adam (1883–1977)

A member of the Inklings, and Fellow of Magdalen College, Oxford*, and Dean of Divinity there from 1929. In 1938 he was elected Professor of Poetry at Oxford. He became Canon of Westminster Abbey in 1942. Among his publications were *Plato for Pleasure* (1945), *Meet the Greek Testament* (1952) and *Dean Inge* (1960).

God

Throughout his life CSL loved particular things, distinctiveness in people and places, books and conversations. This was an affinity he shared with his mentor, George MacDonald*. In CSL's book, *Miracles**, which is essential for understanding his view of God, many connections are made between the deep reality of particular things and the underlying factuality – the utter concreteness – of God.

CSL's view of God as the utterly concrete thing, the basic fact, was part and parcel of the supernaturalism that marks all his writings. CSL stressed the danger that our theoretical reasoning – which has to be abstract – can easily draw us from the particularity of the world. God is present to us first of all in given things, facts which resist being grasped fully in abstractions. Often CSL felt picture language, myth and stories came closer to grasping the concreteness of reality.

Like George MacDonald*, CSL saw God essentially as 'the glad creator' and hence regarded the incarnation as the central miracle, springing from God's involvement with his creation. Christian faith, beginning as it does with concrete historical events, endorses and delights in the reality and 'thereness' of the universe.

For many readers of CSL, he is most memorable for the fresh images of God and Christ that he created, enabling people in our modern world to see again the meaning of God's reality. These images include Aslan*, the Emperor-over-sea, Maleldil, the Old One, the Landlord, and even the pagan insights of the character of the Westwind, the God of the Mountain in *Till We Have Faces*. CSL's delight in God's creation was at the heart of his fantasy writing, and his theology of romance. (*See* CHAPTER 6.)

In JRRT's mythology of Middle-earth*, the name of God, creator of the world, is Ilúvatar. He is also called Eru, 'The One'. Ilúvatar means 'Father of All'. In *The Ainulindalë* is recorded how, when he created the angelic beings, he revealed to them the themes of creation in music. As his agents they helped to realize the vision in the making of the world. JRRT always endeavoured to invent his sub-created world in accord with Christian teaching. So Ilúvatar, like the biblical God, is creator out of nothing, with all else being creature. (*See* CHAPTER 6; CHRISTIAN MEANINGS IN THE FICTION OF JRRT.) As most of JRRT's fiction has a pre-Christian setting, he gives himself less scope than CSL to explore the nature of God, though he demonstrated that much could be revealed about him and his creation, for example about his providence. JRRT's published letters however give many insights into his understanding of God, which is thoroughly Trinitarian.

Though superficially, God seems absent from the events of Middle-earth*, in fact its history is the outworking of the themes of the music at the beginning of creation. Consequently, providence is a constant reality throughout the tales of Middle-earth. The presence of the will of Ilúvatar, the creator, emphasizes JRRT's idea of sub-creation*. In reading the fiction, the reader is aware of the mind and will of the teller and maker of the tale (JRRT). In making and telling stories, JRRT believed, we exercise a God-given right to be a sub-creator. If done with skill and integrity, our creation parallels the primary world. It is part of 'the seamless web of story'. The human creator parallels the divine creator, though on a sub-scale.

In JRRT's mythology, elves and humans are called 'The Children of Ilúvatar' as they were the special and direct creations of God, not the handiwork of the demiurgic angels. Their destiny had an element of mystery to it. The elves were to be forever tied up with the world, whereas the destiny of mortals beyond death was to be greater. These sorts of theological and philosophical themes constantly preoccupied JRRT as he invented his mythology. They contributed to his inability to complete his work.

CW's contribution to an understanding of the creator undoubtedly centres on God's relationship to time. CW worked out some of the imaginative and theological possibilities raised by the idea of all temporal events being present simultaneously to God.

See also JOY; MYTH

God in the Dock (CSL, 1970)
See UNDECEPTIONS (1971)

Graal, The (Holy)
See Grail, The (Holy)

Grab and Grace (1941)
Sequel to The House by the Stable*. In this play CW portrays grace as a mischievous boy, playing tricks on sin and pride; appearing as an image of light to the Accusers, and to the pagan Assantu as 'Father and Eater'.

Grail, The (Holy)
(Spelled 'Graal' in CW's War in Heaven*.) The wine-cup from which Jesus and the disciples drank at the last supper, said in late Arthurian legend to have been used by Joseph of Arimathea to receive the blood of the crucified Christ; then (in several accounts) brought to Britain by Joseph. In Arthurian legend, the Grail represents purity and perfection. The Knights of the Round Table quested for it. Launcelot was unsuccessful because he had committed adultery with Guinevere. Three of Arthur's purest and noblest knights, Galahad, Bors and Perceval, were granted a vision of the Grail.

The Grail legends draw from Christian tradition, Celtic myth, and pagan fertility mythology. The legend of the Dolorous Blow in Malory's Morte D'Arthur, which results in a wounded knight and a blighted land, and can only be redressed by Galahad's 'achievement' of the Sankgreal (Holy Grail), generated much future myth. It resonates in, for example, T.S. Eliot's The Waste Land and some children's play songs (cf. Iona and Peter Opie, The Lore and Language of Schoolchildren, 1959, passim). Cf. also Digory's quest in CSL's The Magician's Nephew*, and, for an example of the image of goodness redeeming a blighted land, Michael Ende, *The Neverending Story* (1979: Eng. tr. 1983).

CW devoted a chapter to 'The Grail' in the incomplete 'The Figure of Arthur'*. He discusses the identification of the act of the Eucharist with Jesus; it was an offering and a feeding, 'there was a kind of exchange in it'. The church came to discuss the nature of the Eucharist late; CW lists a number of theologians who raised the issue around the tenth to twelfth centuries. In the thirteenth century Innocent III implicated the whole church, rather than the priest alone, in the act of Communion. By the time of the Council of Lateran in 1215, the Eucharist had become one of the 'formulating doctrines'. But this doctrine unlike the others had to do with the visible. And it was a doctrine that provoked ritual. In 1264 Urban IV instituted the Feast of Corpus Christi, which for CW represents the culmination of the doctrine of the Sacred Body. 'The Act . . . United all contraries in a mystery of exchange . . . The [elements] were the material centre of Christendom; and they were the very Act that made them so.' CW concludes by observing that now 'almost any article connected with the Act served for its symbol'; the Grail might have been a dish. He mentions the Celtic myths of 'vessels of plenty and cauldrons of magic' and rejects the notion that these are the origins of the Grail tradition. The Eucharist, he argues, pre-dates the fables. And the Eucharist is much bigger than any petty myth. The biblically founded image of the Grail, by contrast, served as a poetic and epic image that possessed far superior strength, precisely because 'the Grail contained the very Act which was related to all . . . existence'.

In the final extant chapter of 'The Figure of Arthur' – 'The Coming of the Grail' – CW examines the European literary Grail traditions, and suggests two influences on twelfth-century writers: the theological discussion of the sacraments, and the crusades: 'the thought of the Eucharist and the thought of Jerusalem were in the minds of most men'. He considers the variations of Arthurian myth that lie behind Malory's work. He suggests that there were five stages: (a) the invention of the Grail's history; (b) the connection, most clearly through Merlin, with Arthur; (c) the invention of the Dolorous Blow; (d) the development of the love of Launcelot and Guinevere; (e) the invention of Galahad.

CW examines each of these in detail and goes on to describe how later writers made the Grail a definite, tangible object; no longer 'a grail' but 'the Grail', and 'the Holy Grail'. He recounts the legend of Joseph of Arimathea, to whom the resurrected Jesus entrusted the Grail. And he shows how the legend of the Grail becomes involved with the legendary history of Britain through Merlin, 'a prophet of the Grail'.

What then, concludes CW, is the achievement of the Grail? It is to live in the world where the incarnation and the sacrament(s) happen; to live beyond them, to be as conscious of them as of oneself. The fragment concludes with a discussion of the Matter of Britain and the world of Arthur's kingdom. *See also* CHAPTER 5

Great Dance, The

In medieval cosmology, one of three central elements: the others being the Great Chain of Being, and the system of correspondences*. The dance is a central theme in *The Greater Trumps**, where it is symbolized by the table of moving figures and enacted by the intervention of Love and of Law. The image is, in CW, an affirmation both of the harmony of the celestial spheres and also the Co-inherence* of all things. 'The name of the Dance is Charity, and only the saints really understand it. All evil represents some violating of the steps' (Thomas Howard, *The Novels of Charles Williams*, p. 253).

This concept is expounded in three classic studies. CSL's *The Discarded Image**: *An Introduction to Medieval and Renaissance Literature* (1964) is based on his Oxford lectures and draws on a wide range of medieval texts as sources. E.M.W. Tillyard, with whom CSL crossed swords in *The Personal Heresy: A Controversy** (1939), wrote a brilliantly succinct chapter in his *The Elizabethan World Picture* (1943). Both writers acknowledge the classic study of the Great Chain, setting the entire image into context, by the American critic Arthur O. Lovejoy, *The Great Chain of Being* (1936).

CSL takes up CW's medieval idea of the Great Dance powerfully in the climax to his *Perelandra**.
See also MUSIC

Great Divorce, The (CSL, 1945)

Like *The Screwtape Letters**, also by CSL, this story was first serialized in a religious periodical, and also concerns the relation of heaven and hell. The story opens in hell, with CSL standing in a bus queue on a pavement in a long, shabby street. Anyone in hell who wishes can take a bus trip to heaven, or at least its outlands. CSL takes such a trip with a varied collection of ghosts. Upon arrival in heaven the passengers find it painfully solid, hard and bright in comparison to hell. Much of the story is taken up with encounters between solid people and ghosts, who were friends, relations, or spouses on earth. Even though the solid people try to persuade the wraiths to stay, for CSL universalism is ruled out by the reality of human will. CSL's portrayal of the damned adds to Sartre's brilliant comment, 'Hell is other people', the reality that hell is also oneself.

CSL handles the question of salvation and damnation very sensitively. In both *The Screwtape Letters* and *The Great Divorce*, CSL highlights practical matters of the Christian life like family problems, selfishness, disagreement, greed and the persistence of bad habits.

Greater Trumps, The (CW, 1932)

CW's fifth novel shares many themes with its predecessors, such as romantic love*, Co-inherence*, the way of Exchange, substitution, the ability of good to conquer evil* even when evil is projected in magical power, and a sense of absolute spiritual principles inherent in the created cosmos. Moral choices and commitments are shown to have absolute implications.

Lothair Coningsby (significantly, an officer in law) has been bequeathed an ancient pack of Tarot* cards, in which his daughter Nancy's fiancé, Henry Lee, is extremely interested – and which, he shows Nancy, have strange powers. He shows Nancy how by holding the appropriate cards their corresponding elements can be made to appear. Nancy is successful in creating a quantity of soil.

The Coningsbys spend Christmas at the Lees' home. The Coningsbys encounter Joanna, Henry's deranged great-aunt, and her servant Stephen; Joanna believes she is the goddess Isis, doomed to wander in search of her dead child, Horus. Sybil Coningsby, Lothair's sister, is able to reason with her.

Henry's grandfather, Aaron, is of gypsy descent. In a secret room in his house he has an ancient model of a table on which golden figures, representing the symbols of the Tarot pack, perpetually dance. This is why Henry desires the pack of cards, for he believes it to be the original pack. If cards and table could be brought together, great and arcane knowledge would be revealed. Henry sees the possibility that he and Nancy, in the persona of the Lovers in the Tarot pack, could in a sense enter the dance and so acquire even deeper knowledge.

Henry's dilemma is that of persuading Lothair to give up the cards (promised already to the British Museum) without violence, which is forbidden. The solution Aaron proposes is to loose the cards' powers against him, releasing to the full the same forces that created soil for Nancy. Nancy, though she does not know of the plot against her father, is willing to join Henry in his quest for knowledge.

While Lothair is out of doors a great snowstorm arises. Nancy sees Henry at its centre and realizes that he is causing it with the cards. She struggles with him, and most of the pack is lost; the storm cannot now be controlled. Sybil rescues Lothair, Nancy's brother Ralph rescues Joanna and Stephen. Nancy confesses to Sybil, who suggests that Nancy's love for Henry may yet enable the table of dancers to restore order. They succeed in doing so, using the Greater Trumps that are all that remain of the pack. Nancy realizes the sublime mystery and power of love.

At this point Joanna seizes Nancy, intending to sacrifice her to free the lost child whose heart she believes she can hear beating in Nancy's, but Lothair interrupts the sacrifice. In the confrontation that follows Lothair's identification with Law and Sybil's with Love are victorious. Joanna summons the power of fire in the cards and brings about their final destruction. The novel ends with Sybil's pausing of the dance, and the superimposition upon the images of unleashed power and anarchic primal forces of the overarching controlling power of Love, personified in the last pages by the themes of Christmas, the resurrected child, and the Messiah.

There are considerable links with CW's preceding novel, *The Place of the Lion**, which also deals with correspondences between earthly objects and spiritual absolutes.

The novel uses the prototypes of the Tarot pack – for example Henry appears at times as the Hanged Man, Aaron as the Hermit, Sybil as the Priestess; the Moon Card is the basis of the description of the stilling of the storm; the Juggler and the Fool play crucial roles. There is continuous resonance with medieval religious models, not least the Great Dance* (see for example, E.M.W. Tillyard, *The Elizabethan World Picture*, 1943, ch. 8; CSL, *The Discarded Image*, 1964, passim; and Arthur Lovejoy, *The Great Chain of Being*, 1936, passim).

'Great war' (between CSL and OB)

See BARFIELD, OWEN

Grief Observed, A (CSL, 1961)

Originally published under a pseudonym, N.W. Clerk (*see* NAT WHILK), this slim book sets out CSL's pilgrimage through bereavement after losing his wife, Joy Davidman Lewis*. *A Grief Observed* complements his study, *The Problem of Pain**. He uses the device that it is written in four manuscript books as a kind of journal of grief, just as he uses the device of letters in *Letters to Malcolm**. Whereas *The Problem of Pain* explores suffering generally and theoretically, the journal observes it specifically and personally (or existentially). Like the earlier book, *A Grief Observed* affirms the presence of God in the deepest human darkness, even when he long seems absent.

Biographically, *A Grief Observed* reveals the quality of relationship between CSL and Joy Davidman Lewis. He remembers: 'She was my daughter and my mother, my pupil and my teacher, my subject and my sovereign; and always, holding all these in solution, my trusty comrade, friend, shipmate, fellow-soldier.'

Hadfield, Alice M.

Biographer of CW: *An Introduction to Charles Williams* (1959), and *Charles Williams: An Exploration of his Life and Work* (1983). She is also the author of other books including a retelling of the stories of King Arthur. Hadfield had access to a large amount of correspondence and other information, including letters written to and from CW's two great loves, his wife Florence and his 'second love' Phyllis Jones*. But she was also a close friend of CW, who shared with her some of his most private thoughts and to whom he explained much of his more elusive and complex ideas. 'I met him while working in my first jobs at the Oxford University Press, as editor of the *Oxford Dictionary of Quotations*, then being compiled, and later also as the Librarian . . . I worked with him, went to his evening lectures, heard him talk about his ideas and his books, and exchanged letters with him during the war. I am glad to say that I was among his friends until the end of his life.'

Hardie, Colin (1906–98)

A Scotsman and member of the Inklings, Colin Hardy was born in Edinburgh and earned a double first class degree at Balliol College, Oxford. After a period researching and teaching he became, in 1933, Director of the British School at Rome. In 1936 he was elected a Fellow and classical tutor at CSL's college, Magdalen. He had a particular interest in the works of Homer and Virgil. In 1945 he became a Roman Catholic, which coincided with a burgeoning interest in Dante. From 1967 to 1973 he was Public Orator at Oxford University. One of his last speeches was upon the occasion of JRRT's award of an honourary Doctorate of Letters on 3 June 1972.

It was during the Second World War that he was invited into the circle of the Inklings.

Harwood, Alfred Cecil (1898–1975)

A lifelong friend of CSL's who first met OB* when OB was a scholar at Christ Church, Oxford*. Both were introduced to CSL in 1919 through a mutual acquaintance, Leo Baker. Harwood was, like OB, an anthroposophist*. In 1931, Warren Lewis* described him in his diary as a 'pleasant, spectacled, young looking man, with a sense of humour of a whimsical kind, to whom I took at sight . . . we found ourselves seeing everything with much the same eye'. After CSL's death he was for many years joint executor of his estate with OB, and then a trustee.

Havard, Dr Robert E. 'Humphrey' (1901–85)

Affectionately known as the 'Useless Quack', he was the doctor of JRRT and CSL, and member of the Inklings. Some of his recollections are recorded by the Oral History Project of the Wade Center at Wheaton College. The son of an Anglican clergyman, 'Humphrey' Havard studied medicine after graduating in chemistry at Oxford in 1922 and became a doctor. In 1934 he took over a medical practice in Oxford with surgeries in Headington and St

117

Giles (near 'The Eagle and Child' public house, haunt of the Inklings). It was soon after this that he got to know CSL and was invited to the Inklings. He and CSL took to each other instantly.

It was years later that Havard says he woke up one morning to find his friends famous. He appears briefly as a character in *Perelandra**. In 1943 he volunteered for the Royal Navy Reserve, and became a naval surgeon. When he returned to Oxford (because of his wife's breast cancer) he was dubbed 'the Red Admiral' by the Inklings because he now sported a red beard, and turned up to a meeting in uniform. 'Hugo' Dyson called him 'Humphrey' because he couldn't remember his name. Havard converted to Roman Catholicism in 1931, influenced by Ronald Knox. He had five children. His wife succumbed to her cancer in 1950. Havard is one of the best sources for insight into the character of the Inklings and their meetings. As far as Havard was concerned, CSL was the axis of the group, though CSL himself denied this when Havard suggested that without him the group would split up. All the group recognized CSL as being the dominant personality, but there was no authoritarianism. According to Havard, the group had a critical Christianity. All of them, in one way or another, were dissatisfied with the church as it existed here and now, but not with Christian doctrine.

Havard recalled that the Inklings were inclined to laugh in a good-natured way at the idea of CSL doing radio broadcasts. They did not take him that seriously. They had no idea that he was going to develop into the figure that he is today. CSL was simply one among many. They either liked or didn't like what he read to them; usually they liked it, and would say so. None in the group was aware of being anything special. They were simply a group of friends. There were no rules, and 'no subscription except CSL's hospitality'. According to Havard the Inklings' meetings had a free and easy atmosphere – as informal a gathering as he had ever attended. Members said what they thought 'without let or hindrance'. Havard also recalled CW with affection. What struck Havard about him was his charm and laughter. 'He was always full of laughter, ready to join in any joke that was going. He would throw his arms back and his head to the ceiling, chuckling with joy. But when it came to reading his work, I couldn't understand a word of it.' He felt that others in the group shared his view, except CSL. But even he protested at the obscurity, saying on one occasion, 'Charles, you're impossible.' JRRT, he recalled, had intense reservations about CW 'dabbling in the occult'. Havard observed that this in fact strained the friendship between CSL and JRRT. '[CSL] was fascinated by CW, and rightly; he [had] a very extraordinary charm. You couldn't be in the same room with him without being attracted to him.' Havard felt that he had a 'curious, rather mixed character'. In some way he 'wasn't fully integrated'. On the friendship of CSL and JRRT, and its eventual cooling, Havard observed: 'The surprising thing, really, is that they became such close friends, rather than that differences appeared and separated them.'

Dr Havard appears to some extent in fictional form in the redhaired and redbearded character of Rupert Dolbear in 'The Notion Club Papers'*.

FURTHER READING

Robert E. Havard, 'Philia: Jack at Ease', in *C.S. Lewis at the Breakfast Table* (edited by James T. Como, 1979); Marion Wade Center Oral History Project.

He Came down from Heaven (CW, 1938)

Published as the fifth in a series entitled 'I Believe: A Series of Personal Statements', this was CW's first book of theology. It is in two parts: first, how God relates to humanity; second, how human beings relate to each other. He begins with a discussion of heaven, a non-negotiable that like God himself is the backdrop against which human activities proceed. Terms like 'choosing' or 'accepting' God are alien to CW, who here as elsewhere deals in terms of obedience, of submission to the divine Will, of acceptance only in the sense of accepting what God is and desires (though not mute, zombie-like acceptance: see below). He develops this in the context of romantic love, and introduces the concepts of affirmation* and rejection; to know something is good is to know other things are not: 'This also is Thou; neither is this Thou.' Contradictions proliferate, as does mystery; in chapter 3 he turns to Job, comparing his arguing and contending with God to the way of Ecclesiastes, who said it was no use to rail against God. The comparison, according to CW, is between the sensible received wisdom of Ecclesiastes and the tempestuous, stormy Job-like realities of the poets and mystics. The incarnation is a similar uncomfortable, dangerous state. The gospel is 'a state of being, but not a state of being without which one can get along very well . . . It is intensely dangerous, and yet easily neglected.' The original choice of Adam, and the remedy of God, he says, mean that we can now 'know evil as an occasion of heavenly love' – provided, and only if, repentance is part of that knowledge.

His writing on Dante* in the chapter on romantic love was to be followed later by *The Figure of Beatrice**. (The chapter, incidentally, includes a long quotation from CSL's *The Allegory of Love**.) CW expounds the way of romantic love, pointing out that though it can be followed without invoking the name of God, its demands are only met by Christianity. He cites three 'principle attacks' of hell in this way: 1) the assumption that it will be everlasting; 2) the assumption that it is personal; and 3) the assumption that it is sufficient. His dealing with these points is poignant in view of his earlier love for Phyllis Jones*: analysing Dante's discussion of love in *The New Life* and *The Divine Comedy*, he points out how, in Paradise, Dante is found by Beatrice and the old love rekindles:

> Here, surrounded by angels, prophets, evangelists, virtues, Romantic Love is seen to mirror the Humanity and Deity of the Redeemer... All the exchanges of love lie open. But really, though he had imagined it more clearly and more strongly, he had not known anything different, in essence or in principle, when the face of the Florentine girl flashed her 'good morning' at him along the street of their city.

The chapter on 'The Practice of Substituted Love' gathers three of CW's chief concerns – Co-inherence*, Exchange and substitution. He devotes much of the chapter to explaining that *exchange* must result in *change*. This change, in individuals, he argues, is seen by exchange of qualities, so that, for example, 'this man's patience shall adorn that man'. Thus he moves to his last chapter, 'The City', where he describes a city* that inheres by a network of *caritas*, of joyous love; a city that is and that shall be, in which God is the light and the only excluded ones are those who love lies. In that city the only reason a thing is loved is that God loves it, and the abiding principle is glory. Foreshadowing heaven, possessing some of heaven's characteristics, it is a gift given to those who have nothing; an exchange of glory for poverty. The city is to be lived, not talked. He ends by noting that the city is a prescription as well as a reality, and reminding his readers of 'the threat which must inevitably accompany the coming of the heavenly thing onto earth: "Blessed is he whosoever shall not be offended at me."'

In 1950 Faber and Faber published a combined edition of this book and CW's *The Forgiveness of Sins*, which Bles had published in 1942. The book is dedicated to the Inklings. CW explains, 'I propose ... first to examine how forgiveness is presented in Shakespeare; afterwards how it appears in the theology of the Christian Church; and finally, how it operates, or should operate, among men.' In the latter he argues that forgiveness is applicable '(i) to things which need not be forgiven; (ii) to things which can be forgiven; (iii) to things which cannot be forgiven.' Characteristic CW themes of mutuality, the City*, and Co-inherence* – expressed as the communion of saints – leads him to a conclusion in which responsibility of forgiveness towards one's neighbour is argued in a passage reminiscent of the conclusion to CSL's essay 'The Weight of Glory'.

Healing

As a counter to the ever-present effects of evil* and the Fall* this theme is persistent particularly in JRRT's fiction. Healing powers are often a quality of gifted people, whether Maiar, elves or humans – such as Melian, Gandalf, Lúthien, Beleg (in the tale of Túrin Turambar*), or Aragorn. It is also a property of certain places such as the Pools of Ivrin, Lórien or Fangorn Forest. Healing can also be instituted as an expression of care, as in the Houses of Healing in Minas Tirith.

When Beren was grey and exhausted by his journey to Doriath across the Nan Dungortheb the sight of Lúthien's beauty, and her singing, brought healing to him – the power of romantic love*. Lúthien's healing powers are often exercised (*see BEREN AND LÚTHIEN THE ELF-MAIDEN, THE TALE OF*), as when she healed Beren of the evil wound he received from Carcharoth. Her greatest healing deed was when, by her sacrifice, she brought Beren back from the dead.

One of the principal healers in *The Lord of the Rings** is the future king, Aragorn. The power of healing was part of his true kingship, a kingship that was Christ-like (*see* CHRISTIAN MEANINGS IN THE FICTION OF JRRT). One of his ancient names was *Envinyatar*, the Renewer. His healing hands are laid on Faramir, the Lady Eowyn and the Hobbit, Merry. The healing process took great skill and persistence. In this restoration an old prophecy was fulfilled: 'Life to the dying/In the king's hand lying!'

In CW, healing is central to the Arthurian poems (the healing of the Dolorous Blow), and is often seen in inversion, as for example the healing gifts of Simon the Clerk. On a deeper level, the healing of relationships both between God and man and between human beings is very much part of the working of the Co-inherence*.

Henry VII (CW, 1935)

One of the short biographies commissioned by Arthur Barker. CW found it a difficult book to write, and struggled to complete 70,000 words: 'The real title of the book ought to be "The King Without a Face".'
See also BIOGRAPHIES OF CHARLES WILLIAMS

Heroes and Kings (CW, 1930)

This collection of CW's poems was printed at the suggestion of Hubert Foss, a colleague at the Oxford University Press and the composer of the music to CW's masques. At Foss's suggestion, 300 copies were printed of an 80-page book, finely printed and bound, illustrated by Norman Janes. The printers were Henderson and Spalding, associates of Foss, and the imprint was the Sylvan Press. Of the 300 copies, 250 were offered for sale.

It contains poems that were the beginning of the Arthurian cycle that was to continue in *Taliessin through Logres*, *The Region of the Summer Stars*, and the unfinished *Advent of Arthur* (*see* ARTHURIAN POEMS).

History

History preoccupies both CSL and JRRT, and CW wrote popular historical biographies. OB explored historical changes in human consciousness.

In much of his literary criticism, CSL was a literary historian. In an important essay, 'Historicism' (1950), first published in book form in *Christian Reflections**, he expressed his attitude to the study of history. This essay contains both an affirmation and a denial concerning the meaning of history.

On the one hand, CSL believes absolutely that human history is 'a story written by the finger of God'. On the other hand, he firmly rejects all claims to know the inner meaning and patterns of history by means of mere rational observation of events. Writing history is of course worthwhile, but grand philosophies of history (historicisms) are doomed to futility. Thinkers such as Hegel, Marx, and even Augustine, have worked out such grand schemes. He comments: 'If by one miracle, the total content of time were spread out before me, and if, by another, I were able to hold all that infinity of events in my mind and if, by a third, God were pleased to comment on it so I could understand it, then, to be sure, I could do what the Historicist says he is doing. I could read the meaning, discern the pattern.'

CSL wants instead to emphasize trust in God and an openness to ordinary human reality – the 'primary history' in which God reveals himself in the moment by moment experience of life to each one who seeks him. That this view of history doesn't lead to scepticism about the value of culture is clear from another key essay, 'Learning in War-Time', where he points out the abiding value of scholarship.

JRRT affirmed the value of history by exploring it through invented history. History, real or feigned, resonates with our lives and is therefore constantly applicable. For JRRT myth and history meet in the Gospels (*see* MYTH). CW composed a history of the church, *The Descent of the Dove**, and wrote a number of historical biographies. OB in turn explored significant changes in human consciousness, particularly in his *History in English Words** and *History, Guilt and Habit**.

History, Guilt and Habit (OB, 1979)

An excellent introduction to OB's thought which is lucid and distils his earlier work of over 50 years. Chapter 1 draws on his lifelong interest in history, as in *History in English Words** (1926). For OB, language itself records the history of, and changes in, human consciousness. Chapter 2 focuses upon idolatry*, the theme of *Saving the Appearances** (1957). He employs this concept to highlight the main heresy of the modern world of scientism* and technocracy. He points out a serious one-sidedness in contemporary knowledge and virtue, a theme that complements CSL's *The Abolition of*

*Man**. Chapter 3 reflects OB's belief that a 'Romanticism come of age' gives hope for a future reconciliation between humanity, nature* and God*. The imagination* has a key role to play in restoring a perception of the inside of things as well as their surfaces. In an older age (*see* OLD WEST) perceptions were images – symbolically portraying the actual world. The modern mistakenly worships the image. This idolatry misplaces the image, thus the surface, for the reality. This leads to a reduced reality, stripped of qualities like beauty and love. Paradoxically it denies the very human consciousness that is able to make such a truth-claim. (In CSL's parallel analysis, this is the problem of naturalism.)

Whereas for CSL and JRRT a critique of the modern world is based upon Christian orthodoxy, OB finds an affinity with his approach in anthroposophy*. There is considerable overlap however between OB, CSL and JRRT. In their core ideas not only do they share a deep preoccupation with language, but also a profound sense of great loss in the modern consciousness. They all sought to rehabilitate insights from an older world, in the belief that such values constitute the irreplaceable character of our humanity.

In *History, Guilt and Habit* OB argues that, though we can distinguish between thinking and perception, we are not to divide them. This is because consciousness includes perception as well as thinking. Knowledge is both subjective and objective. Our ordinary perception is of the actual world – the world of molecules and particles disclosed by science is not more real.

OB points out that changes in human consciousness are therefore also changes in the actual world. Consciousness is not on the 'outside', but rather on the 'inside' of the world. But perception is not as such based on a particular philosophy. Rather, it is founded on historically entrenched habits of thought – habits that are to us unconscious. For this reason the study of changes in consciousness in history is different from a history of ideas.

This interpenetration of thinking and perceiving is a fact of consciousness. It is easier to see the interpenetration in language than in consciousness itself, for it is impossible of course for consciousness to stand outside its consciousness. Language, according to OB, reveals a varying proportion of thinking and perceiving – for instance, poetic language is more perceptual than prose, and prose more conceptual than poetry (*see also* POETIC DICTION).

History in English Words (OB, 1926)

This, OB's second book, is a meditation on the etymology of key words, tracing changes in human consciousness, changes OB regarded as an 'evolution of consciousness'*. For OB, a history of consciousness must be very different from a history of ideas, as he points out in *History, Guilt and Habit**. Consciousness is intimately related to perception as well as to the products of thinking. Once upon a time, there was a feeling thinking and a perceiving word. The etymology of words often gives a glimpse of an ancient unity of consciousness, as OB tries to show. Cultural and historical changes might be better explained by shifts in consciousness than by changes in intellectual ideas.

OB explained the background to the book in an interview with G.B. Tennyson in 1992:

> I . . . found that by tracing the changes of meanings of words, you do get an insight into the kind of consciousness that our ancestors had, which was very different from our own, and by writing a book dealing with individual words in some detail, I could bring that out . . . What I was anxious to point out, and what I thought was brought out by these etymological observations was that it wasn't just people in the past who think like us but have different ideas, but who didn't think like us altogether at all. They had a different kind of thinking. That impressed itself on me fairly early . . . Which of course is another way of formulating the concept of the evolution of consciousness.

History of the Lord of the Rings (JRRT)

A series of four books, part of *The History of Middle-earth**, which collect early drafts of *The Lord of the Rings**. The books are *The Return of the Shadow**, *The Treason of Isengard**, *The War of the Ring** and *Sauron Defeated**.

History of Middle-earth

Strictly, Middle-earth is only part of the world, or Ea. Before the change in the world, after the destruction of Númenor, the Undying Lands of the West, including Valinor, were physically part of the world. The history of elves and humans incorporates events in Valinor. The history can be divided into four Ages.

Much of JRRT's fiction concerned the history, annals, languages and chronology, and geography of Middle-earth. He intended to make an inwardly consistent sub-creation*. There were a number of major tales which stood (or were intended to stand) independently of the history, with that history as an imaginatively appealing backdrop. The tales were those of Beren and Lúthien the elf-maiden*, Túrin Turambar*, Tuor and the Fall of Gondolin*, the Voyage of Eärendil the Mariner, *The Hobbit** and *The Lord of the Rings**. JRRT may of course have intended to create others.

JRRT also invented a beautiful cosmological myth, portraying events before the creation of the world.

See also CHAPTER 4

History of Middle-earth, The (JRRT)

The title of a series of volumes of unfinished or preliminary material edited and published after JRRT's death by his son, Christopher*, who also provides a detailed commentary. The volumes are *The Book of Lost Tales**, *The Lays of Beleriand**, *The Shaping of Middle-earth**, *The Lost Road**, the four books of *The History of the Lord of the Rings**, *Morgoth's Ring**, *The War of the Jewels**, and *The Peoples of Middle-earth**.

Hobbit, The (JRRT, 1937)

This children's story belongs to the Third Age of Middle-earth*, and chronologically precedes *The Lord of the Rings**. It came out on 21 September 1937. JRRT himself recalls the story beginning many years earlier, when he came across a blank page on an exam he was marking. On it he wrote the now famous words: 'In a hole in the ground there lived a hobbit'. The writing of the book probably began in 1930 or 1931. CSL was shown a draft before the end of 1932. JRRT's eldest sons remember the story being told to them before the 1930s. Perhaps various oral forms of the story merged into the more finished written draft. What is significant is that *The Hobbit* begins as a tale told by JRRT to his children.

It is also clear that at first the story was independent of his burgeoning mythological cycle, *The Silmarillion*, and only later became drawn into the single invented world and history. The tale introduced hobbits into this world and history, dramatically affecting the course of events.

A party of dwarves, 13 in number, are on a quest for their long-lost treasure, which is jealously guarded by a dragon. Their leader is the great Thorin Oakenshield. They employ Bilbo Baggins as their burglar to steal it, at the recommendation of the wizard Gandalf the Grey. The reluctant Mr Baggins would rather spend a quiet day with his pipe and pot of tea in his comfortable hobbit-hole than partake in any unrespectable adventure.

The dwarves become increasingly thankful for the fact that they employed him, despite initial misgivings, as he gets them out of many scrapes. He seems to have extraordinary luck, but there is an underlying sense of providence at work in events. At one point in the adventure Bilbo is knocked unconscious in a goblin tunnel under the Misty Mountains, and left behind in the darkness by the rest of the party.

Reviving, Bilbo discovers a ring lying beside him in the tunnel. It is the ruling ring that forms the subject of *The Lord of the Rings*, but Bilbo is to discover only its magical property of invisibility at this stage. After putting the ring in his pocket, Bilbo stumbles along the black tunnel. Eventually, he comes across a subterranean lake, where Gollum dwells, a luminous-eyed corruption of a hobbit, his life preserved over centuries by the ring he has now lost for the first time. After a battle of riddles, Bilbo escapes, seemingly by luck, by slipping on the ring. Following the vengeful Gollum, who cannot see him, he finds his way out of the mountains, on the other side.

Bilbo's discovery of the ring provided JRRT with the link between *The Hobbit* and its large sequel, *The Lord of the Rings*. However it proved necessary for JRRT to partially rewrite chapter 5 of the former book to provide proper continuity between the two works over the great significance of the ruling ring. He drafted this in 1947, in the midst of composing *The Lord of the Rings*. The new edition, incorporating the revised chapter, first appeared in 1951.

In the story the plucky Bilbo eventually leads the party successfully to the dragon's treasure, and the scaly monster perishes while attacking nearby Lake-town. Bilbo and Gandalf in the end journey back to the peaceful Shire. Bilbo has refused most of his share of the treasure, having seen the results of greed. The events have changed him for ever, but even more, the ring he secretly possesses will shape the events recorded in *The Lord of the Rings*.

Significant information about the background to 'The quest of Erebor' (the events of *The Hobbit*) is found in *Unfinished Tales** (published posthumously in 1980). There we learn of the reluctance of the dwarves to take along a hobbit, the great persuasion Gandalf had to muster for Thorin, and the place that providence played in the unfolding of events.

What is striking about the book is JRRT's skill in adjusting the scale of his great mythology of the earlier ages of Middle-earth to the level of children. Names for instance are simple, in complete contrast to the complexities of *The Silmarillion*. Erebor is simply The Lonely Mountain. Esgaroth is usually called Lake-town. Elrond's home in Rivendell is described as the Last Homely House west of the Mountains.

Holy Grail
See GRAIL, THE (HOLY)

Hooper, Walter (b. 1931)
Described by *The Independent* (7 March 1994) as Lewis' other American (the first being Joy Davidman Lewis*), Walter Hooper was born in Reidsville, North Carolina. He was educated at the University of North Carolina in Chapel Hill. After serving in the US Army, he read theology at Virginia Episcopal Seminary. He taught English at Christ School, Arden, North Carolina, 1960–61, and then at the University of Kentucky in Lexington, 1961–63.

After corresponding for a while, Lewis invited Walter Hooper to visit him in Oxford. They met on 7 June 1963, and Hooper attended his first meeting of the Inklings a few days later. That summer, in poor health, Lewis accepted Hooper's offer of secretarial assistance. 'There followed the happiest period of my life', Mr Hooper told the author, 'for Lewis was a thousand times more interesting than his books. But the privilege was of short duration. I was in Kentucky teaching one final term before returning to Oxford when Lewis died.'

When Hooper did return to Oxford in 1964, the Lewis estate hired him to collate and edit Lewis's literary legacy. Hooper has been working since 1964 as the literary adviser to the estate, during which time he has edited a number of Lewis' posthumous publications. In 1974 he and Roger Lancelyn Green co-authored the first authorized biography of Lewis.

Formerly an Anglican, Walter Hooper became a Roman Catholic in 1988. He is the author of the definitive *C.S. Lewis: A Companion and Guide* (1996). Walter Hooper has undoubtedly contributed more than any other individual to Lewis' popularity throughout the world by his unstinted devotion to the publication of Lewis' works, many of which would have otherwise been neglected.

Hopkins, Gerard Manley (1844–89)

CW contributed a critical introduction to the second edition of the *Poems* (1930). Hopkins' nephew, Gerard (Gerry) Hopkins, was a colleague at the Oxford University Press.

Horse and His Boy, The (CSL, 1954)

Set in the period of Narnia's Golden Age, most of the story unfolds in the cruel southern land of Calormen. Cor, a lost prince of the friendly country of Archenland, knows nothing of his true origin, but has a strange longing to travel to the northern lands. The story also concerns a high-born Calormene girl, Aravis, who runs away from home to flee an unpleasant marriage. Both children independently encounter Narnian talking horses, in captivity in Calormen, who tell them about the freedom of Narnia's pleasant land, and who escape with the children. When passing through Calormen's capital, Tashbaan, Aravis uncovers a treacherous plot to conquer Archenland and Narnia, led by the spiteful Prince Rabadash, foiled in his suit of Queen Susan of Narnia. Both the sceptical Narnian talking horse Bree and the disdainful Aravis have to encounter Aslan*.

House by the Stable, The (CW, 1939)

A nativity play written by CW for Ruth Spalding's drama group in Oxford. It tells how Pride was driven out of the house of Man, having been responsible for the banishing of Joseph and Mary to the stable. Although the characters are types rather than personalities the play is more than a mystery play, and there are some effective passages including the dicing for the soul of Man. CW wrote a sequel, *Grab and Grace*, in which sanctification is described as a comic farce, Pride once again being driven out under the guise of Self-Respect. The characters play out a readily grasped theology: Faith and Pride are unable to live together, for example. Like Bunyan's *The Pilgrim's Progress*, these plays by personalizing traits and characters turn theology into high drama.

House of the Octopus, The (CW, 1945)

Based on characters and themes from the Arthurian poems*, this is a missionary play written for the United Council for Missionary Education. It tells of a Christian island outpost invaded by enemy forces who plan to weaken the faith of the people as a means of conquest. The pagan Assau represents an interesting perversion of Exchange: 'I wish not to be eaten, but to eat others;/I wish to grow great and thrive on others'. It is a rejection of exchange. By contrast the motives of the island priest, Anthony, are quite the reverse: 'Grant this, blessed Spirit, and bless/me to my task, whatever their present wants'.

Howatch, Susan (b. 1940)

Already a best-selling novelist because of her *Penmarric* series, Susan Howatch has more recently written a sextet of novels portraying the Church of England in the twentieth century. In them, like the novels of CW, substantial theological discussion is intertwined with very readable narratives to the detriment of neither; she might be regarded in some ways as the heir to part of CW's achievement. The novels (which average around 600 pages each) are technically superior to those of CW (whose characters are often sketchily drawn and whose plots are sometimes perplexing, with subplots launched and later abandoned); but they discuss several related themes. For example, the central issue in *Glamorous Powers* (1988) – the worthy use of supernatural spiritual gifts – is the same as that faced by Chloe Burnett in *Many Dimensions**.

Ideas, Platonic

CSL, JRRT, OB and CW drew inspiration from Plato's philosophy of ideas. In OB's terms, they represented an ancient unity of thinking and perception that we have greatly lost, seeing glimpses in poetry and dreams. Plato's analogy of the cave was particularly an inspiration for CSL's idea of the

Shadowlands, portrayed in the Narnian Chronicles *The Silver Chair** and *The Last Battle**, and elsewhere (as in the solid matter of the outskirts of heaven in *The Great Divorce**). JRRT draws upon Plato for his magnificent creation myth that opens *The Silmarillion**, *The Ainulindalë*. CW displays the reality of the ideas or principles behind creation in *The Place of the Lion**, described by CSL as a blend of Genesis and Plato.
See also PLATO

Idolatry

OB explored modern idolatry in *Saving the Appearances** (1957) and *History, Guilt and Habit** (1979). For him, idolatry marks the failure to perceive the inner nature of things, abstracting the external sense-object. It marks a lack of participation in our knowledge of the world. Scientism is a dominant modern example of idolatry. In CSL's *De Descriptione Temporum** he follows OB's concept of idolatry in characterizing our times as the period of the machine. He locates the great divide between the Old West* and the Post-Christian West in the last century on the basis of the machine becoming an archetype. He deliberately refrains from locating the change simply in terms of ideas, although these are important. There are parallels, too, between OB's *Saving the Appearances* and CSL's *The Discarded Image**, in that CSL gives high place to changes in consciousness in effecting our perception of nature – changes which lead to the 'discarding' of the medieval model of the cosmos. Our thinking and science is not neutral because of our suscept-ability to idolatry. OB wrote that idolatry 'results when man begins to take his models – his representations – literally' (*Saving the Appearances*, p. 51).

Image

For CW, the images of everyday life were things in which God was to be found; the way of affirmation* is a sacramental awareness of the in-Goddedness of images, a similar idea to Gerard Manley Hopkins' 'inscape' by which the most ordinary thing could be seen to possess a unique quality that made it what it was and defined what it was not. The way of the affirmation of images is important in many of CW's writings (*see DESCENT OF THE DOVE*, and passim). Describing CW's writing on Dante*, Dorothy L. Sayers* said that the key word in his criticism was 'image'.

Imagination
See CHAPTER 6

Immortality
See DEATH

'Imram' (JRRT)

A poem concerning the voyage of St Brendan. JRRT altered the story to fit his invented mythology. The poem was intended to be part of the (unfinished) 'The Notion Club Papers'*, which was to feature time-travel like *The Lost Road**. 'Imram' is Gaelic for 'voyage'. The poem mentions the Lost Road, a 'shoreless mountain' (Meneltarma) marking 'the foundered land' (Númenor), a mysterious island (Tol Eressëa) with a white Tree (Celeborn), and a beautiful star (Eärendil) marking the old road leading beyond the world.

'Imram' was published in *Time and Tide*, 3 December 1955.

Intello d'Amore: An Introduction to Romantic Theology (CW, 1924)

A change of title for *Outlines of Romantic Theology* (1924)*, by CW, suggested by a publisher's reader at Faber and Gwyer (later Faber and Faber, who published several of his novels). CW approved of the change.

Iron Crown Enterprises (ICE)

Now defunct game publisher based in Virginia, USA, who published a range of Tolkien-based board games (notably *Fellowship of the Ring*), fantasy role playing games (notably *Middle-earth Role Playing* and the *Lord of the Rings Adventure Game*) and a collectible card game, *Middle-earth: The Wizards* and its sequels. The games are now out of print, though a second-hand market exists. The company's products are marked by meticulous research, often developing areas of Middle-earth lore left unexplored by Tolkien: the text of the role playing games is very literate and sympathetic to Tolkien's style, and the artwork, which is often very fine, builds on Tolkien's own. The games illuminate and comment on Tolkien's work as much as books can, and in some cases, in ways that books cannot.

ICE launched a number of newsletters and clubs based on Tolkien's world. A series of fantasy multi-choice novels include titles from Tolkien; a series of Narnia fantasy game books was withdrawn for licensing reasons. Both series, though less distinguished than the role playing games, are well-produced and competently written and illustrated.

In a market where acquisition of a sought-after marketing licence often leads to disappointing products being published, ICE's work stands out and has a great deal to offer Tolkien enthusiasts who may not have thought of the games industry as relevant to Middle-earth. The equivalent Narnia products, though entertaining, are much less significant as resources.

Islam

See CHAPTER 5; *MANY DIMENSIONS*

James, Montague Rhodes (1862–1936)

Medievalist, palaeographer and linguist, James (who became Provost of Eton College) was also a writer of horror stories in the tradition of Sheridan Le Fanu. CW shows traces of his influence, especially in his learned characters and his sense of the identification of evil* with particular places and buildings. In *War in Heaven** the character of Gregory Persimmons has significant similarities to that of Karswell in 'Casting the Runes' (*More Ghost Stories*, 1911), whose evil as an occultist is demonstrated by gratuitous mental and spiritual terrorizing of the local children – and who is thought to have been based, like several of CW's characters, on Aleister Crowley.

James I (CW, 1934)

See BIOGRAPHIES BY CHARLES WILLIAMS

Jerusalem

See CHAPTER 5

Jones, Phyllis

The object of CW's romantic devotion for several years (during which he was married to Florence), Phyllis (frequently referred to by CW as 'Celia') was 15 years younger, and a librarian at Oxford University Press offices. The love was not returned: in fact she married an older colleague and went to live abroad. No sexual relationship developed, though CW writes frankly (and sometimes by implication) of the strong physical attraction he felt for her.

Joy in CSL and JRRT

The quality of joy is central to CSL's thought, experience, and writing. This longing for beauty or joy he learned from gazing at the Castlereagh Hills of Belfast from his nursery windows. Towards the end of his life CSL personified the imaginative longing in a character in *Till We Have Faces**. Because myths and other-worldly tales can often define this longing for beauty, CSL defended and wrote this type of literature throughout his distinguished career.

There is a relationship between love and zest for life and the desire for beauty that constantly fascinated CSL. CSL's own imaginative creations such as *The Chronicles of Narnia** sprang from this love of life. The creation of another world, he believed, is an attempt to reconcile human beings and the world, to embody the fulfilment of our imaginative longing. Imaginative worlds, wonderlands, are 'regions of the spirit'. Joy for CSL is the key both to the nature of human beings and to their creator.

CSL saw this unquenchable longing as a sure sign that no part of the created world, and thus no aspect of human experience, is capable of fulfilling fallen humankind. In *Surprised By Joy** CSL reported his sensations of joy, some of which were responses to natural beauty and others of which were literary or artistic responses, in the belief that other people would recognize similar experiences of their own. 'Joy', wrote CSL, 'is the serious business of Heaven.'

In attempting to imagine heaven, CSL discovered that joy is 'the secret signature of each soul'. CSL's portrayal of joy can be seen as providing valuable data of a key human experience, data which have philosophical and religious importance.

Sehnsucht, seen as a yearning or longing that is a pointer to joy, was for CSL a defining characteristic of fantasy. Like CSL, JRRT desired to embody that quality in his work. Though associated with CSL, joy is distinctive too in JRRT's fiction, and deeply valued by him, as his essay 'On Fairy Stories' makes clear. It is a key feature of such stories, he believes, related to the happy ending, or *eucatastrophe*, part of the consolation they endow. JRRT believes that joy in the story marks the presence of grace from the primary world. 'It denies (in the face of much evidence, if you will) universal final defeat and in so far is *evangelium*, giving a fleeting glimpse of Joy, Joy beyond the walls of the world, poignant as grief'. He adds: 'In such stories when the sudden "turn" comes we get a piercing glimpse of joy, and hearts desire, that for a moment passes outside the frame, rends indeed the very web of story, and lets a gleam come through.'

In an epilogue to the essay, JRRT gives more consideration to the quality of joy, linking it to the Gospel narratives, which have all the qualities of an other-worldly, fairy story, while at the same time being primary world history. This doubleness intensifies the quality of joy, identifying its objective source.

In JRRT, there is not only the quality of joy linked to the sudden turn in the story, the sense of *eucatastrophe*, but also this joy as inconsolable longing, in CSL's sense. Dominating the entire cycle of his tales of Middle-earth* is a longing to obtain the Undying Lands of the uttermost West. The longing is often symbolized by a longing for the sea, which lay to the west of Middle-earth, and over which lay Valinor, even if by a hidden road.

Such longing is sharply portrayed in Galadriel, who, since the rebellion of the Noldor, had been forbidden to return to the West from Middle-earth. Her longing is poignantly captured in her song. Though a Wood Elf, Legalas grows to long for the sea and the west. In *The Silmarillion**, Turgon of Gondolin instructs mariners to seek a way to the West in the hope that the

Valar, the lords of the West, might help him. One of them, Voronwë, is gripped by the longing of his people, and, in the purposes of providence, leads Tuor to Gondolin. On a more homely level, Sam is gripped with longing for all things elvish before he is chosen to aid Frodo in the quest to destroy the One Ring.

Judgement at Chelmsford (CW, 1939)

A historical pageant by CW commissioned for the twenty-fifth anniversary of the diocese of Chelmsford. It was postponed because of the war and was not performed until 1947. Its use of time as different aspects of the same event has some links with the concept of simultaneity by which the plots of several of CW's novels are constructed.

Kirkpatrick, W.T. (1848–1921)

Born on 19 January 1848, in Carrickmaddyroe, Broadmills, Co. Down. CSL described him as the greatest single intellectual influence on his life, according to Walter Hooper. For CSL, in his autobiography *Surprised by Joy**, he was the 'Great Knock' who forced him to think logically. Kirkpatrick was CSL's private tutor between 1914 and 1917. Before his retirement he had been headmaster of Lurgan College, in Northern Ireland, where he had tutored CSL's father, Albert.

Kolbitar, The

An informal reading club initiated by JRRT soon after he became a professor at Oxford* to explore Icelandic literature such as the *Poetic Edda*. The name meant those who crowd so close to the fire in winter that they seem to 'bite the coal'. CSL attended meetings, as did Nevill Coghill*. It pre-dated the Inklings.

'Lalage'

See Lang-Sims, Lois

Lang-Sims, Lois ('Lalage')

Lang-Sims is a writer whose work has several qualities in common with those of CW. Her novel *The Contrite Heart* (1968) has some similarities to his novels, and *Canterbury Cathedral* (1979), a history, shares CW's concern with the spiritual qualities of place and history. Her *Christian Mystic* (1980) is considered to owe a great deal to CW by Glen Cavaliero, who introduces *Letters to Lalage* (1989) – the collected correspondence between CW and Lang-Sims.

In September 1943 Lois Lang-Sims wrote to CW after reading his *The Figure of Beatrice**. She asked him who was supposed to be the object of love in 'the Dantean experience'. An extended correspondence and friendship followed from this, which demonstrates the almost hypnotic fascination that CW, then 30 years her senior, exerted upon his admirers. Like H.G. Wells, he was said to have been very attractive to women, though there is no suggestion that he was ever unfaithful to his wife, Michal. On the other hand, Lang-Sims recounts extraordinary episodes in which CW declared that she must be 'punished' and beat her on the buttocks, and also moments when he grasped her in very close physical embrace. At pains to point out that even on such an occasion CW showed no sign of sexual desire for her, she suggests that it was for him a similar spiritual discipline to that of the pursuit of sexual transcendence in some religions and even the ascetic practices of the medieval cult of love. She had no difficulty in separating out this aspect of their relationship from CW's remorseless flirting and teasing, though she does consider that he was in some sense manipulative of her devotion to him. Whether this was responsible for the fact that she began to feel herself in love with him is not explicitly discussed in the letters or her notes on them.

Lang-Sims' accuracy over matters of detail has been questioned by some reviewers, and she is imprecise in some crucial areas; in particular her implication that CW may have tended towards sadism must be read with some caution. CW's earlier passion for Phyllis Jones* need not suggest that he had not, two decades later, managed to control his romantic yearnings for unavailable women. In light of the suggestion of sadism, too, it is worth mentioning that Alice Hadfield has suggested that CW himself overstated the case in his writings.

Last Battle, The (CSL, 1956)

Based upon biblical prophecies of the end of the world, this story by CSL tells the end of one world, the world of which Narnia* is a part, how all worlds are linked, and how the great talking lion Aslan* is the key to this link.

The Last Battle tells of the passing of Narnia and the beginning of the New Narnia. It recounts the attempt of Shift, the talking ape, to delude the creatures of Narnia that Aslan* has returned. In fact, the true Aslan does return.

As in all the stories, children from our world find themselves in Narnia to help or to rule. All go into Narnia, though only Eustace and Jill are active and centre-stage participants in the final battle against evil*, helping Tirian, Jewel and the loyal Narnians.

Each Narnian Chronicle illuminates a central Christian doctrine, in this case, biblical teaching about end times.

Lays of Beleriand, The (JRRT)

This is the third volume of *The History of Middle-earth**, edited by Christopher Tolkien* from his father's unfinished writings. It mainly consists of substantial unfinished narrative poems, one telling the story of Túrin Turambar*, and the other, the tale of Beren and Lúthien, the elf-maiden*. These are two of what JRRT regarded as the four narratives that stood independently of the complex annals of the First Age of Middle-earth. (The others were the tale of Tuor and the Fall of Gondolin*, and the story of Eärendil, the Mariner.)

The Túrin poem, entitled 'The Lay of the Children of Hurin', consists of two versions, both unfinished. It was a bold experiment in alliterative verse, which JRRT confessed he wrote 'with pleasure'. Unlike the summary tale published in *The Silmarillion* it has vividness and what CSL elsewhere called 'realism of presentation'. The poem is early, begun around 1918, so some names differ from the final *The Silmarillion*. Gwindor for instance is called Flinding go-Fuilin.

It is valuable to read this poem in conjunction with the long prose version (alas, also incomplete) in *Unfinished Tales*. These, along with the summary in *The Silmarillion*, will help the reader to have a fuller enjoyment of one of JRRT's greatest stories.

The Beren and Lúthien poem, entitled 'The Lay of Leithian' (meaning 'release from bondage'), is also in two versions, the first much longer than 'The Lay of the Children of Hurin', and the other quite brief. It is written in octosyllabic couplets, a form JRRT uses with great power and effectiveness. JRRT abandoned the first version in 1931, returning to it in 1949 or 1950 and beginning the second version. At this time he still hoped that *The Silmarillion* might be published. As with the Túrin poem, this beautiful poem, telling the love story of Beren and Lúthien and the quest* for the Silmaril, adds reality to the summary version in the published *The Silmarillion*.

CSL, in the early days of his friendship with JRRT, provided diplomatic and ingenious criticism of the unfinished poem. CSL's commentary is reproduced as an appendix to *The Lays of Beleriand*.

'The Lay of Leithian'

A long, unfinished poem telling the tale of Beren and Lúthien the elf-maiden*, published in *The Lays of Beleriand** by JRRT.

'Lay of Aotrou and Itroun, The' (JRRT, 1945)

A narrative poem published in *The Welsh Review* (Volume 4, No. 4, December 1945). The title means 'Lord and Lady', and the poem was inspired by the Celtic legends of Brittany (which has close linguistic links with Wales). A childless lord obtains a potion from a Corrigan, a fairy enchantress. Twins result, but in payment, the Corrigan demands that he marries her. He refuses, and there is no happy ending. Sin has real consequences.

Leaf by Niggle (JRRT, 1945)

First published in January 1945 in *The Dublin Review*, this short allegory was republished in *Tree and Leaf**. The allegory, an unusual form for JRRT, is also untypical in having autobiographical elements.

Niggle, a little man and artist, knew that he would one day have to make a journey. Many matters got in the way of his painting, such as the demands of his neighbour, Mr Parish, who had a lame leg. Niggle was soft-hearted, and rather lazy.

Niggle was concerned to finish one painting in particular. This had started as an illustration of a leaf caught in the wind, then had become a tree. Through gaps in the leaves and branches a forest and a whole world opened up. As the painting grew (with other, smaller paintings tacked on) Niggle had had to move it into a specially built shed on his potato plot. Eventually Niggle fell ill after getting soaked in a storm while running an errand for Mr Parish. Then the dreaded Inspector visited to tell him that the time had come for him to set out on the journey.

Taking a train his first stop (which seemed to last for a century) was at the Workhouse, as Niggle had not brought any belongings. He worked very hard there on various chores. At last, one day, when he had been ordered to rest, he overheard two voices discussing his case. One of them spoke up for him. It was time for gentler treatment, he said. Niggle was allowed to resume his Journey in a small train which led him to the familiar world depicted in his painting of long ago, and to his tree, now complete. 'It's a gift!' he exclaimed.

Niggle walked towards the familiar forest (which had tall mountains behind). He realized that there was unfinished work here, and that Parish could help him – his old neighbour knew a lot about plants, earth and trees. At this realization he came across Parish, and the two of them worked busily together. At last, Niggle felt that it was time to move on into the mountains. Parish wished to remain behind to await his wife. It turned out that the region they had worked in together was called Niggle's Country, much to their surprise. A guide led Niggle into the mountains.

Long before, back in the town near where Niggle and Parish had lived before the journey, a fragment of Niggle's painting had survived and had been hung in the town museum, entitled simply, 'Leaf by Niggle'. It depicted a spray of leaves with a glimpse of a mountain peak.

Niggle's Country became a popular place to send travellers as a holiday, for refreshment and convalescence, and as a splendid introduction to the mountains.

JRRT's little story suggests the link between art and reality. Even in heaven there will be place for the artist to add his or her own touch to the created world. It also demonstrates JRRT's own attitude to his work.

Letters of C.S. Lewis

CSL's letters are in the process of being published as *The Collected Letters* in three volumes. Many of his letters, however, have already been published. *Letters of C.S. Lewis* (1966), edited, with a memoir, by his brother, Warnie Lewis*, grew out of his unpublished biography. It can be examined at the Wade Center. *Letters to an American Lady* (1967), edited by Clyde S. Kilby, is a collection of letters to a lady CSL never met, Mary Willis Shelburne. A large collection, *They Stand Together*: The Letters of C.S. Lewis to Arthur Greeves* (1914–63), edited by Walter Hooper, is made up of letters to one of CSL's closest Ulster friends, Arthur Greeves. *Letters to Children* (1985), edited by Lyle W. Dorsett and Marjorie Lamp Mead, contains a foreword by Douglas Gresham, one of the sons of Joy Davidman Lewis*. In 1989, *Letters: C.S. Lewis and Don Giovanni Calabria*, was published, edited and translated by Martin Moynihan.

A revised and enlarged edition of the *Letters* edited by W.H. Lewis was brought out in 1988, edited by Walter Hooper, and containing some changes to Warnie Lewis' sometimes free editing. This is therefore not strictly a replacement for the 1966 volume, which is worth obtaining if possible.

Letters of J.R.R. Tolkien, The (1981)

This substantial 463-page book is a selection of JRRT's letters from the mid-1930s (when he was in his mid-40s), as *The Hobbit** was being prepared for the press, to just before his death in 1973 at the age of 81. Only eight letters come from the period before that. The collection was edited by Humphrey Carpenter, JRRT's biographer, with the assistance of Christopher Tolkien*, JRRT's son, to whom a number of the letters are addressed.

The letters greatly concern JRRT's fictional works, including their development and interrelationship. Much is also revealed of the life and personality of this remarkable and complex man. Far from mentally inhabiting an 'unreal' world of imagination*, the letters unveil JRRT's sharp observation and critique of the foibles of the modern age.

Much like his close friend CSL, JRRT probably would have been happy to be seen as a specimen or even relic of the almost lost age of 'Old Western Man'. Like CSL, he was able successfully to look at, and write for, our modern age with command and pertinence. The letters constantly give clues to JRRT's thought and worldview, unlike CSL almost totally expressed in his fiction (but *see* 'ON FAIRY STORIES'). His deep Christian faith is evident in the letters, where in one place he answers a child's letter (letter 310) about 'the purpose of life' (*see* CHRISTIAN MEANINGS IN THE FICTION OF JRRT).

As deep as his Christian insight is his love for language. He was a philologist* by profession. His genius with language is nowhere more evident than in his creation of names for people and places in Middle-earth*. Many of the letters concern his invented languages, including elvish.

Mainly since the cult popularity of JRRT's fiction in the 1960s, numerous interpretations of his work have appeared in journals and books. These letters have embedded in them JRRT's own interpretation of, and commentary on, his work. An author's own view of his or her work is not necessarily the final say, or the best, but because of the unique nature of JRRT's invention, his comments provide a framework and standard for understanding his work. Without the letters interpretation would be much more difficult, especially as so much of JRRT's work is unfinished. The letters reinforce the fact that JRRT's work demands to be taken seriously, in the terms in which it was written, including its linguistic inspiration.

Letters to Malcolm: Chiefly on Prayer (CSL, 1964)

Malcolm is an imaginary friend of CSL's to whom he writes 22 letters on the theme of prayer, and much else, including heaven and the resurrection of the body. In the book, CSL writes as having known Malcolm from undergraduate days. Some have felt that CSL's theological writings lack an experiential depth (but display a shyness of spiritual experience). This last book concerns one of the most experiential subjects of the Christian life, and CSL handles it with great power. From the moment of his conversion to theism CSL was a thoroughgoing supernaturalist, and thus the question of petitionary prayer made in time to a God outside of space-time was a central one to him. He saw it as God's prerogative to change actual events in the light of the prayers of his people.

The letter format allowed CSL to explore and speculate on prayer in a manner impossible in a more didactic book. Prayer, for CSL, was necessary for our understanding of our relation to our Father creator.

Letters to Lalage (1989)

See Lang-Sims, Lois

Lewis, Clive Staples (1898–1963)

Known to his friends as 'Jack' (he didn't like 'Clive Staples'), CSL was born in the outskirts of Belfast on 29 November 1898, and died in his Oxford*

home, the Kilns, almost 65 years later on 22 November 1963. He was equally a scholar and a storyteller. The story of his early life, his conversion from atheism to Christianity, and his awareness of joy* and longing for a fulfilment outside his own self, is told in his autobiography *Surprised by Joy** and his allegory *The Pilgrim's Regress**.

His published letters, especially *Letters of C.S. Lewis**, and *They Stand Together**, and *Brothers and Friends: The Diaries of Major Warren Hamilton Lewis*, give vivid insights into his life. A selection from his diaries, *All My Road Before Me*, records the years between 1922 and 1927. CSL was devoted to his brother Warnie. The two brothers were brought together by their common interest in creating imaginary worlds as boys, particularly Boxen*, and also by the death of their mother of cancer. Mrs Flora Lewis died when CSL was nine. Their father never got over the loss and relations between father and sons became more and more strained as time went on. CSL portrays his father, Albert Lewis, as having little talent for happiness, and withdrawing into the safe monotony of routine. A.N. Wilson, however, believes the picture CSL painted of his father as a 'comic character' to be one-sided. The richest heritage he gave to CSL was, literally, a houseful of old books which the gifted boy explored unimpeded.

In the year of his mother's death, CSL was sent off to Hertfordshire to join his brother at a school dubbed 'Belsen'. This title seems no great exaggeration. The brutal headmaster was several years later certified insane. In 1910 CSL was moved first to Campbell College, Belfast, and the next year to Cherbourg House ('Chartres') in Malvern, and later Malvern College ('Wyvern'), Worcestershire. He was never happy, however, until he was finally sent to a private tutor in Bookham called W.T. Kirkpatrick*.

His brother Warnie wrote, in his introduction to *Letters of C.S. Lewis*: 'The fact is he should never have been sent to a public school at all. Already, at 14, his intelligence was such that he would have fitted in better among undergraduates than schoolboys; and by his temperament he was bound to be a misfit, a heretic, an object of suspicion within the collective-minded and standardising Public School system'. Characteristically, CSL wrote his first article entitled 'Are Athletes Better than Scholars?' for a school magazine.

His private tutorage under the Irishman W.T. Kirkpatrick was one of the happiest periods of his life. Not only did he rapidly mature and grow under the stringent rationality of this teacher, but he discovered the beauty of the English countryside and the appeal of fantasy writers such as William Morris. Full of the discovery of George MacDonald's* *Phantastes*, CSL wrote about its power to Arthur Greeves, his lifelong Ulster friend, in 1915: 'Of course it is hopeless for me to try to describe it, but when you have followed the hero Anodos along the little stream of the faery wood, have heard about the terrible ash tree ... and heard the episode of Cosmo, I know you will agree with me.' In *Surprised By Joy*, CSL describes the effect as 'baptising his imagination'.

The Great War had broken out, and its shadow loomed over CSL's peace. Warnie was already on active duty. CSL was not old enough to enlist until 1917. He spent his nineteenth birthday on the front line. In spring 1918 CSL was wounded in action and was eventually discharged after a spell in hospital. During all this time he had been writing poetry and preparing a book of poems, *Spirits in Bondage**, for publication.

At the Front he had lost a billet-mate called 'Paddy' Moore. Before his death, CSL had apparently promised him that, should anything happen to him, he would take care of Paddy's widowed mother and sister.

CSL in fact looked after Mrs Janie Moore until her death in 1951. It is possible that he had at first an affair with her, as argued without robust evidence by his biographer, A.N. Wilson. His sense of duty is enough reason, however, for his commitment to her. Her troublesome personality was a thorn in the flesh both to him and later Warnie, who joined the Kilns household in 1931.

By 1923 CSL had confirmed his brilliance by gaining a triple first at Oxford* University. By this time he was already deep in the 'great war' with his friend OB*, a dialogue which greatly shaped his thinking. He won a temporary lectureship in philosophy at University College. Then Magdalen College appointed him as a Fellow, lecturing and tutoring in English. He was an Oxford don until 1954, when Cambridge University invited him to the new Chair of Medieval and Renaissance Literature, where he described himself as an 'Old Western Man' in his inaugural lecture. CSL's pupils included such figures as the critic Kenneth Tynan, George Sayer*, the poet John Betjeman*, Harry Blamires, and novelist and poet John Wain*.

In the early Oxford days JRRT also became one of CSL's lifelong friends. They would criticize one another's poetry, drift into theology and philosophy, pun or talk English department politics.

Because JRRT, along with 'Hugo' Dyson*, helped to force CSL to reconsider the claims of Christianity, he was first 'cornered' by theism and then biblical Christianity. The movement of CSL's thinking at this time is vividly captured in his book *Miracles**. He later confessed:

> I never had the experience of looking for God. It was the other way round; He was the hunter (or so it seemed to me) and I was the deer. He stalked me like a redskin, took unerring aim, and fired. And I am very thankful that that is how the first (conscious) meeting occurred. It forearms one against subsequent fears that the whole thing was only wish fulfilment. Something one didn't wish for can hardly be that.

Another significant friendship was forged in 1936 when CSL read CW's *The Place of the Lion** while CW was reading the proofs of *The Allegory of Love** for Oxford University Press. The two men exchanged letters and soon met up, with CW being introduced to the Inklings.

In 1952 CSL met an American woman, Helen Joy Gresham (*see* LEWIS, HELEN JOY DAVIDMAN), with whom he had corresponded for some time. She was a poet and novelist who had been converted from atheism and Marxism to Christianity partly through reading CSL's books. When she was free to remarry, and was dying of cancer, CSL married her in a Christian ceremony in 1957. Previously they had had a Register Office (state) wedding to provide her with British citizenship, for her protection, and that of her sons.

She came home to the Kilns to die in summer 1957, but had a miraculous remission. In fact she lived until 1960, and was able to have a final holiday in Greece with CSL. The happiness that had come to him so late in life, and his subsequent bitter bereavement, is recorded in his *A Grief Observed** and has been made into two successful films based around a similar script by William Nicolson, both entitled *Shadowlands*.

CSL never got over the loss, and this was combined with constant worry about his unassuming brother's alcoholism. The last book he saw to press, *Letters to Malcolm: Chiefly on Prayer**, affirmed his hope in heaven.

As well as *The Chronicles of Narnia** for children, CSL wrote a classic science-fiction trilogy, a novel (*Till We Have Faces**), other fiction, literary criticism, cultural criticism, ethics, theology and poetry. He was the epicentre of the Inklings, and was influenced by George MacDonald. To some extent he appears in fictional form in the character of Philip Frankley in JRRT's unfinished 'The Notion Club Papers'.*

See also CHAPTER 1; LITERARY CRITIC, CSL AS A

FURTHER READING

All My Road Before Me: The Diary of C.S. Lewis 1922–27 (ed. Walter Hooper, 1991)

Humphrey Carpenter, *The Inklings: C.S. Lewis, J.R.R. Tolkien, Charles Williams and their friends* (1978)

Lyle W. Dorsett, *And God Came in: The Extraordinary Story of Joy Davidman Lewis – Her Life and Marriage to C.S. Lewis* (1983)

Colin Duriez, *The C.S. Lewis Encyclopedia: A Complete Guide to His Life, Thought and Writings* (2000)

Roger Lancelyn Green and Walter Hooper, *C.S. Lewis: A Biography* (1974)

Douglas Gresham, *Lenten Lands: My Childhood with Joy Davidman Lewis and C.S. Lewis* (1989)

William Griffin, *C.S. Lewis: The Authentic Voice* (1988)

Walter Hooper, *C.S. Lewis: A Companion and Guide* (1997)

Letters of C.S. Lewis (1966)

C.S. Lewis, *The Pilgrim's Regress* (1933, 1943)

C.S. Lewis, *Surprised By Joy: The Shape of My Early Life* (1955)

George Sayer, *Jack: C.S. Lewis and His Times* (1988)

Jeffrey D. Schultz and John G. West Jr (eds), *The C.S. Lewis Readers' Encyclopedia* (1998)

Brian Sibley, *Shadowlands: The Story of C.S. Lewis and Joy Davidman Lewis* (1985)

They Stand Together: The Letters of C.S. Lewis to Arthur Greeves (ed. Walter Hooper, 1979)

W.H. Lewis, *Brothers and Friends: The Diaries of Major Warren Hamilton Lewis* (ed. Clyde S. Kilby and Marjorie L. Meade, 1982)

A.N. Wilson, *C.S. Lewis: A Biography* (1990)

Lewis, Helen Joy Davidman (1915–60)

CSL's wife, and subject of his book, *A Grief Observed**, written after her death from cancer at the age of 45. Joy Davidman Lewis was a poet and novelist, and also published a theological study of the ten commandments, *Smoke on the Mountain*. Joy Davidman had been converted from Marxism to Christianity partly through reading CSL.

A short time after making his acquaintance, Joy Davidman came to live in Oxford with her two young sons. She and CSL became on close terms. The friendship with Joy further eroded CSL's friendship with JRRT, an erosion which had begun with CSL's devotion to CW. It is likely that the writing of *Till We Have Faces** was influenced in style and content by Joy. The title of CSL's autobiography, *Surprised By Joy** (1955) had a second meaning, whether intended or not, to his friends.

In the autumn of 1956 they learned that Joy had terminal cancer. A bedside Christian wedding ceremony took place on 21 March 1957. Joy came home to the Kilns to die. After prayer for healing, she had an unexpected reprieve. The cancer eventually returned, but the Lewises were able to have a trip to Greece in the spring of the year of her death, a journey much desired by both of them.

FURTHER READING

Joy Davidman, *Anya* (Jarrolds, 1943)

Joy Davidman, *Letter to a Comrade* (Yale University Press, 1938)

Joy Davidman, *Smoke on the Mountain* (Hodder and Stoughton, 1955)

Joy Davidman, *Weeping Bay* (Macmillan, 1950)

Lyle Dorsett, *And God Came In: The Extraordinary Story of Joy Davidman Lewis – Her Life and Marriage to C.S. Lewis* (1983)

Douglas Gresham, *Lenten Lands* (London: Collins, 1989)

William Nicholson, *Shadowlands* (play-script, 1991)

Brian Sibley, *Shadowlands: The Story of C.S. Lewis and Joy Davidman Lewis* (1985)

Lewis, Warren Hamilton 'Warnie' (1895–1973)

CSL's only brother, lifelong friend, and member of the Inklings from its inception. Like his brother he was a gifted writer, producing a number of books on French history. He contributed to *Essays Presented to Charles Williams**. His diaries provide a unique and essential insight into CSL's life, and meetings of the Inklings. A selection has been published as *Brothers and Friends* (1982), which, inexplicably, is only published in North America.

Warnie Lewis began his military career when he entered the Royal Military academy shortly before the outbreak of the First World War. After the war he served in Sierra Leone, and Shanghai, before retiring from the army in 1932 with a pension. He joined the unusual household run by his brother and Mrs Janie Moore at the Kilns, in Oxford. This short note cannot do justice to Warnie Lewis' immeasurable importance to CSL, an importance that can be seen through his elegantly written diaries. Warnie Lewis devoted himself to the task of editing the CSL family papers and, after CSL's death, prepared a powerful memoir of his brother, now housed in the Wade Center, Wheaton (with a copy in the Bodleian Library, Oxford). An abridged version of the *Memoirs* is published in *Letters of C.S. Lewis**.

Lindsay, David (1878–1945)

His *A Voyage to Arcturus* (1920) is today recognized as a minor masterpiece of science fiction, though its first edition sold under 600 copies, making it difficult for Lindsay to sell subsequent work. CSL, hearing of it, found great difficulty in obtaining a copy. When he did, it greatly influenced his own science-fiction trilogy, particularly *Out of the Silent Planet**, and his unfinished 'The Dark Tower'*.

Lindsay's 'Tormance', located in far-off Arcturus, perhaps gets its name from a contraction of 'torment' and 'romance'. In an essay 'On Stories', which appeared in *Essays Presented to CW**, CSL wrote that David Lindsay's

> Tormance is a region of the spirit. He is the first writer to discover what 'other planets' are really good for in fiction. No merely physical strangeness or merely spacial distance will realize that idea of otherness which is what we are always trying to grasp in a story about voyaging through space: you must go into another dimension. To construct plausible and moving 'other worlds' you must draw on the only real 'other world' we know, that of the spirit.

David Lindsay's other tales of fantasy were *The Haunted Woman* (1922), *Sphinx* (1923) and *Devil's Tor* (1932). He also wrote a historical novel, *The Adventures of M. de Mailly* (1926). In 1970 a memorial volume appeared, *The Strange Genius of David Lindsay*, including articles by Colin Wilson and E.H. Visiak (who finds parallels between *A Voyage to Arcturus* and Milton's *Paradise Lost*).

Lion, the Witch and the Wardrobe, The (CSL, 1950)

This is the first tale of Narnia* that CSL wrote. Four children, Peter, Edmund, Susan and Lucy Pevensie, are evacuated from war-time London to stay with Professor Digory Kirke (who, as a boy, had visited Narnia, as recounted in *The Magician's Nephew**). Three of them join forces with the talking animals who are loyal to Aslan*, the great talking lion, creator of Narnia. Aslan pays the terrible cost of the traitor Edmund's treachery by sacrificing his own life to break the witch's magic. Narnia is freed, Aslan returns to life, the witch is destroyed, and the creatures that she had turned to stone are unpetrified by the lion.

Literary critic, CSL as a

CSL was an outstanding literary critic, being invited to the newly created Chair of Medieval and Renaissance Literature at Cambridge University in 1954 as a result of his work in these periods. Prior to that he was for almost 30 years Fellow and tutor in English at Magdalen College, Oxford. His main works of literary criticism are: *The Allegory of Love: A Study in Medieval Tradition** (1936); *Rehabilitations and Other Essays** (1939); with E.M.W. Tillyard), *The Personal Heresy: A Controversy** (1939); *A Preface to 'Paradise Lost'**; (1942, with CW), *Arthurian Torso** (1948); *English Literature in the Sixteenth Century, excluding Drama** (1954); *Reflections on the Psalms** (1958); *Studies in Words** (1960); *An Experiment in Criticism** (1961); *The Discarded Image: An Introduction to Medieval and Renaissance Literature** (1964); *Studies in Medieval and Renaissance Literature* (1966, edited by Alistair Fowler); *Spenser's Images of Life** (1967) and *Selected Literary Essays* (1969).

Much of CSL's critical work was on Spenser, Chaucer, the Arthurian tales, Milton, and Dante*, as well as on myth*, allegory*, world models, meaning, story, metaphor, linguistics and fairy stories. He also wrote key essays on John Bunyan, Jane Austen, Shelley and William Morris, many of them collected in *Selected Literary Essays*.

CSL advocates and demonstrates the close reading of texts, where readers and critics have a first-hand experience of an author's work. CSL argues that 'we invariably judge a critic by the extent to which he illuminates reading we have already done'. It was important, believes CSL, for a student and reader of English Literature to be acquainted with Anglo-Saxon. As well as classical languages, CSL himself was able to read German, French and Italian, and this enriched his critical work. Complementary to this textual concern is a historical engagement. He is always interested in the intellectual and cultural currents of a period.

CSL feels that the extrinsic features of the literary work are essential to consider, such as its worldview, including the model of reality and the universe it embodied, and authorial intention. The work, however, is *poiema* as well as *logos*, something made as well as something said. He emphasizes the interrelationship of literary works, particularly in what he perceives as a unified period before the rise of the stranglehold of modernism, a period he sees as stretching from ancient pagan times to sometime in the nineteenth century. CSL identified modernism (expressed for example in a machine mentality) as a social and cultural embodiment, not simply as a set of theoretical ideas. In this he reflected OB's analysis of 'idolatry', for instance in OB's *History, Guilt and Habit**.

Literary works illuminate each other, contributing to a symbolic language and iconography. CSL is not a narrow specialist. For CSL there is a vast ancient continuity. Therefore he is not simply seeking to rehabilitate the medieval period but the entire pre-modernist period. He has a strong polemical purpose. In his fiction and theology CSL paints the inner world using allegory, symbol, or myth – just like the medievals and (if OB is correct) the entire ancient western world. His fiction and literary work are therefore of a piece.

In his literary criticism he maintains both continuity and discontinuity with the present (he is a pre-modernist who has a post-modern appeal). He is thus valuable in giving a transcendent perspective on our times. His early rejection of 'chronological snobbery'* allowed this freedom. His preoccupation with story and metaphor as a condition of all good thinking was fought out in opposition to modernism and its characteristic naturalism. Furthermore, his literary and related criticism fuels his imaginative writing. There are often parallels, for instance, between his works of criticism and particular fictions. The pattern is established in the inspiration that allegory gives to the writing of *The Pilgrim's Regress* (1933): his *Preface to 'Paradise Lost'** (1942) naturally leads to *Perelandra** (1943); *The Abolition of Man** (1943) theoretically treats the themes of *That Hideous Strength** (1945); his many explorations of myth and pre-Christian paganism result in *Till We Have Faces** (1956); and it could perhaps be argued that his consideration of Spenser's *The Faerie Queene* over many years provides a pattern for the imaginative eclecticism yet coherent unity of the Narnian Chronicles* (1950–56).

CSL's uniqueness and particularity are not easy to capture. It is easier to show him as a child of his times – an upper-middle-class Ulsterman, a reluctant product of the British public school system, and a brilliant scholar of the type best nurtured by a traditional university setting like Oxford, which encouraged cross-disciplinary exploration. There are contemporaries similar to him, such as OB and JRRT, and many other Christian writers which belong to what Harry Blamires called a 'minor Christian literary renaissance' in the 1930s. However, like JRRT and OB, his great friends and mentors, he is remarkably relevant to the context that confronts us at the cusp of the millennium. Post-modernity has proved a haven for the unique anti-modernism of CSL and his closer mentors.

See also PHILOLOGY, JRRT AND

FURTHER READING

Peter Barry (ed.), *Issues in Contemporary Critical Theory* (Macmillan, 1987)
Colin Duriez, 'Into the Library: Composition and Context', in Tom Martin (ed.), *Reading Literature with C.S. Lewis* (Baker Book House, 2000)
David Lodge (ed.), *20th Century Literary Criticism: A Reader* (Longman, 1972)
Tremper Longman, *Literary Approaches to Biblical Interpretation* (Apollos, 1987)

Literary criticism of Charles Williams

CW's literary criticism includes *Poetry at Present* (1930); *The English Poetic Mind** (1932); *Reason and Beauty in the Poetic Mind* (1933); *Religion and Love in Dante** (1941); *The Figure of Beatrice** (1943); *Arthurian Torso** (1948). He also wrote individual essays on Milton, Landor, Pope and others.

Logres

In CW's Arthurian poems, Britain: the head or brains of the map of the body. Arthur's Logres, originally disordered, is to be brought by Taliessin to the order and unity of the rest of the empire – a mission that Taliessin is given after his journey to Byzantium*.

See also CHAPTER 5

Lord of the Rings, The (JRRT, 1954–55)

This great tale of the Third Age of Middle-earth* is written in six parts. Each of the three volumes published contains two of the parts. The volumes are: *The Fellowship of the Ring**, *The Two Towers**, and *The Return of the King**. The evolution of the work is traced in the four parts of *The History of the Lord of the Rings**, edited by Christopher Tolkien*.

The Lord of the Rings is a heroic romance, telling of the quest to destroy the one, ruling Ring of power, before it can fall into the hands of its maker, Sauron, the dark lord of the title. As a consistent, unified story, it stands independently of the invented mythology and historical chronicles of Middle-earth. Events of the past provide a backdrop and haunting dimension to the story.

As a work of literature, the merits and demerits of *The Lord of the Rings* have been extensively discussed by scholars. Among its admirers were the poet W.H. Auden*, and JRRT's friend, CSL. In a review written upon the publication of the third volume, CSL pointed out the beauty of the structure of the work:

There are two Books in each volume and now that all six are before us the very high architectural quality of the romance is revealed. Book I builds up the main theme. In Book II that theme, enriched with much retro-spective material, continues. Then comes the change. In III and V the fate of the company, now divided, becomes entangled with a huge complex of forces which are grouping and regrouping themselves in relation to Mordor. The main theme, isolated from this, occupies IV and the early part of VI (the latter part of course giving all the resolutions). But we are never allowed to forget the intimate connection between it and the rest. On the one hand, the whole world is going to the war; the story rings with galloping hoofs, trumpets, steel on steel. On the other, very far away, miserable figures creep (like mice on a slag heap) through the twilight of Mordor. And all the time we know the fate of the world depends far more on the small movement than on the great. This is a structural invention of the highest order: it adds immensely to the pathos, irony, and grandeur of the tale (*Of This and Other Worlds*, 1982).

Some critics less enthusiastic than CSL have pointed out what they regard as flaws in the work: the change of tone from *The Hobbit*-like opening to the seriousness of the quest; a lack of moral seriousness (in that the good char-acters do not wrestle with evil*); the adolescent quality of many of the characters, who never grow up; unconvincing battle scenarios; the distrac-tion of having to read half a book before the tale of Frodo and Sam continues; and so on.

Considered structurally, however, the opening is not a flaw, but sets the scene of homeliness, so important to JRRT. Out of this humble context, the unexpected heroes, Frodo and Sam, arise. The charge of a lack of moral seriousness does not hold once the subtlety and range of JRRT's examina-tion of evil is explored. On JRRT's character portrayal, it is important to realize that this is not meant to be novelistic. *The Lord of the Rings* is a heroic romance. Characters are known according to type, and in JRRT type can be dwarf, hobbit, ent and elf, as well as varieties of the human. And so the discussion can go on.

One mark of the quality of *The Lord of the Rings* as literature is its lin-guistic basis. JRRT makes use of his invented languages in names, and also in imaginative possibility. Language is the basis of the background mythology. Another mark of its literary quality is JRRT's success in integrating the wealth of symbolism of his work. Quest, the journey, sacrifice, healing*, death*, and many other symbolic elements are beautifully incarnate in the book. The very landscapes through which the travellers pass are symbolic, suggesting moods which correspond to the stage of the journey, and to the phase of the overall story. The terrors of Moria, the archetypal underworld, contrast for example with the refreshment to the spirit of Lórien. Always, these landscapes are fully part of the movement of the book, aesthetically shaped and integrated.

JRRT's greatest achievement is the embodiment of myth* in literature. It was an amazing achievement to create living myth. JRRT shared this ability with George MacDonald*. It is a further achievement to successfully make myth incarnate in literary form. In MacDonald the myth remains outside literary form, extraliterary, as CSL points out. Had JRRT completed his work on *The Silmarillion**, all the evidence suggests that there would have been several stories in which this literary achievement of embodying myth was repeated, stories like 'The Tale of Beren and Lúthien the Elf-Maiden'*, which are already powerful as myth.

See also THE WAR OF THE RING

Lost Road and Other Writings, The (JRRT, 1987)

This is the fifth volume in the series, *The History of Middle-earth**, in which Christopher Tolkien* has collected together and edited unfinished material by his father.

Under pressure to produce a sequel to the popular *The Hobbit**, JRRT at the end of 1937 reluctantly set aside his mythology and tales of the First and Second Ages of Middle-earth*. This fifth volume completes the presentation and commentary on his invention up to that time.

At this point, JRRT had composed later versions of 'The Annals of Valinor' and 'The Annals of Beleriand', and a greatly amplified version of *The Silmarillion** was nearly complete. He had also started work on the history of the downfall of Númenor and the change in the world which resulted from this. All this material is included. There is also an account of the development of the elvish languages, 'The Lhammas' ('Account of Tongues'), supposedly written by Rumil.

JRRT was also wrestling with the problem of the narrative framework of *The Silmarillion*. One of the most interesting sections of this book is his unfinished tale of time-travel, 'The Lost Road', which, if it had been successful, would have provided such a framework. JRRT tried to absorb his earlier framework, whereby the traveller Aelfwine was told the tales of the First Age, into the story of 'The Lost Road'. As it happened, the telling of *The Lord of the Rings** provided some kind of resolution to the problem of the narrative framework for *The Silmarillion*.

JRRT never prepared a sustained elvish vocabulary, but did construct an etymological dictionary of word relationships. This is included in the book under the title, 'The Etymologies'.

See also PHILOLOGY, JRRT AND

Love

See CHAPTER 6; *FOUR LOVES, THE*; *HE CAME DOWN FROM HEAVEN*; *OUTLINES OF ROMANTIC THEOLOGY*

McCallum, Ronald B. (1898–1973)

A member of the Inklings and Fellow of Pembroke College, Oxford*, until 1955, when he was elected Master of Pembroke.

MacDonald, George (1824–1905)

The Scottish writer George MacDonald was born in Huntly in rural Aberdeenshire, the son of a weaver. CSL regarded his own debt to him as inestimable. JRRT's attitude to the fantasist was more ambivalent, and often critical. Yet there were many affinities. The theme of death* is central to the fiction of both JRRT and MacDonald.

The Scot's thinking about the imagination* has a number of striking similarities with JRRT's. The goblins in JRRT's children's story, *The Hobbit**, are reminiscent of the goblins in MacDonald's *Curdie* stories for children, not as terrifying and malicious as the orcs of *The Lord of the Rings** and *The Silmarillion**. There are hints of rudimentary 'sub-creation'* in MacDonald. His distinctive great-great-grandmother figures have an elven quality that could belong to JRRT's world. He has powerful feminine images of spirituality and providence that are akin to JRRT's Galadriel and Varda.

Like JRRT and CSL, MacDonald lost his mother in boyhood, a fact that touched his thought and writings. His views on the imagination anticipated those of CSL as well as JRRT, and inspired G.K. Chesterton. He was a close friend of Charles Dodgson (Lewis Carroll) and John Ruskin, the art critic. His insights into the unconscious mind pre-dated the rise of modern psychology. Like CSL and JRRT he was a scholar as well as a storyteller. George MacDonald made a brief and memorable appearance in CSL's *The Great Divorce**, for CSL regarded him as his 'master'.

MacDonald's sense that all imaginative meaning originates with the Christian creator became the foundation of CSL's thinking and imagining. Such a view is also central to JRRT. Two key essays, 'The Imagination: Its Functions and its Culture' (1867) and 'The Fantastic Imagination' (1882), remarkably foreshadow JRRT's famous essay 'On Fairy Stories'*. JRRT's views on imagination persuaded CSL of the truth of Christianity one night in 1931. Many years before CSL had stumbled across a copy of MacDonald's *Phantastes* (1858), resulting in what he famously described as a baptism of his imagination.

M

George MacDonald wrote almost 30 novels, several books of sermons, a number of abiding fantasies for adults and children, short stories, and poetry. His childhood is beautifully captured in his semi-autobiographical *Ranald Bannerman's Boyhood* (1871). He never lost sight of his humble childhood and adolescence, living in a cottage so small that he slept in an attic. He was a happy boy, riding, climbing, swimming and fishing – and reading while lying on the back of his beloved horse. We catch many glimpses of the countryside he knew and loved in his writings.

George MacDonald entered Aberdeen University in 1840, and had a scientific training. For a few years he worked as a tutor in London. Then he entered Highbury Theological College and married. He was called to a church in Arundel in Sussex, where he fell into disfavour with the deacons, who reduced his small salary to persuade him to leave. Some of the poorer members, however, rallied around with offerings they could ill afford. Then he moved to Manchester for some years, preaching to a small congregation and giving lectures. The rapidly growing family were always on the brink of poverty. Fortunately, the poet Byron's widow, recognizing MacDonald's literary gifts, started to provide financial help. The family moved down to London, living in a house then called 'The Retreat', near the Thames at Hammersmith, later owned by William Morris.

Many famous writers and artists came to visit the MacDonalds, as well as people who shared a concern for London's desperate and crowded poor. One friend was Charles Dodgson, who let the MacDonald children hear his story, *Alice in Wonderland*. As a result of their enthusiasm he decided to publish it. One of MacDonald's sons, Greville, remembered calling a cab for the poet Tennyson.

For a time George MacDonald was Professor of Literature at Bedford College, London. Because of continued ill-health, the family eventually moved to Italy, where MacDonald and his wife were to remain for the rest of their lives. There were, however, frequent stays in Britain during the warmer months, and a long and successful visit to the United States on a lecture tour. One of his last books, *Lilith* (1895) is among his greatest, a fantasy with the same power to move and to change a person's imaginative life as *Phantastes*.

In her book, *The Stars and the Stillness*, Kathy Triggs points out the paradox of a leading nineteenth-century writer being virtually forgotten today, and hazards some reasons for this. We live in a post-Christian world where MacDonald's values are alien. Television and other claims on our time deprive us of the leisure to tackle his lengthy novels. Yet, she points out, we lose out on so much if we neglect to read him. His theological insights are still needed today. He was the master of ageless symbolism in his imaginative work: a fact that so captured CSL, bringing him face to face with the quality of holiness, though he didn't acknowledge it for many years.

Despite neglect, MacDonald's children's stories and fantasies for adults have always remained in print. Most of his novels are now available in facsimile and some can be downloaded in electronic form via the Internet.

FURTHER READING

R.N. Hein, *The Harmony Within: The Spiritual Vision of George Macdonald* (Chicago: Cornerstone Press, 1999)

C.S. Lewis, *George MacDonald: An Anthology* (Bles, 1946)

Greville MacDonald, *George MacDonald and his Wife* (Allen and Unwin, 1924)

Michael Phillips, *George MacDonald: Scotland's Beloved Storyteller* (1987)

William Raeper, *George MacDonald* (Lion, 1987)

Elizabeth Saintsbury, *George MacDonald: A Short Life* (1987)

Kathy Triggs, *The Stars and the Stillness: A Portrait of George MacDonald* (Lutterworth, 1986)

Macgowan, John (1726–80)

A Baptist minister and author of *Infernal Conference; or Dialogues of Devils*, a forerunner of CSL's *The Screwtape Letters**, though CSL never read it. There are striking similarities of aim, and one devil is the uncle of another. John Macgowan wrote several other popular works, including *Death: A Vision* and a life of the biblical character Ruth.

Magician's Nephew, The (CSL, 1955)

This tale by CSL tells of the creation of Narnia* by Aslan*. It also tells us about the Edwardian childhood of Professor Digory Kirke, who owned the big country house with the wardrobe in *The Lion, the Witch, and the Wardrobe**, and about how the London gas lamp post came to be in Narnia at all. Also it speaks of the origin of the White Witch, and explains the arrival of evil* in Narnia – showing the evil as older than that world.

Digory and his dying mother are staying with his Uncle Andrew and Aunt Letty in London, his father being in India. He makes friends with Polly Plummer, his neighbour, and the two are tricked into an experiment with magic rings by the Uncle, a mad scientist. Digory awakens the White Witch from a spell, despite warnings from Polly.

Polly, Digory and the Witch, along with Frank, a London cabby, and his horse, and Uncle Andrew, end up in an empty world of Nothing, in time to hear Aslan's creation song. At the words and music of the lion's song mountains, trees, animals and other creatures come into being to make Narnia and the world of which it is part. The sequence is reminiscent of the creation passage from JRRT's *The Silmarillion**, with which CSL was familiar in unfinished form.

Aslan gives Digory the opportunity of undoing the evil* he had brought into Narnia. His task is to find a magic apple, the seed of which would produce a tree to protect the young world from the Witch for many years. Polly joins him on the adventure, which requires journeying into the mountains of the Western Wild to find a delightful valley. In a garden there, on a hilltop, grows an apple tree with the magic apples. Upon the children's return, Aslan allows Digory to bring back an apple from the tree that immediately sprang up from the apple's seed. This will restore his dying mother. CSL's own mother, Flora Hamilton Lewis, died when he was a boy in Edwardian Belfast.

Later, after the great tree fell, Digory had it made into a large wardrobe, the very same wardrobe that features in *The Lion, the Witch and the Wardrobe*.

Manuscript, Masque of the (CW, 1927)

See Masques, Two

Many Dimensions (CW, 1931)

Written by CW in 1930, *Many Dimensions* has thematic links with its predecessor *War in Heaven**; it concerns the presence and the pursuit of an arcane object invested with supernatural meaning and powers. Sir Giles Tumulty, the archaeologist and antiquarian who appeared in the previous novel, has acquired a circlet of ancient twisted gold encompassing a stone cube bearing Hebrew letters – the Tetragrammaton, the unspeakable name of God. It is the last surviving remnant of the crown of King Suleiman ben Daood (Solomon, son of David) of Jerusalem. This characteristically Williamsian object is expounded in the opening pages of the novel, as Tumulty, his nephew Reginald Montague, and Prince Ali Mirza Khan, secretary to the Persian ambassador, discuss the stone. It has the power to transport the person who possesses it anywhere, by the mere power of thought.

The novel has the same readability as *War in Heaven* – the reader wants to know how the tale will turn out, an interest that carries one through the more abstruse pages. There is an especially interesting discussion of time travel, knotty but understandable to non-specialists. For example, if you use the stone to take you into the past, you will arrive there without the stone, because if you did not you would not truly be in the past – because in the past, you did not have the stone. So you are condemned to live out the intervening time again, until you reach the point at which the time travel began. But as that has 'already' happened, you will make the same choice: so using the stone for time travel condemns the user to an eternal retreading of the same tract of time. Of such speculations much of the novel consists, but CW succeeds in making them integral to the developing plot and its dramatic compulsion. The discussion is similar to that by J.W. Dunne in *An*

Experiment in Time (1927) – a popular science author who was known to the Inklings; CSL cites him in the fragment 'The Dark Tower' (c. 1938).

Tumulty has acquired the stone from its Persian guardians – the 'Keepers' – in dubious circumstances. He has invited Prince Ali Mirza Khan of the Persian Embassy in London to authenticate the stone. The Prince does so, and on his return to the Embassy informs Hajji Ibrahim, a descendant of the Keepers, that the stone is genuine.

Tumulty and his nephew, stockbroker Reginald Montague, are enthralled by the financial possibilities of the stone. Devices incorporating chips of it, enabling instantaneous travel for those who owned them, could be sold, raising huge sums in royalties and threatening the abolition of existing large travel industries. Industries and governments alike would have to deal with its owners.

Montague approaches another of his uncles, the Lord Chief Justice Lord Arglay, inviting him to invest in a new company to exploit the stone (it transpires in due course that Bruce Cumberland, Permanent Official at the Foreign Office, has also been approached). Arglay, who has recently engaged a secretary Chloe Burnett to help him as he writes his book *A Survey of Organic Law*, is sceptical but agrees to consider the matter, despite his acute mistrust of Tumulty. Reginald demonstrates the stone's power of transport. Arglay tests it himself; Chloe, who has a deep disquiet about the whole business, refuses to do so. She leaves the gathering, and after her departure, experimenting with the stone, the others discover that it is capable of being infinitely divided, each new stone or 'Type' being identical to the first and with identical powers. Soon Arglay and others are in possession of individual Types.

The proliferation of the stone generates much of the excitement of the book, for many characters experience its powers and it seems that the power, once released and multiplied, will be impossible to restrain. Chloe, in an encounter with Hajji Ibrahim, learns of the ancient history of the stone, and is told that it embodies within itself the end and purpose of all human strivings and longings: the End of Desire. In the wrong hands, it might bring about that End by 'chaos and madness'; but were Chloe to offer her soul to the stone, she may not be destroyed and the Repose of the End would be achieved – for Ibrahim recognizes that Chloe is one whom Allah shall bring to 'the Resignation'. Allah, for the Muslim characters in *Many Dimensions*, represents Unity and Protection, two names CW gives to the Godhead. Arglay represents law (not least by his Office), and Tumulty's name is a crude metaphor for what *he* is. At an early stage of the novel, Chloe is marked out for spiritual destiny and service, in contrast to the hopes of Frank Lindsay, her suitor, who desires her.

Tumulty's associate is Abel Palliser, a psychologist; the more Arglay discovers about Palliser, the more uneasy he becomes; he has an uneasy feeling that the pair will be 'playing with victim after victim'. And he decides to oppose them. He goes to Hajji Ibrahim, where he learns more of the stone's history and of Ali Khan's total commitment to regaining it. He uses his Type of the stone to observe Tumulty, and witnesses a young man being doomed by Tumulty to be locked in a time warp, by use of the stone. In later discussion, the Hajji reveals that he regrets the dividing of the stone more than the victimization of the man: a significant pointer to the profound difference that the incarnation makes between the Islamic and the Christian faiths.

The stone becomes more widely known. Lord Birlesmere, the Foreign Secretary, becomes interested, and through him, the government. Angus Sheldrake, an American millionaire, buys a Type from Reginald for 73,000 guineas; he recognizes its commercial possibilities and is attracted by the romance of its history. Chloe and Frank, exploring the nearby countryside, trespass on Sheldrake's land at the very moment his wife rematerializes from a test of the stone's powers. Subsequently the stone is lost in a hedge, where it is found by Oliver Doncaster, who is staying in a nearby village; he refuses to surrender his find.

It is at the village that the stone first demonstrates healing powers, attracting enormous publicity in a series of miracles, which prompts the Persian Embassy to warn the government that disastrous results may ensue. But Lord Birlesmere points out that the difficulties of regaining possession are now immense.

CW now develops his theme in several directions. The mayor of the town of Rich is used to develop the theme that the powers of the stone should be used for the good of all. Ali Khan is prepared to restore the stone to its rightful guardians, using any means available to him. Chloe, who refuses more than once to use the stone in any self-interested way (the theological issue is similar to that in the [much later] Susan Howatch's* *Glamorous Powers*), moves inexorably in the novel towards that point where she will offer herself to the stone as the means of the stone drawing all its Types back into itself and the 'restoring of the Unity'. 'You will be of one chief use,' says Lord Arglay. 'You will discover all that is possible of the nature of the stone.'

The theme of that discovery and self-offering provides the theological core of the novel, around which the minor themes revolve – Tumulty's destruction by being drawn into the centre of the stone itself; the confounding of all in the novel who would loot the Unity for personal profit; Lord Arglay's eventual abandoning of government office, and rising importance of his book – his 'attempt to formulate once more by intellect the actions of men'; counterfeiting attempts; the death of Ali Khan at the hands of the stone itself, and several more. Ali Khan's death comes when Chloe, having already refused to exploit the stone for her own purposes, lies fearful in her bed as Ali breaks into her room searching for the stone. Let the stone do as it wills, says Chloe – the nearest she will go to exploiting the stone for herself. She is protected; Ali Khan's body is found at dawn, burnt as if by lightning.

All lesser motives are drawn away from Chloe. Frank, forced to choose between her uncompromising purity of motive and his own shady dealings with the General Secretary of the National Transport Union, chooses the latter. Throughout her pilgrimage to the End of Desire (a self-offering that must be unconditional, which is why the Muslims cannot do it as Muslims – the Unity is above such divisions), Lord Arglay, the embodiment of justice, protects and supports her.

Reginald is murdered. Garter Browne, the Home Secretary, leads a government attempt to make the public lose confidence in the stone. Chloe's act of self-offering leads to her death at the end of a nine-month coma, culminating in the restoration of the stone (the Hajji's dearest wish); a poignant theme of loss is expounded as the Mayor of Rich contemplates the miracles that will now never happen, and Lord Arglay begins the search for a new secretary. For Chloe, her becoming one with the stone is a greater good than any that human benefactors might have found her. Her role is increasingly described in specifically Christian terms, as CW, with considerable skill, expounds the difference between the Islamic concept of the Unity and the Christian concept of God in Christ.

Masques, Two (CW, 1927, 1929)

The 'Amen House Masques' – *The Masque of the Manuscript* and *The Masque of Perusal* – were privately printed occasional pieces, displaying CW's light touch in verse and his liking for allocating amusing nicknames to colleagues. There is said to have been a third, but it was neither performed nor printed.

Mathew, Gervase (1905–76)

One of the Inklings, and a contributor to *Essays Presented to Charles Williams**. Educated at Balliol College, Oxford, he joined the Catholic order of Dominicans in 1928 and was ordained a priest in 1934. He lectured in modern history, theology and English at Oxford, and wrote books on Byzantium and medieval England.

Maynard, Theodore

Maynard was a Catholic poet who reviewed CW's *Poems of Conformity* very harshly; he accused him initially of being a 'satanist', a term he later withdrew. He also reviewed, for G.K. Chesterton's *The New Witness*, Dorothy L. Sayers'* *Catholic Tales and Christian Songs* (1918). This, he considered, reduced Christianity down to paganism. Sayers responded by persuading her friend Muriel Jaeger to write to the periodical under assumed names, initiating an aggressive debate; one of the readers who joined in was a poet who pointed out that Maynard's 'patronising clericalism' had been already displayed towards CW, 'whose truly noble poetry he vilified from the same viewpoint'. CW wrote a reply, adroitly affirming both Maynard and Sayers, and said that he had liked 'most' of *Catholic Tales* and had read and admired particularly 'The Mocking of Christ'. Sayers and Jaeger tired of the joke shortly afterwards and let the 'Maynard Controversy' die (Barbara Reynolds, *Dorothy L. Sayers: Her Life and Soul*, 1993, pp. 81–82).

'Mercy, Under the'

A common blessing, epigraph or signature phrase between the Inklings, and Companions of the Co-inherence*. 'A phrase that appears frequently in [CW's] writings, as it did in his conversation. He liked to refer to the Divinity by Its Attributes: the Mercy, the Protection, the Omnipotence' (Lois Lang-Sims*, *Letters to Lalage*). In *Many Dimensions**, Chloe Burnett often uses the similar invocation 'Under the Protection'.

Mere Christianity (CSL, 1952)

One of the most well-known of CSL's books, *Mere Christianity* is a revised and enlarged edition of three previous books of talks given on BBC radio, *Broadcast Talks* (called *The Case for Christianity* in the USA) (1942), *Christian Behaviour* (1943) and *Beyond Personality* (1944). It is straightforward and lucid, and its contents are captured in its part-titles: 'Right and wrong as a clue to the meaning of the universe', 'What Christians believe', 'Christian behaviour', and 'Beyond personality: or first steps in the doctrine of the Trinity'.

His feelings about the first set of talks were recorded in a letter. The broadcasts, he wrote, were pre-evangelism 'rather than evangelism, an attempt to convince people that there is a moral law, that we disobey it, and that the existence of a Lawgiver is at least very probable and also (unless you add the Christian doctrine of the Atonement) that this imparts despair rather than comfort'.

Metaphysical thrillers

CW's description of his fiction, as distinct from 'supernatural thrillers'.

Middle-earth

JRRT's sub-created world (*see* SUB-CREATION) that features in *The Silmarillion**, *The Hobbit**, and *The Lord of the Rings**.
See also CHAPTER 4

Miracles: A Preliminary Study
(CSL, 1947; revised new edition, 1960)

This book, which reveals more than any other CSL's view of God* and nature*, was intended for people for whom the question of miracles is real. It is not couched in the specialist language of theology or philosophy, though it has an enormous amount to contribute to both theology and philosophy of religion. The book was substantially revised and improved after chapter 3 in the first edition, 'The Self-Contradiction of the Naturalist' was criticized by philosopher Elizabeth Anscombe at the Oxford University Socratic Club*. The first part of the book, consisting of the first seven chapters, describes two basic attitudes of thought about life, the universe and everything. The first, which CSL felt was now habitual in the modern person, he called Naturalism. This materialistic view sees the natural universe as all that is; nature is 'the whole show'. Nothing else exists. The possibility of miracles is ruled out in advance; seeking evidence for a miracle is as silly as looking for Santa Claus. For CSL, the Naturalist sees nature as a pond of infinite depths made up of nothing but water. The central point is that, if Naturalism is true, miracles are impossible. If Supernaturalism is true, miracles are possible, and, indeed, to be expected.

CSL points out two insurmountable difficulties with Naturalism: the realities of reason and conscience. For CSL, both conscience and reason provide an analogy for the way a miracle imposes itself upon the natural order. Both conscience and reason are testimonies to the reality of the supernatural world.

After this preparation, CSL proceeds to his main theme, the biblical miracles, particularly the incarnation of Christ.

Modern world, the
See POST-MODERNISM

Monsters and the Critics and Other Essays, The (JRRT, 1983)

A collection of general essays on linguistic or literary topics. They are all lectures given over a long period of time, from the mid-1930s to JRRT's retirement in 1959 as Merton Professor of English Language and Literature. The collection includes the seminal pieces 'Beowulf: The Monsters and the Critics'*, the now famous essay defending the artistic unity and integrity of the great Old English poem, and 'On Fairy Stories'*, an Andrew Lang lecture delivered at the University of St Andrews on 8 March 1939, presents the heart of JRRT's thinking about fantasy, sub-creation*, and the nature of fiction. It provides a key into his work, and that of CSL and George MacDonald*.

Moore, Mrs Janie King (1872–1951)

The woman adopted by CSL almost as a mother in fulfilment of an apparent promise made to her son, a billet-mate of CSL's during the Great War. Mrs Moore, along with her surviving child Maureen, shared CSL's household from soon after the war. With typical generosity, CSL focused on her virtues, praising her hospitality. His brother, 'Warnie', was less charitable; he could not understand how CSL put up with her. He shared the household from the early 1930s, thus knowing Mrs Moore in domestic life for almost 20 years. As far as Warnie was concerned, 'Minto', as she was dubbed, was CSL's thorn in the flesh. He sketched out her life and character in a journal entry a few days after her death for posterity in *Brothers and Friends: The Diaries of Major Warren Hamilton Lewis* (entry, 17 January 1951).

Since the publication of A.N. Wilson's biography of CSL, there has been speculation that CSL and Mrs Moore were lovers, with the affair ending at the time of CSL's conversion to Christianity. While this is of course possible, there is no robust evidence that has been uncovered to point one way or another. A.N. Wilson does not take into account CSL's strong sense of duty, which could explain his commitment to looking after Mrs Moore. CSL's Ulster background makes such a virtue in CSL plausible.

Morgan, Father Francis

The guardian of JRRT and his brother Hilary, appointed by their mother, Mabel Tolkien. Father Morgan was a Roman Catholic parish priest, attached to the Birmingham Oratory, founded by John Henry Newman. He provided friendship and counsel for the fatherless family. Half-Welsh and half-Spanish, he was an extrovert, whose enthusiasm helped to better the lot of the JRRT family. With the boys often ill, and the mother developing diabetes, Father Morgan hit on the plan of moving them to Rednal, in the countryside, for the summer of 1904. It was like being back at their beloved Sarehole. Mabel Tolkien died there later that year, and Father Morgan was left with the responsibility of the boys. He helped them financially, found them lodgings in Birmingham, and took them on holiday. An improvement in lodgings meant that JRRT met his future wife, Edith Bratt, another lodger. Father Francis (like King Thingol with Beren and Lúthien) disapproved of their love, fearful of distraction, and ordered JRRT to make no committment to Edith until he was 21. It meant a long separation, but JRRT was loyal to his benefactor, the only father he had known. When JRRT wrote of their eventual engagement, Father Francis accepted it without a fuss. When their first son was born, Father Francis travelled from Birmingham to baptize him. Sometimes he joined the growing family on their seaside holidays at Lyme Regis.

Morgoth's Ring (JRRT, 1993)

Volume 10 of *The History of Middle-earth** traces the evolution of *The Silmarillion** from the completion of *The Lord of the Rings** in 1949 until JRRT's death. Edited by his son Christopher Tolkien, a member of the Inklings, it draws upon unpublished papers to show this development. The task is completed in Volume 11, *The War of the Jewels**. Volume 10 follows the narrative up to Morgoth's theft of the precious Silmarils.

Mr Bliss (JRRT, 1982)

This is a children's story, illustrated in colour throughout by JRRT, about a man, noted for his tall hats, who lives in a tall house. In 1932 JRRT bought a car (he later abandoned car ownership on principle, because of the environmental effect of massive car ownership and production). The consequences of having a car suggested the story of Mr Bliss' adventures after buying a bright yellow car for five shillings. The story was shown to JRRT's publishers in 1937, when the publication of *The Hobbit** had created a demand for more from the pen of the professor. Colour printing costs, however, were prohibitive. JRRT eventually sold the manuscript to Marquette University, in the United States. It was not until after JRRT's death that the book was published. Several of its illustrations are of high quality.
See also PICTURES

Music

Music and song are a central theme running through JRRT's tales of Middle-earth*. His mythology begins with the *Ainulindalë*, the music of the Ainur. Before the creation of the world, its character and development is expressed in music. The presence of evil* in the world is prefigured in a discord introduced by Morgoth (Melkor), a discord which Ilúvatar is able to harness into a greater ultimate harmony.

The Hobbit* and *The Lord of the Rings** are replete with songs, all integral to the story. JRRT wrote major sections of *The Silmarillion** in verse which, though not song, is closer to music than prose, which is true of all poetry. Modern composers like Donald Swann and Stephen Oliver have been able to set songs from Middle-earth to music with great effect. A love of song is characteristic of elves and hobbits. Tom Bombadil's very speech is song.

Song is also part of the narrative action in key stories of the First Age. In the tale of Beren and Lúthien the elf-maiden*, the elven-king Finrod Felagund battles with Sauron in song, and the singing of Lúthien destroys Sauron's tower at Tol Sirion. In Doriath, her singing had enchanted Beren, as her mother's singing had enchanted her father, Thingol, in earlier days. In the tale of Túrin Turambar*, after Túrin finds healing at the Pools of Ivrin, he is able to make a song for his lost friend, Beleg, and is thus able to act once more, in defiance of the enemy.

In the Third Age, this direct power of song only seems to be retained by Galadriel. Her lament in Lórien, sung while the Company of the Ring were there, mentions this power. She can sing of leaves and of wind, and they appear.

The power of song is the magical power lying behind creation, an idea CSL took up in the creation of Narnia in *The Magician's Nephew**.
See also ROAD GOES EVER ON, THE; GREAT DANCE, THE

Mystical Way

A common description of what CW called the way of the rejection of images. He emphasized that it must be practised in conjunction with the way of affirmation, for both are two sides of the same coin.

Myth

CSL, like his friend JRRT, placed the highest value on the making of myth – or mythopoeia – in imaginative fiction and poetry. Some stories are outright myths – as is the story of Cupid and Psyche retold by CSL in *Till We Have Faces**. Other stories have what CSL called a 'mythical quality'. Examples he gave were the plots of Dr Jekyll and Mr Hyde, H.G. Wells' *The Door in the Wall*, Kafka's *The Castle*, and the conceptions of Gormenghast in Mervyn Peake's *Titus Groan* and of the Ents and LothLórien in JRRT's *The Lord of the Rings**.

Myth, according to CSL, is always fantasy, dealing with the impossible and preternatural. James Frazer had documented many myths of dying and rising gods throughout the world, a phenomenon that much exercised CSL. As he grew as a Christian thinker, he continued to reflect on such myths. At the heart of Christianity, CSL believed, is a myth that is also a fact – making the claims of Christianity unique. But by becoming fact, it did not cease to be myth, or lose the quality of myth. CSL was indebted to his friends JRRT and 'Hugo' Dyson* for convincing him that the Gospels demonstrated myth become fact – a point JRRT brings out in his essay 'On Fairy Stories'*. JRRT's view of myth is captured in a poem written to CSL at the time his scepticism about Christian belief was shattered. JRRT's belief that God in his grace had prefigured the gospel *evangelium* in human stories, a view shared by CSL, was a kind of natural theology.

JRRT sharply distinguished myth from allegory*, though he did believe in the applicability, and need to apply, stories. CSL, who thought rather similarly (though was more 'allegorical' than JRRT), expressed this distinction of myth and allegory. CSL concentrates on the aspect of recovery:

The value of the myth is that it takes all the things we know and restores to them the rich significance which has been hidden by the veil of familiarity. The child enjoys his cold meat, otherwise dull to him, by pretending it is buffalo, just killed with his own bow and arrow. And the child is wise. The real meat comes back to him more savoury for having been dipped in a story; you might say that only then is it real meat. If you are tired of the real landscape, look at it in a mirror. By putting bread, gold, horse, apple, or the very roads into a myth, we do not retreat from reality: we rediscover it. As long as the story lingers in our mind, the real things are more themselves. This book applies the treatment not only to bread or apple but to good and evil, to our endless perils, our anguish and our joys. By dipping them in myth we see them more clearly. I do not think he [JRRT] could have done it in any other way.

Both CSL and JRRT aspired to myth-making in their fictional creations. They had a theology of myth (*see* CHAPTER 6).

Myth of [Francis] Bacon, A (CW, c. 1930)

According to John Heath-Stubbs, this play is known to have existed in at least two copies, now destroyed. It was performed in 1932 at Downe House School*, where CW frequently lectured and which included among its pupils Anne Bradby, later Ridler* – a distinguished poet and writer on CW and niece of Humphrey Milford, CW's publisher at Oxford University Press. The play was produced following a 1930 talk by CW at Downe House on Bacon, and led to a commission from Arthur Barker for a short biography of Bacon, published in 1933.

Myth of Shakespeare, A (CW, 1929)

The first of CW's books to achieve reasonable sales (it was printed in April and reprinted in July; in 1936 it was reissued in the Oxford Bookshelf series), this verse play was the result of a suggestion 'and largely on the plan' of A.C. Ward of the City Literary Institute, who wanted it for a Shakespeare festival. It was published by Oxford University Press. The play is a verse setting for a number of biographical sketches and quotations from the plays, acted out as if taking place in Shakespeare's imagination. CW contributes (as he himself points out) no critical theory, appraisal or critical judgements. The play was omitted from OUP's 1963 *Charles Williams: Collected Plays*.

'Mythopoeia' (JRRT)

A poem by JRRT in rhyming couplets addressed to a pre-Christian CSL, defending fantasy and myth* as a means to truth, against CSL's materialism. Similar ideas are set out in his essay 'On Fairy Stories'*. The poem is written as from Philomythus to Misomythus (from lover to distruster of myth). It is included in the second edition of *Tree and Leaf** (1988).

Narnia

See CHAPTER 3

Narnia, The Chronicles of (CSL)

Seven tales for children by CSL which cover almost half of the twentieth century and over two and a half millennia of Narnian years from its creation to its final days. In chronological order the titles are: *The Magician's Nephew**, *The Lion, the Witch and the Wardrobe**, *The Horse and his Boy**, *Prince Caspian**, *The Voyage of the 'Dawn Treader'**, *The Silver Chair** and *The Last Battle**. In reading order, it is preferable to read *The Lion, the Witch and the Wardrobe* first.
See CHAPTER 3

Narrative Poems (CSL, 1969)

CSL wrote both lyrical and narrative verse, and originally hoped to make his name as a poet. This volume contains four stories, including *Dymer**, *Launcelot*, *The Nameless Isle*, and *The Queen of Drum* – about the escape of a queen from a dictator into fairy land.

Natural law

See ABOLITION OF MAN, THE

Natural theology

See CHAPTER 6

Nature in CSL and JRRT

'In our world,' said Eustace, 'a star is a huge ball of flaming gas.'

'Even in your world, my son,' replied the old man, 'that is not what a star is but only what it is made of.' (*The Voyage of the 'Dawn Treader'*)

Like his friend, OB, CSL believed that, as Ransom remarked to Merlin in *That Hideous Strength**, 'the soul has gone out of wood and water'. The world's history is one of humankind's separation from God* on the one hand and nature on the other. This view led to CSL's opposition to scientism (but not true science). Our separation from nature came from our wish to exalt ourselves and thus to belittle all else. Christians, CSL believed, should recognize God's continued activity in the fecundity of natural things like trees, grass, flowers and shrubs. JRRT, another great friend of CSL, also held this view.

For CSL, what fixed the reality of the natural world for ever was the incarnation of God himself as a fully human being in a fully real human body. The environment of his resurrected body, and those of his followers in the future, could be called a new Nature, though CSL prefered to call this environment 'heaven'.

Integral to CSL's thinking is a link between ordinary reality and imaginative creation. CSL therefore found himself as much on the defensive about fantasy as about his lifestyle (he told the American *Time* magazine that he liked monotony). Closely linked to CSL's zest for ordinary reality, for nature, was his attention to the details of life and experience. In *Out of the Silent Planet**, CSL brilliantly manages to create talking animals that are acceptable to adult readers. CSL's letters are also full of references to animals. Nature, said CSL, has the air of a good thing that has been spoiled, and he vividly illustrated this in his short story, 'The Shoddy Lands'.

The natural world of God's creation imposes a fundamental limit on the human imagination*. CSL believed that evil* – whether from human beings or demons – always results in the disruption or even the destruction of nature. In 1947, CSL wrote, 'The evil reality of lawless applied science . . . is actually reducing large tracts of Nature to disorder and sterility at this very moment.'

In his studies, *The Problem of Pain** and *Miracles**, he goes deeper into the meaning of nature as God's creation. In *Miracles* he contrasts this Christian view with what he calls Naturalism, the belief that nature is all that is. As well as in *Miracles*, he expounds on a biblical view of nature in *Reflections on the Psalms**. Ultimately, there was, for CSL, an inevitable connection between nature and joy*, as in nature heaven itself is foreshadowed:

> The settled happiness and security which we all desire, God withholds from us by the very nature of the world: but joy, pleasure, and merriment, He has scattered broadcast. We are never safe, but we have plenty of fun, and some ecstacy. It is not hard to see why. The security we crave would teach us to rest our hearts in this world and oppose an obstacle to our return to God: a few moments of happy love, a landscape, a symphony, a merry meeting with our friends, a bathe or a football match, have no such tendency. Our father refreshes us on the journey with some pleasant inns, but will not encourage us to mistake them for home. (*The Problem of Pain*, chapter 7)

Like CSL, JRRT also believed that worlds of the imagination are properly based upon the humble and common things of life. Again like CSL, JRRT believed that nature is better understood as God's creation. When the storyteller is building up a convincing 'Secondary World', he or she in fact is engaged in sub-creation*; creating, as it were, in the image or as a miniaturization of the 'Primary World'. Such storymaking surveys the depth of space and time. It is the imaginative equivalent of the reason's attempt to capture reality in a single, unified theory.

Sub-creation, the storytelling at least of humankind (that of elves is different), reflects the brokenness of God's original creation. The Fall* theme is intrinsic. JRRT clarified this theme in the light of the claims of Christian revelation (see CHRISTIAN MEANINGS IN JRRT). To give just one example of the effect of the Fall: evil always results in the disruption or even the destruction of nature. JRRT's work is full of symbolic landscapes of a spoiled world: the devastation of Ard-galen, the ruin of Beleriand, the drowning of Númenor, the desolation of Smaug – to name just a few. He even takes the basis of life – light – and employs it symbolically to show the mischief that wickedness causes, particularly the malice of Morgoth.

JRRT uses his own sub-creation of Middle-earth* as a mirror of nature. There are considerable complexities in the structure of his world. Genetically, for example, there are differences between elves and humans, even though the two races can intermarry fruitfully. As a result of these differences one race is immortal and the other must face the mystery of death. Elves are tied to the natural order in a way that humans are not. Nevertheless (and, in JRRT, because of this), elves represent the higher aspect of human nature. Another example of complexity in JRRT's portrayal of his world is its geography. At the drowning of Númenor the very shape of the world is changed, becoming the sphere that is familiar to us. Though an invented world, JRRT supposes that it is our Primary World in its pre-Christian history, especially as regards northern Europe.

This sense of familiar location is intensified by JRRT in his creation of the Shire, and of Tol Eressëa in early versions of *The Silmarillion*. The Shire, and the original Tol Eressëa, are homely places associated with JRRT's experience of the West Midlands at the turn of the century. This identity of the West Midlands was strengthened for JRRT by his study of medieval English literature. Favourite works such as *Pearl* were written in a rich West Midlands English.

As well as this large-scale 'homeliness', JRRT was fond of creating homely places such as the Cottage of Lost Play, Bag End, Crickhollow, the house of Tom Bombadil, the Prancing Pony pub, and Rivendell. By a powerful transposition, JRRT portrayed a homeliness in his idea of the hero, an idea which he took from the Bible. His real heroes, such as Bilbo Baggins and Sam Gamgee, are taken from ordinary life. Even more 'heroic' heroes, like Beren, are in the opinion of the wise, weak and frail. The great king Aragorn must be disguised as a humble ranger for much of his life to be prepared for the great tasks required of him.

JRRT had a great love for nature as a garden. His brother Hilary was a market gardener, and JRRT was an amateur gardener. His knowledge of flora is an important element in his fiction. He, of course, created Elanor, Athelas and Evermind. His love for the tree became a central theme in his work. In Middle-earth, the tree is the crown of the flora of creation.

Nat Whilk

Anglo-Saxon for 'I know not whom', used by CSL as a pseudonym, usually in the form of the initials 'N.W.' In the first edition of *A Grief Observed** he called himself 'N.W. Clerk'. Clerk is Middle-English for 'scholar'. Playing on his pseudonym, CSL quotes the medieval authority 'Natvilcius' in *Perelandra** regarding eldila.

Negative way

See AFFIRMATION, WAY OF

New Book of English Verse, The (ed. CW, 1935)

An anthology compiled at the request of Victor Gollancz, the *New Book* announced its publisher's two rules of selection as '(1) that it should contain nothing that was in the *Oxford Book of English Verse* or the *Golden Treasury*, (2) that every poem included should be of poetic importance.' Charles Williams was editor and Lord David Cecil, Ernest de Selincourt and E.M.W. Tillyard were associate editors – there were some disagreements over selection, notably on Wordsworth and Clare, but by and large it was CW's project. The substantial introduction is an important statement of his view of poetry. He points out that he has added a third criterion of his own; a preference for poetry that 'contained a certain critical comment', for example parody.

He explains that an anthology covering, as this does, more than a few years has to deal with the process of 'continual readjustment of standards', and alerts his readers to the tendency to 'blur', through loss of critical contrast aided by fashions in scholarship. He discusses 'cant', the 'great and everlasting enemy of poetry', which prompts reactions before the reader has had the opportunity to react – a symptom, in CW's opinion, of bad writing, and something to which even the greatest poets are sometimes prone: 'Shelley's "aerial music" has sometimes a dubiously habitual sound about it'.

> The language of poetry is bound to be ceremonial, however direct. It is when versifiers (that is, ceremonialists) use such a language without the intensity it should convey and concentrate that Cant begins to exist; it is when ceremony is willingly accepted as a substitute for intensity that it triumphs.

N

CW next identified 'the Celian moment', which he illustrated with a poem by Marvell that celebrated 'the moment that contains, almost equally, the actual and the potential "in all love and Nature's store".' He charts it through successive generations of poetry until it finds fulfilment in Milton and Wordsworth. Though such as these went beyond Shakespeare, CW argues, Shakespeare gave the Celian moment 'new perfection', surpassable only by Dante. (NB that 'Celia' is the name that CW gave to Phyllis Jones*, his 'second love'.)

The anthology ends at the death of Gerard Manley Hopkins, a point CW calls 'the moment of the close of the myths', when myths, far from merely falling into disuse, were overtaken by a new use of myth*, metaphor and knowledge. Since Hopkins' death, comments CW, divinities have yielded to knowledge: 'the most important things now in our self-consciousness are the conscious knowledge of our consciousness and our revolt against our knowledge. Yet the future is hopeful, for 'a new vision of an extreme subject-ivity with a freer objectivity is, it seems, approaching.'

Among the acknowledgements CW placed the names of advisors including R.C. Goffin and T.S. Eliot*, and concluded by expressing his gratitude to his wife.

'New Shadow, The' (JRRT)

A story intended to be set in the Fourth Age, abandoned by JRRT. It was to tell of events about 100 years after the death of Aragorn, where people had soon become bored with goodness. There were secret revolutionaries involved in Satanism (whether extolling Sauron or Morgoth, JRRT does not say), and boys of Gondor played at being orcs.

Noises that Weren't There, The (CW, 1943)

An unfinished novel by CW, parts of which were used in *All Hallows' Eve**.

'Notion Club Papers, The' (JRRT)

An incomplete work published in JRRT's *Sauron Defeated**. In a letter to his publisher in July 1946, he mentioned having written three parts of this. He said that it took up material employed in the unfinished 'The Lost Road'*, but in an entirely different frame and setting.

Tolkien supposes that the papers were found early in the twenty-first century, and constitute the minutes of discussion of the Notion Club in Oxford between 1986 and 1987 – the years of the great storm.

JRRT wrote the unfinished papers between 1945 and 1946. Along with the Notion Club Papers was a new version of the Númenorean legend – 'The Drowning of Anadûne'. The Papers are a second attempt (the first being 'The Lost Road') at time travel, in response to a challenge that CSL and

JRRT set themselves: to write a time or space travel story. CSL's response was his space trilogy.

'The Lost Road' has elements of an idealized portrait of the father–son relationship between JRRT and his son Christopher. Similarly, 'The Notion Club Papers' idealizes the Inklings. Neither contains direct biography or autobiography. Both however concern the discovery of clues to the lost world of Númenor through strange words seemingly discovered by Tolkien-like people exceptionally sensitive to language. The later work appreciates the value of a group or community of people in building up together an imaginative picture of the past. The insights into the past achieved imaginatively are in a curious way as objective as the seemingly hard facts of traditional history. This objectivity is demonstrated by the intrusion of a great storm in late twentieth-century Oxford which derives from the calamity which befell Númenor. The world of Númenor – specifically its terrible destruction – in fact intrudes into the future western world in the summer of 1987. (Interestingly, there was a great storm – a hurricane – in Britain that Autumn!)

As well as language, the Inklings-like discussions of the Notion Club concern the status of dreams, and time and space travel via that medium. Behind it is an exciting exploration of the place imagination* has in putting us in contact with objective reality, resisting the view that imagination is purely subjective and individualistic.

Christopher Tolkien – who was a member of the Inklings at the time JRRT created this idealized picture of them – assures us from his intimate knowledge that there is no direct correspondence between characters in the Notion Club and actual Inklings. However there are hints of actual characters, e.g. parallels between Dolbear and Dr Humphrey Havard*, and between Dyson* and Arry Lowdham.

The extent that the picture is idealized can be discovered by comparing 'The Notion Club Papers' to Humphrey Carpenter's superb reconstruction of an Inklings evening in his study of the Inklings (part 3, chapter 3). Discussion (as is revealed in Warren Lewis' diary) ranges far and wide, which was very much to CSL's taste. The Notion Club discussions are very much more focused around linguistic and dream issues, more to JRRT's own taste (not that CSL and others wouldn't have been interested in these issues – in fact the Papers were read to the Inklings). However, despite being idealized, they do acknowledge the value of a community of like-minded thinking and imaginating. There is not the isolation of 'The Lost Road', with only the father and son.

Old West

JRRT was by profession a philologist, teaching Old English and Middle English, very much in connection with the literature of the period. His work was intimately related to his construction of the languages, peoples and history of Middle-earth*. From the burgeoning creation of elvish languages he reconstructed a forgotten world. Actually, he invented a world as if it were a forgotten world, patterned on the philologist's construction of forgotten contexts and earlier forms from vestiges of old languages. JRRT particularly explored the possibility of a forgotten, old western world in his unfinished tales of time travel, *The Lost Road** and 'The Notion Club Papers'*. The same concept is implicit in the theme he returned to again and again, that of Aelfwine's voyage to the utter west by the lost road, where he hears the forgotten tales of Middle-earth – or rather the tales of the cosmos to which Middle-earth belongs.

The instincts of a philologist are captured in the figure of the Cambridge philologist Elwin Ransom, in CSL's science-fiction story, *Out of the Silent Planet**. Ransom has been kidnapped to Malacandia (Mars), and in terror escapes his captors. He fears an alien life form called a *sorn*, until a startling event takes place, which dramatically overturns his perceptions. He encounters another animal, which he realizes is language-using.

> In the fraction of a second which it took Ransom to decide that the creature was really talking, and while he still knew that he might be facing instant death, his imagination had leaped over every fear and hope and probability of his situation to follow the dazzling project of making a Malacandrian grammar. *An Introduction to the Malacandrian language – The Lunar Verb – A Concise Martian–English Dictionary* ... the titles flitted through his mind. And what might one not discover from the speech of a non-human race? The very form of language itself, the principle behind all possible languages, might fall into his hands. Unconsciously he raised himself on his elbow and stared at the black beast. (Chapter 9)

Ransom's thought, 'what might one not discover from the speech of a non-human race?' is the kind of notion that would naturally arise in JRRT's mind. Indeed, the creation of elvish languages – non-human languages of a kind – were for him an explanation of the dazzling possibilities of language for illuminating our knowledge of reality, both natural and supernatural, seen and unseen.

The character of Elwin Ransom, in CSL's story, is actually based upon JRRT, his close friend. Elwin means 'Elf-friend', like the name Aelfwine. JRRT was aware of this resemblance, writing several years later to his son

Christopher: 'As a philologist I may have some part in [Ransom], and rec-ognize some of my opinions Lewisified in him' (letter 77). Ransom is both CSL's voice in the story and representative of JRRT.

The affinity between CSL and JRRT that allowed CSL to fictionalize this friend, and allowed his friend modestly to recognize this fictional treatment, is not simply a linguistic one. Philology is undoubtedly an important element in *Out of the Silent Planet*, as it is in the foundation of all JRRT's fiction. Equally important however, and present in both theory and fiction, is a commitment to the Old West, and a related antipathy to modernism. What the friends would have viewed as Old Western values are embodied in Elwin Ransom, values they each endorsed.

These Old Western values are embedded in the portrayal of Ransom, both positively and negatively. Positively they are displayed in Ransom's perception, which is pre-modernist and essentially medieval. CSL, like JRRT and also CW, loved the Renaissance and medieval cosmos, its imaginative model of reality, and it is this world-picture that is smuggled into the minds of modern readers as they enjoy CSL's story.

Negatively, Ransom's pre-modernist values are expressed in contrast to the attitudes of Professor Edward Weston, a scientist who represents all that CSL dislikes about the modernist world. CSL is not against science or scien-tists, but the cult of science, or scientism*, found in modernism (*see* POST-MODERNISM). Weston is the person responsible for kidnapping Ransom, an act he considers completely justifiable. He has disdain for all values of the Old West. His guiding value is the survival of humanity at any cost.

CSL famously defended the Old West in his inaugural lecture on taking up the Chair of Medieval and Renaissance literature at the University of Cambridge in 1954, a seat JRRT helped him gain (*see DE DESCRIPTIONE TEMPORUM*). JRRT, along with their mutual friend OB, was responsible for helping along the procession which led CSL to become aware of a dramatic shift from the Old to the Modernist West, a shift which made the change from medieval to Renaissance culture insignificant by comparison.

OB was responsible for ridding CSL of his earlier 'chronological snobbery', an abiding vice of the modern world. CSL, in his autobiography, *Surprised by Joy**, called this 'the uncritical acceptance of the intellectual climate common to our age and the assumption that whatever has gone out of date is on that account discredited'.

JRRT, in turn, was responsible for pointing out to CSL that the values of pre-Christian paganism were not merely of aesthetic interest, but were life and death matters reflecting an objective state of affairs.

As a result of JRRT's arguments, CSL came to the conclusion that simi-larities between Christian teaching and ancient myths can argue for the truth of Christianity as well as against it. At the heart of Christianity, CSL came to believe, is a myth that is also a fact – making the claims of Christianity unique (*see* MYTH). JRRT's fiction, significantly, largely has a pre-Christian setting. Of CSL's corpus, only his novel *Till We Have Faces**, has such a setting. It is such a significant work, however, that it underlines the deep affinity between the two men.

JRRT, of course, embodies his love of and commitment to the Old West in his mythology. Most obvious of all is the geographical – Valinor and Númenor symbolically embody the values of the Old West (*see* CHAPTER 4). Quests for the Undying Lands figure often in the tales of JRRT's sub-created world. Eärendil, for instance, seeks the blessed realm of Valinor in order to intercede for the threatened peoples of Beleriand. The tapestry of tales essentially begins and ends with quests for the West. After the awakening of the elves they are called on a great journey to the Uttermost West, Aman, by the Valar, their guardians. Then, at the end of the Third Age of Middle-earth, after the War of the Ring, the ring-bearers pass from Grey Havens West over the Great Sea by the Straight Road to seek the Undying Lands beyond the world. In our own history, JRRT imagines Aelfwine's journey west to Tol Eressëa, where he hears the elven tales. In the unfinished 'The Lost Road'* and 'The Notion Club Papers'*, the lost western island of Númenor figures prominently in the setting of our world.

JRRT's tales in their own manner embody anti-modernist themes as powerfully as any stories written by CSL, disclosing his Old Western values. Anti-modernism can be seen clearly, for instance, in JRRT's treatment of the related themes of possession and power, themes central to his work.

In our time, modernism increasingly seems to be collapsing in on itself like a stellar black hole. The anti-modernism of JRRT and CSL is now acceptable to an extent that would have astonished them. It is not really surprising that the popularity of their writings is greater than ever – as a poll by one of the UK's largest chains of bookshops revealed in 1998. The current phase of post-modernism is difficult to characterize, but, like pre-modernism, is identified in relation to what CSL called the hideous strength of modernism. It is interesting that even back in 1954, CSL defined the Old West by placing it in contrast to modernism. The great divide lay, he believed, somewhere in the last century. It was as much a sociological and cultural divide as a shift in ideas. However, with the recent rise of a new paganism, CSL and JRRT would probably caution against assuming that this is the same as the pre-Christian paganism they loved and explored, much as they might have welcomed features of it. The new paganism we are experiencing today is on our side of the great divide, not on the other side, the side of the Old West. Both CSL and JRRT found values in pre-Christian paganism that prefigured the Christian values that they championed. CSL warned, in his inaugural Cambridge lecture:

Christians and Pagans had much more in common with each other than either has with a post-Christian. The gap between those who worship different gods is not so wide as that between those who worship and those who do not ... A post-Christian man is not a Pagan; you might as well think that a married woman recovers her virginity by divorce. The post-Christian is cut off from the Christian past and therefore doubly from the Pagan past.

All is not gloom perhaps. The continuing popularity of CSL's and JRRT's pre-modernism – their sustained rejection of modernism in favour of Old Western values – suggests the existence of a continuity between the Old West and now, despite the Great Divide. It indicates a strong, though small, stream that has never been eradicated, despite JRRT's and CSL's fears. To this stream belong other Inklings like CW, as well as many other writers. The values that the two friends were attacking are still all-powerful, however, continuing to represent a hideous strength.

FURTHER READING

Colin Duriez, 'Tolkien and the Old West', in *Digging Potatoes, Growing Trees: 25 Years of Speeches at the JRRT Society's Annual Dinners*, Vol. 2 (The JRRT Society, 1988)

'On Fairy Stories' (JRRT, 1947)

This lecture is the key source for JRRT's thinking and theology behind his creation of Middle-earth and its stories. He links God and humanity in two related ways. In the first he, as an orthodox Christian, sees humans – male and female – as being made in the image of God. This makes a qualitative difference between humans and all other things which exist in the universe. Our ability to speak, love and create fantasy originates in this imageness of God. The second way JRRT links God and humanity is in similarities that exist by necessity between the universe of God's making and human making. Human making derives, that is, from our being in God's image.

The actual course of JRRT's essay does not so starkly highlight these two related links between God and humanity, but they underlie both the essay and JRRT's fiction.

'On Fairy Stories' was originally given as a lecture at St Andrews University. It is concerned to rehabilitate the idea of the fairy story, which had been relegated to children's literature, and fantasy* in general. To regard fairy stories as trivial, suitable only for telling to children, failed to do justice either to such stories or to real children.

JRRT, who had by then written much of *The Silmarillion**, and published *The Hobbit** attempted to set out a structure which belonged to good fairy tales and fantasies. This structure demonstrated that fairy tales were worthy of serious attention.

Fairy tales, he pointed out, were stories about faerie: 'the realm or state where fairies have their being'. Listeners who had read his essay, 'Beowulf: The Monsters or the Critics'*, may have noticed a similarity here with JRRT's portrayal of the Old English poem. JRRT had spoken of the poet making his theme 'incarnate in the world of history and geography'. Fairy tales were fantasy, allowing their hearers or readers to move from the details of their limited experience to 'survey the depths of space and time'. The successful fairy story in fact was 'sub-creation'*, the ultimate achievement of fantasy, the highest art, deriving its power from human language itself. The successful writer of fairy story 'makes a Secondary World which your mind can enter. Inside it, what he relates is "true": it accords with the laws of that world.'

In addition to offering a Secondary World, with an 'inner consistency of reality', a good fairy tale has three other key structural features. In the first place, it helps to bring about in the reader what JRRT called recovery – that is, the restoration of a true view of the meaning of ordinary and humble things which make up human life and reality, things like love, thought, trees, hills and food. (*See also* HEALING.) Second, the good fairy story offers escape from one's narrow and distorted view of reality and meaning. This is the escape of the prisoner rather than the flight of the deserter. Third, the good story offers consolation, leading to joy* (connected to the longing CSL called *sehnsucht*).

The consolation, argued JRRT, only had meaning because good stories pointed to the greatest story of all. This story had all the structural features of a fairy tale, myth, or great story, with the additional feature of being true in actual human history. This was the gospel, the story of God himself coming to earth as a humble human being, a king, like Aragorn, in disguise, a seeming fool, like Frodo and Sam, the greatest storyteller entering his own story.

JRRT's fundamental idea of the consolation is related to his view of nature*, which was deeply theological. He saw nature in terms of a natural theology* which was sacramental. His own created elves – which are the central concern of *The Silmarillion*, and his invented languages – were natural creatures or, at least, their destinies were tied up with the natural world. Elves are his name for fairies, and thus are central to this essay. His main fiction, like this essay, was concerned to rehabilitate the fairy tale, and to provide consolation for his readers. The three features of recovery, escape and consolation, focus on the effect that good fairy tales have on their readers. The effect of a work of literature on its reader is an important dimension of literary meaning. CSL explored such effects in relation to story in his *An Experiment in Criticism**. His ideas in this late book were hammered out in meetings of the Inklings, and JRRT would have been in substantial agreement with them. Thus, to explore the themes of JRRT's essay and fiction further, it is important to read this book of CSL's.

See also MYTH; CHAPTER 6

Order of the Golden Dawn

A secret society of which CW was a member for several years. 'There is hardly a legitimate occult order in Europe or America that has not borrowed directly or indirectly from the Golden Dawn' (Francis Regardie). And quite apart from its influence in occult circles, the order attracted a number of distinguished writers.

The order began as a Rosicrucian movement. As recently as 1801 it seems there were no Rosicrucians in England. The Societas Rosicruciana, founded in Anglia in 1865, appears to have been the first Rosicrucian secret ritual society. There were Rosicrucian lodges in freemasonry, and another strand feeding into the making of the Order of the Golden Dawn was theosophy. Some early members were freemasons, theosophists and cabbalists. The order they joined was founded in Paris as a secret society, struggled to survive, and was relaunched in London by A.E. Waite, a poet with a strong interest in the occult. In 1917 he invited CW to become a member. CW was 31, a published poet, and it is not clear why he wanted to join; but the experience and knowledge he gained appeared in several of his books. The incantation of the Tetragrammaton by Simon the Clerk in *All Hallows' Eve** is a rite of the order, and Simon himself is modelled on the notorious Aleister Crowley, once a member of the order but thrown out for extreme behaviour. Other members were of great interest to CW. Evelyn Underhill*, novelist and Christian mystic, was a member; CW's edition of her letters was published in 1945, when he had left the order; he is quite dismissive of it in his Introduction. Another member was W.B. Yeats.

CW's name in the order was 'Frater Qui Sitit Veniat', and he remained a member for at least 11 years, though some have suggested he may have stayed even longer.

Though his precise motives for joining are unclear, it is unlikely that he was interested in the notion of gaining power as an adept. All his subsequent writings condemn such aspirations, and in the book in which one would have expected a deep knowledge of the occult to have been evident – *Witchcraft** – he writes with little interest in the rituals and ceremonies and sees the whole movement as a perversion.

See ANTHROPOSOPHY

FURTHER READING

R.A. Gilbert, *The Golden Dawn: Twilight of the Magicians* (Aquarian Press, 1983)
Frances A. Yates, *The Rosicrucian Enlightenment* (Routledge and Kegan Paul, 1972)

Original participation

The Inklings sometimes discussed primitive human beings, and pre-Christian paganism is explored as a central theme in JRRT's tales of Middle-earth*. Enlightened paganism is also a common theme in CSL, as in *Till We Have Faces**. OB's thinking is constantly captured by a vision of an ancient unity, by definition embodied both in perception and language, a unity we have lost. Key to this vision was a sense of what OB called 'original participation', a sense we can glimpse at times through dreams, poetry and myth. He believed that this primitive awareness was 'pre-logical' and 'pre-mythical'.

OB defines original participation as the belief that 'there stands behind the phenomena, and on the other side of them from me, a represented which is of the same nature as me . . . of the same nature as the perceiving self, inasmuch as it is not mechanical or accidental, but psychic and voluntary' (*Saving the Appearances*, 1957, p. 42). He explained that human beings, in this primitive state, feel themselves to be 'a functioning member of the natural world, as a finger is a member of the physical body' (*Romanticism Comes of Age*, 1944, p. 230).

OB's concept inspired CSL particularly, but also JRRT. CSL shows how animal consciousness presents a hint of this original human participation in his affectionate portrayal of Mr Bultitude the bear in *That Hideous Strength**:

> Mr. Bultitude's mind was as furry and as unhuman in shape as his body . . . One of our race, if plunged back for a moment in the warm, trembling, iridescent pool of that pre-Adamite consciousness, would have emerged believing that he had grasped the absolute for the states below reason and the states above it have, by their common contrast to the life we know, a certain superficial resemblance. Sometimes there returns to us from infancy the memory of a nameless delight or terror, unattached to any delightful or dreadful thing, a potent adjective floating in a nounless void, a pure quality. At such moments we have experience of the shallows of that pool. But fathoms deeper than any memory can take us, right down in the central warmth and dimness, the bear lived all its *life*.

See EVOLUTION OF CONSCIOUSNESS

Orpheus: A Poetic Drama (OB)

Written by OB in the 1930s, and performed at the Little Theatre, Sheffield, England, 1948. OB recalls discussing his urge to write a play in verse with CSL. His friend suggested, in something like these words: 'Why not take one of the myths and simply do your best with it – Orpheus for instance?'

OB followed Virgil's* presentation of the myth of Orpheus and Eurydice in his fourth *Georgic*, exploring the insights of a pre-Christian imagination*, as CSL was to do in his retelling of the myth of Cupid and Psyche in *Till We Have Faces**. There are Christian echoes in OB's treatment, themes of fall and redemption, but also an exploration of consciousness, participation and the imagination's role in human growth. He includes the loves of *eros* and *agape* (*see THE FOUR LOVES*). In the drama OB also explores the nature of myth* itself, a central preoccupation of the Inklings.

Orpheus represents a rare excursion into fiction on OB's part. Other fictions include *The Silver Trumpet**, *This Ever Diverse Pair**, and an unpublished novel and novella.

Outlines of Romantic Theology (CW, written 1924)

An unpublished prose work, posthumously published in an edition by Alice Hadfield (1990) based on a surviving copy of CW's typescript. It is one of several books on the theme of romantic love* that CW wrote at the time of, and in the years immediately following, his marriage to Florence in 1917. Influences on the book, Hadfield suggests, are Dante* and Malory, and Coventry Patmore who wrote poetry on married love. Although CW seems to have lost interest in publishing the book, it is a valuable insight on his early thinking about a theme that was to be at the heart of his major works.

CW argues that romantic love between men and women can help us to understand better the ways of God. Theologians have tended to overlook romantic love as expository source material, though they have often used natural phenomena, ethical issues and human reasoning. But why ignore the experience that human beings universally share? And what can we learn as we consider it? It is a book that draws on CW's experience of love as he contemplated marriage (and there are clues in *The Silver Stair** that he and Florence may have planned a much earlier marriage and postponed it), and now was married.

He begins by defining 'romantic theology' and the principles of romantic love; goes on to consider the New Testament and then the Mass in romantic theology; adds a chapter on 'dangers and safeguards' followed by another on 'doctors and documents'; and concludes with a brief survey of 'other aspects'.

One of the reasons why CW did not pursue publication (Faber and Gwyn were very interested in publishing it but requested some changes which in principle CW was willing to implement) may well be that his marriage was encountering problems, and he had fallen in love with Phyllis Jones*.
See also RELIGION AND LOVE IN DANTE

Out of the Silent Planet (CW, 1938)

The first volume of CSL's science-fiction trilogy. Dr Elwin Ransom, a philologist don from Cambridge University, is kidnapped while on a walking holiday in the Midlands and taken to Malacandra (Mars) by Devine and Weston, the latter a famous physicist and materialist. They are under a misapprehension that the unseen ruler of Malacandra wants a human sacrifice – a fantasy created by their dark minds.

After escaping his captors Ransom is at first terrified and disoriented by the red planet and its diversity of terrain and inhabitants – various forms of rational life related in a harmonious hierarchy. The inhabitants – sorns (or, more properly, seroni), hrossa, and pfifltriggi – turn out to be civilized and amiable. Ransom, as a linguist (modelled on JRRT), is soon able to pick up the rudiments of their language.

In *Out of the Silent Planet* CSL imaginatively recreates the medieval picture of the cosmos he later set out in his book, *The Discarded Image**. In Deep Heaven, the planets are guided by spiritual intelligences, or Oyarsa. Our planet is the Silent Planet, Thulcandra, because it is cut off from the courtesy and order of Deep Heaven by a primeval disobedience.

See also OLD WEST

Oxford

City and county town of Oxfordshire, England, where, with exceptions at various times, the Inklings lived and met. It was CSL's home from immediately after the Great War until his death in 1963. It was JRRT's home from 1925, when he was elected Rawlinson and Bosworth Professor of Anglo-Saxon, to his death in 1973, except for a few retirement years in Poole. CW was evacuated there with the Oxford University Press' London office during the Second World War. It was in Oxford that the Inklings met, sometimes at the Eagle and Child public house (mainly on Tuesdays), often on Thursday evenings at CSL's room in Magdalen College, and sometimes in JRRT's rooms at Exeter College.

University teaching has been carried on at Oxford since the early years of the twelfth century, perhaps as a result of students migrating from Paris. The university's fame quickly grew, until by the fourteenth century it rivalled any in Europe.

University College, where CSL was an undergraduate, is its oldest college, founded in 1249. CSL taught philosophy for one year at University College during the absence of its tutor, then, in 1925, he was elected Fellow and tutor in English Language and Literature at Magdalen College. With his appointment to the Chair of Medieval and Renaissance Literature in 1954 he commuted to Cambridge usually for part of the week during term times.

During most of CSL's life in Oxford he lived at the Kilns, on the outskirts of Oxford, at Headington. Originally this was isolated, but is now surrounded by a housing estate, where a street is named after him.

JRRT was associated with three Oxford colleges: Exeter, Pembroke and Merton. Between 1911 and 1915 he was an undergraduate at Exeter College, studying first Classics then English language and literature. In 1925 he returned from Leeds University to become Professor of Anglo-Saxon, with Pembroke as his college. After he changed chairs to become Professor of English Language and Literature in 1945, he became a Fellow of Merton College. A professor's first responsibility was to the whole Oxford faculty.

The Tolkien family lived in a succession of houses in suburban Oxford. In 1925, JRRT bought a house at 20 Northmoor Road, in the north of the city, and then, in 1930, moved to a larger house next door, number 22. It was the mutilation of a favourite poplar tree in the street that inspired JRRT's story, *Leaf by Niggle**. In 1947 the family moved to a smaller house in 3 Manor Road, as John and Michael Tolkien had now left home, but this proved too small. The house the Tolkiens moved to in 1950, in Holywell Street, had much more character, but they soon found that the Oxford traffic made living there unbearable. JRRT wrote that 'This charming house has become uninhabitable: unsleepable-in, unworkable-in, rocked, racked with noise, and drenched with fumes. Such is modern life. Mordor in our midst.' Three years later they found a house in Headington, a quiet suburb to the east of the city, near to CSL's home, the Kilns. This was 76 Sandfield Road, where the Tolkiens lived until 1968, when they moved to Poole in Dorset. After Edith's death in 1971, JRRT was able to move back to Oxford, living in college rooms in 21 Merton Street. He lived there from March 1972 until his death the following year.

With the outbreak of the Second World War the London office of Oxford University Press was evacuated to Oxford, bringing CW with it. He lodged at the home of Professor H.N. Spalding at 9 South Parks Road, near the city centre and convenient for the Eagle and Child. The temporary offices of the London branch were housed at Southfield House, Hilltop Road, Cowley, a little more than a mile from the city centre, to the south. Williams died at the Radcliffe hospital (now infirmary) on the Woodstock Road in 1945, the hospital where Joy Davidman Lewis* was to die of cancer 15 years later.

Oxford University Socratic Club (1941–72)

A debating club set up by Miss Stella Aldwinckle (1907–90) to discuss questions about Christian faith raised by atheists, agnostics, and those disillusioned about religion. CSL accepted her invitation to be its first president, a position he held until 1954, when he went to Cambridge. Its committee scoured the pages of *Who's Who* to find intelligent atheists who had the time or the zeal to come and present their creed. Leading Christian thinkers also were main speakers. CSL himself took this position on 11 occasions. As

P

president, CSL usually was expected to provide a rejoinder to the speaker. Lead speakers included CW, D.M. MacKinnon, Austin Farrer*, J.Z. Young, C.E.M. Joad, P.D. Medawar, H.H. Price, C.H. Waddington, A.J. Ayer, J.D. Bernal, A.G.N. Flew, J.Bronowski, Basil Mitchell, R.M. Hare, A. Rendle Short, I.T. Ramsey, Iris Murdock, Gilbert Ryle, Michael Polanyi, J.L. Austin, H.J. Blackham, Michael Dummett, E. Evans-Pritchard, Dorothy L. Sayers*, and other outstanding thinkers from different academic disciplines.

P

Participation

Participation is one of OB's central concepts, closely tied to an original state of unified perception. The concept deeply influenced CSL and attracted JRRT. It had many consequences for our understanding of the nature of language and metaphor (*see POETIC DICTION*). Participation, according to OB, is a 'predominately perceptual relation between observer and observed, between man and nature . . . nearer to unity than dichotomy' (*History, Guilt and Habit*, 1979, p. 26). In this relation mind is not yet detached from its representations; the subject and the object not divorced. OB believes that some of this ancient participation endures in medieval art and thought, the four elements theory, the four humours, and in astrology (*The Recovery of Meaning*, 1977, p. 18). There are some parallels with OB in Michael Polanyi's exposition of a tacit dimension to knowledge (*see* his *Personal Knowledge*, 1958).
See also EVOLUTION OF CONSCIOUSNESS; ORIGINAL PARTICIPATION

Pearl

A fourteen-century alliterative poem, derived from the West Midlands, the area on which JRRT based the Shire. The background of the Christian author of this major work of English literature is unknown, but he (or maybe she) is believed to have written the masterpiece, *Sir Gawain and the Green Knight*. JRRT's translation into modern English, retaining the original form, was published after his death.

Pearl is the only daughter of the narrator, who died less than two years of age. The grieving father has a vision in the garden where she is buried. He sees a river. Paradise lies beyond it, where a girl is seated. It is Pearl, grown to maturity. The poet is comforted as the maiden speaks to him of her blessed state, enjoying as she is the salvation of Christ. She is a pearl lost to him.

JRRT argues that the poem is literally autobiographical and symbolic rather than allegorical, i.e. it has a wideness of application.
See also SIR GAWAIN AND THE GREEN KNIGHT, PEARL AND SIR ORFEO

Peoples of Middle-earth, The (JRRT, 1996)

The twelfth and last volume of *The History of Middle-earth**, unpublished papers edited and expounded by JRRT's son, Christopher. This volume reveals the genesis of the Appendices to *The Lord of the Rings**, as well as issuing two stories that JRRT soon abandoned, including 'The New Shadow'.

Perelandra (Voyage to Venus) (CSL, 1943)

This, the second volume of CSL's science-fiction trilogy, is set on the planet Perelandra (Venus), a paradisal, oceanic world of floating islands as well as fixed lands. Dr Elwin Ransom is transported there to rebuff the attacks of the forces of evil* incarnate in the human form of his old enemy, Weston. Perelandra, Ransom discovers, has its own, green-fleshed equivalent of Adam and Eve. Ransom plays a key part, much to his surprise, in frustrating the devilish plans of the Oyarsa of earth to corrupt the unspoiled world. Eventually Ransom realizes, to his dismay, that he must engage Weston in a physical fight to the death. Just as the sequel *That Hideous Strength** is paralleled by CSL's study *The Abolition of Man**, *Perelandra* is complemented by *A Preface to Paradise Lost**. This is his study of John Milton's great epic poem, dealing with the fall of humanity, and key themes such as hierarchy. *Perelandra* portrays the imaginative splendour of Milton's themes in a way designed to bewitch the modern reader, bypassing our prejudice against the past – what CSL dubbed our 'chronological snobbery'*.

The story climaxes in a vision of the 'Great Dance'* of the universe, in which all patterns of human and other life interweave.

Personal Heresy: A Controversy, The (CSL, 1939)

Jointly authored with E.M.W. Tillyard, a Cambridge literary critic. CSL contributed chapters I, III, and V, and a concluding Note, and E.M.W. Tillyard contributed chapters II, IV, and VI, giving an opposing point of view.

CSL argues against the view that poetry is concerned with providing biographical information about the poet, and that it is necessary to know about the poet to understand the poem. The poet's consciousness is a condition of our knowledge gained through the poem, not the knowledge itself. CSL's analysis bears remarkable similarities to the insights of Michael Polanyi, who was concerned with the structure of consciousness and the way we participate* in knowledge. CSL's position here has implications for all the arts (as his late work, *An Experiment in Criticism**, makes clear). CSL would reiterate the poet Shelley's view, in his brilliant *Defence of Poetry*, that imagination* allows us to see quantities as qualities, and to perceive what we know.

See also LITERARY CRITIC, CSL AS A; *TRANSPOSITION AND OTHER ADDRESSES*

Perusal, Masque of (CSL, 1929)

See Masques, Two

Philology, JRRT and

According to Professor Shippey, in his book *The Road to Middle-earth*, JRRT's fiction results from the interraction between his imagination and his professional work as a philologist. CSL put something of his friend into the fictional character of the philologist, Elwin Ransom, in his science-fiction story, *Out of the Silent Planet**.

The name Elwin means 'Elf friend', and is a version of the name of the central character in JRRT's unfinished story, 'The Lost Road'*. In that story he is named Alboin. From when he was a child he invented, or rather discovered, strange and beautiful words, leading him to the theory that they are fragments from an ancient world. This slightly autobiographical story tells us much about the love which motivated JRRT's work in philology, and how it was intimately tied up with his invented mythology of Middle-earth. OB said of CSL that he was in love with the imagination. It could be said of JRRT that he was in love with language.

In many countries the academic discipline of philology, once strong, is now absorbed into the subject area of linguistics. It combined linguistic, literary and cultural study. *Everyman's Encyclopaedia* attempts a definition: 'Philology is used either (and particularly in Europe) to include both literary scholarship and the linguistic study of literary languages, both text-oriented; or purely to mean linguistics, particularly historical or diachronic linguistics (terms to which it is losing ground).' For a taste of JRRT's professional work, see his *The Monsters and the Critics and Other Essays**, where he remarks, 'Philology is the foundation of humane letters'.

At Oxford, JRRT taught mostly Old English, Middle English, and the history of the English language. This professional work was intimately related to his construction of the languages, peoples and history of the three Ages of Middle-earth*. He commented in a letter that he sought to create a mythology for England, but it might be argued that he also tried to create a mythology for the English language. The earliest expression of the mythology embodied in *The Silmarillion**, a poem written in 1914 about the voyage of Eärendil, was inspired by a line from Cynewulf's Old English poem *Christ*, 'Eala Earendel engla beorhtost' ('Behold Earendel brightest of angels').

In his essay, 'The Oxford English School' (1930), JRRT makes clear that he regarded both literary and linguistic approaches as too narrow to gain a full response to works of art. He felt that this was particularly true of early literary works, very distant from contemporary culture. Philology was a necessary dimension of both approaches. It could give a proper depth of response. Professor Shippey points out that JRRT saw works of literary art philologically, and his own fiction came out of a philological vision.

The philological instinct is demonstrated in the quest for an Indo-European language in the deep past. As the old philologists sought for Indo-European, many JRRT readers try to unravel a proto-elvish language, the ancestor of the two distinct branches of JRRT's invented elvish – Quenya and Sindarin. It is interesting that, while JRRT constructs a plausible family relationship between the two branches of elvish, the two languages that inspired them – Finnish and Welsh – are not related in this way, according to linguists.

It is also interesting, as Professor Shippey points out, that the philologist Jakob Grimm produced collections of fairy tales as well as learned scholarship, just as JRRT's imaginative work sprang out of his philological study.

FURTHER READING

Jim Allan, *An Introduction to Elvish*
Ruth S. Noel, *The Languages of Tolkien's Middle-earth*
T.A. Shippey, *The Road to Middle-earth*

Pictures (1979) collected, with notes, by Christopher Tolkien*

This large-format book contains 48 sections of paintings, drawings and designs by JRRT, mostly relating to *The Hobbit**, *The Lord of the Rings** and *The Silmarillion**. JRRT had great skills as an illustrator. His visualization of settings from his fiction are of particular interest. Those from *The Silmarillion* (such as the illustrations of Nargothrond) are especially valuable due to the unfinished nature of that work. JRRT failed to detail the stories of that period of Middle-earth* as vividly as in *The Lord of the Rings*. The illustrations emphasize the great care JRRT took in visualizing and creating his geography of Middle-earth. We glimpse Tol Sirion, with the shadow of Thangorodrim on the horizon. We see the beautiful city of Gondolin, encircled by mountains. There is a powerful depiction of Taniquetil, its peak in the stars.

From the Third Age of Middle-earth is included JRRT's crayon drawing of the Mallorn trees of Lórien in spring, capturing the numinous quality of the region. There are many other illustrations, including a picture of Hobbiton that was the frontispiece to the original edition of *The Hobbit* in 1937. One of JRRT's illustrations of Mirkwood is based on an earlier painting of Taur-nu-Fuin, illustrating Beleg's finding of Gwindor. The depiction of the elven-king's gate from *The Hobbit* is somewhat reminiscent of JRRT's portrayal of Nargothrond. One of JRRT's beautiful, stylized drawings of trees, reproduced in *Pictures*, is used on the cover of *Tree and Leaf*. A more naturalistic crayon drawing powerfully depicts Old Man Willow.

Pilgrim's Regress: An Allegorical Apology for Christianity, Reason and Romanticism, The (CSL, 1933; new edition, 1943)

Twenty years after writing this book, CSL admitted in a letter: 'I don't wonder that you got fogged in *The Pilgrim's Regress*. It was my first religious book and I didn't then know how to make things easy. I was not even trying to very much, because in those days I never dreamed I would become a "popular" author'.

The Pilgrim's Regress is an intellectual, early twentieth-century version of John Bunyan's great allegory. Instead of Christian, the central figure is John, loosely based on CSL himself. The geography of the story has the human soul divided into north and south, the north representing arid intellectualism and the south emotional excess. A straight road passes between them. John's route strays far off the straight and narrow. The allegory skilfully depicts the intellectual climate of the 1920s and early 1930s.

John is in search of a visionary island, and his quest is a fine embodiment of the theme of joy* which is so central in CSL's autobiography, *Surprised By Joy**. The quest helps John to avoid the various snares and dangers he encounters.

In CSL's new edition of *The Pilgrim's Regress* he provided a detailed foreword and notes to the chapters to help his readers with the obscurer points of the allegory. Read as a quest for joy, and in parallel with *Surprised By Joy*, it yields its main meanings. Clyde S. Kilby's study, *Images of Salvation in the Fiction of C.S. Lewis* (1978), provides help with interpretation of the allegory, including its frequent classical references.

Place of the Lion, The (CSL, 1931)

CW's third novel to be published was described by its publisher (Mundanus, an imprint of Gollancz) as 'a work of genius'. It prompted the start of the friendship between CSL and CW. Lent a copy by Nevill Coghill* in February 1936, CSL wrote a letter of congratulation to its author and received a reply by return. CW had been similarly impressed by CSL's *Allegory of Love**. A meeting soon followed and a deep and lifelong friendship began.

The novel is set in London where Anthony Durrant and his room mate Quentin Sabot, waiting for a bus on the Hertfordshire road, encounter a search party for an escaped lioness. Offering to help, they see the animal in the grounds of a large house where in an encounter with the occupant it appears to transform into a lion; the occupant, Mr Berringer, is unharmed but is left in a coma.

Damaris Tighe, with whom Durrant is in love, is an academic engaged in research on Abelard. Her intellectual pride makes her only intellectually interested in religion (and apparently not emotionally interested in Durrant at all). She agrees to give a lecture, on the subject of 'The Eidola and the Angeli' (The Images and the Angels) – a comparison between Platonic and medieval learning – deputizing for the incapacitated Berringer at his monthly study circle. She first dines with her father who mentions that he has seen an unusual number of butterflies that day, all elusive. (Their disagreement as to whether an appetite for mutton is incompatible with an apprehension of beauty is another significant set of clues to CW's purposes.) Later, at the meeting, her lecture is disrupted by a member of the group, Dora Wilmot, who hysterically declares that a crowned serpent has entered the room. Damaris is infuriated that someone seeing a vision has interrupted the exposition of her carefully argued thesis.

But perhaps the real characters of the novel are the Powers and Principles who emerge, called forth initially by Berringer, as the plot develops: dangerous and mighty, they come from a world of Ideas and arrive in the world of the known and familiar (see also IDEAS, PLATONIC). We have already encountered the Lion, the Butterfly and the Serpent. Their appearance is accompanied by strange aberrations of nature: for example, a 'horrible stench' that first appears in Berringer's house, which itself begins to seem to be losing life and energy, and burdensome hot weather; and it becomes apparent that the Principles are also present in their inversions. For example, the pterodactyl that terrorizes Damaris is the inversion of the eagle with whom Durrant is increasingly associated in the novel and which represents ideal intellect.

It is in Berringer's garden that Anthony and Damaris' father see a great butterfly and a host of other butterflies that appear to pass into the great butterfly, provoking a rapturous response in Tighe and a renewed desire in Anthony for Damaris' conversion.

In a chapter appropriately called 'The Two Camps' (again, CW is liberal with his clues: it is the title of the journal on which Durrant works), it becomes clear that the Platonic visitation serves to divide. Even in the early chapters it is clear that Damaris and Dora Wilmot are on the side of the eidola, Durrant and Sabot on the side of the angelicals. The divide becomes confrontation: Durrant and Sabot are visited by Mr Foster, a member of Berringer's group and a friend of Dora Wilmot, who explains in more detail Berringer's role in the appearance of the Principles. Berringer believed that the world was created by the great Principles who infused themselves in varying degrees into human beings, and that if the Principles were to be brought into the everyday world it may be that the everyday world would be subsumed into that other world. Faced with Foster's desire for, in effect, the annihilation of the world, and with Sabot's timidity and fear, Durrant determines to invoke Authority, govern the Principles rather than abandon himself to them, and take up, under God, the adamic destiny of humanity to be the governing crown of creation. (However, in recognizing this underlying scheme it is important that we do not make the mistake of tying off all CW's loose ends or resolving his many ambiguities.)

A fortnight after the lion's appearance Durrant and Sabot return to Berringer's garden. Durrant is determined to confront the lion, and he gets his wish. Sabot flees, but Durrant stands firm in an encounter that recalls the biblical story of Jacob wrestling with the angel (CW's use of the word 'wrestling' to describe the encounter may be a deliberate allusion.) In the middle of it all Durrant is aware of dinosaurs, and of a great pterodactyl, and of an undulating movement in the surface of the road.

Analysing later, Durrant formally acknowledges himself to be a son of Adam and accordingly takes up the task of governing the Principles. He decides first to investigate what happened in Berringer's circle when Damaris lectured, and goes to see Dr Rockbotham, the physician attending the still-unconscious Berringer, who promises to take him to see Berringer. He next visits Richardson, a young bookseller, and arranges to meet later at Richardson's home. He goes there via Wilmot's house, where Mr Foster is also present. During the visit Wilmot appears to transform into a serpent and attacks Durrant, who escapes and makes his way to Richardson's home. Richardson proves to be spiritual brother to Durrant and a fund of arcane knowledge: he explains the volume of angelical lore by one 'Marcellus Victorinus', by which Berringer had been influenced.

The Place of the Lion is full of images and visions, and like all CW's fiction, the flow of time is less important than the simultaneity of events. For this reason the book is not easily summarized in narrative terms. But all the characters are involved in processes of becoming. In Richardson's house, after a lengthy explanation of Berringer's position, Durrant has a vision of an eagle, the encompassing Principle of which the pterodactyl was a corrupt inversion; the eagle combines the power and terror of all the Principles. Richardson has warned him: 'These are Angels . . . the principles of the tiger and the volcano and the flaming suns of space.' 'You either rule or you don't', he adds with an allusion to 1 Corinthians 6:3.

Damaris' next meeting with Durrant happens after she has encountered on a walk the fugitive, demoralized Quentin Sabot. She upbraids Durrant for allowing his friend to be alone, but he turns the challenge back on to her, pleading with her to come to London. Something has happened, he says; Power is abroad in the world; her rational, academic mind cannot understand it. Damaris fails to recognize the crucial issues at stake in her life, though to her credit she refuses what she sees as a hypocritical flight to London for refuge.

Durrant and the doctor visit Berringer, who is still comatose. Durrant has another vision, this time of a huge pit in Berringer's house. He becomes aware of the world of Platonic ideas and forms made concrete, and again the narrative associates him with the Eagle. Indeed throughout the novel characters align with Principles: Foster desires the strength of the lion, though is without the meekness of the lamb; Wilmot desires the subtlety of the serpent but lacks the wisdom of the phoenix. (She dies, busily preparing poison-pen letters, as the form of the serpent breaks from her body and destroys her in the process.)

The association of Principles with characters, though complex in the narrative, resolves into a simple pattern; Berringer, Foster and Wilmot want to know the Powers in order to feed their own purposes; Durrant desires to engage with the Principles and govern them not from his own need for power but because it is the biblical role of humanity and because what motivates his relationship and actions is love – friendship for Sabot and romantic love for Damaris.

It is Damaris who mediates between the poles of this dichotomy of two camps. Her conversion from her self-centred world of academic rhetoric is the central dramatic theme of the book. It involves encountering the pterodactyl and it involves a vision of Abelard, on whom she is an 'expert' but whose appearance challenges her whole emphasis on intellectual matters. In a moving meeting with Durrant she experiences joy and laughter and, as Durrant tells her later, finally acknowledges all that she had denied before. What he does not point out is the role that his own obedience and commitment to the priestly/adamic task has played in her conversion, for he is probably quite unaware of it.

At the end of the book Berringer's house – and Berringer – are consumed by fire, and into that fire, by Durrant's obedient naming and ordering of the Principles, the Principles return to their proper sphere. Richardson, whose role in the book has been to be the one who rejects images and symbols in a desire to pursue them to their source, is also consumed in the fire which, all consuming done, dies out to leave only a fine ash.

Plato

The famous Greek philosopher, born about 427 BC in Athens, was much admired by the Inklings. He founded idealism in philosophy. His work provided much imaginative inspiration for CSL, though he was not a Platonist. Some forms of Platonism were deeply influential during the medieval period which was CSL's great love, and which was the object of much of his scholarship. Different aspects of Plato's thought have been emphasized at different periods of western history, such as his view of existence or his theory of how we know truth. Belief in the immortality of the soul, as held by CSL, JRRT, CW and the Christian tradition, is not in itself Platonism, nor is imaginative use of the Platonic idea of this world as a 'copy' of a more real one. In his essay, 'Transposition', CSL gives a Christian, but dualistic, account of the relationship between spiritual and natural reality. There is a long tradition of Christian Platonism, in which JRRT and CW can perhaps be placed more easily than CSL.

See also GOD; NATURE IN CSL AND JRRT; CHAPTER 6; IDEAS, PLATONIC

Plays, Collected (1963), ed. John Heath-Stubbs

Published by Oxford University Press, this was the first 'collected' edition of CW's plays, but omitted several early pieces. It included *Thomas Cranmer of Canterbury*; *Judgement at Chelmsford*; *Seed of Adam*; *The Death of Good Fortune*; *The House by the Stable*; *Grab and Grace: or, It's the Second Step*; *The House of the Octopus*; *Terror of Light*; and *The Three Temptations*. Of these, the last two were being published for the first time. Heath-Stubbs contributes a useful introduction.

Poems (CSL, 1964; new edition, 1994)

This volume contains most of CSL's lyrical verse. The new edition includes the early cycle of poems entitled *Spirits in Bondage**. The poems reveal a great variety of themes, including 'Narnian Suite', which is in two parts – 'a march for strings, kettledrums, and sixty-three dwarfs' and a 'march for drum, trumpet, and twenty-one giants'.

See also NARRATIVE POEMS

Poetic Diction (OB, 1928)

Along with this intoxicating freedom from the invisible presuppositions of one's age (*see* CHRONOLOGICAL SNOBBERY), CSL also inherited OB's highly original insights into the nature of poetic language. JRRT also incorporated them into his thinking. These insights were embodied in OB's book *Poetic Diction*.

OB had gone up to Oxford in October 1919, and after graduation began a B.Litt., the thesis of which became *Poetic Diction*. As undergraduates CSL and OB had often walked together or asked each other to lunch, but did not really see a lot of each other until after graduation, when the 'great war' started between them.

OB drew inspiration from anthroposophism* and Rudolf Steiner for his many writings, and his adherence to this view formed the basis for that 'great war' between CSL and himself. His influence on CSL and JRRT was mainly through *Poetic Diction*, though later ideas of OB sometimes appear in CSL's writings. This book concerns the nature of poetic language and a theory of an ancient semantic unity, which require no commitment to anthroposophical interpretations of Christianity. The 'great war' of ideas in fact helped to prepare CSL for accepting orthodox Christianity, rather than any anthroposophist ideas. Significant differences remained between CSL and OB, even though they held an enormous amount in common.

Poetic Diction offers a theory of knowledge as well as a theory of poetry. At its heart is a philosophy of language. OB's view is that 'the individual imagination is the medium of all knowledge from perception upward' (p. 22). The poetic impulse is linked to individual freedom: 'the act of the imagination is the individual mind exercising its sovereign unity' (p. 22). The alternative, argues OB, is to see knowledge as power, to 'mistake efficiency for meaning', leading to a relish for compulsion. He speaks of those who 'reduce the specifically human to a mechanical or animal regularity' as being likely to be 'increasingly irritated by the nature of the mother tongue and make it their point of attack'.

Characteristically he writes:

Language is the storehouse of imagination; it cannot continue to be itself without performing its function. But its function is to mediate transition from the unindividualized, dreaming spirit that carried the infancy of the world to the individualized human spirit, which has the future in its charge. If therefore they succeed in expunging from language all the substance of its past, in which it is naturally so rich, and finally converting it into the species of algebra that is best adapted to the uses of indoctrination and empirical science, a long and important step . . . will have been taken in the . . . liquidation of the human spirit. (p. 23)

This fighting talk anticipates much of CSL, as in his *The Abolition of Man* (1943). Indeed many of CSL's preoccupations, and those of the Inklings, are anticipated in OB's book. Some are undoubtedly the fruit of the many conversations and letters between the two men.

Knowledge as power is contrasted with knowledge by participation* (a key word in OB). One kind of knowledge 'consists of seeing what happens and getting used to it' and the other involves 'consciously participating in what is' (p. 24). The proper activity of the imagination is 'concrete thinking' – this is 'the perception of resemblance, the demand for unity' (the influence of Coleridge* can be seen here). There is therefore a poetic element in all meaningful language. CSL elaborates this same point about the poetic condition of meaning in thought in *Selected Literary Essays*, and in the chapter 'Horrid Red Things', in *Miracles** – a chapter which tries to capture the core of OB's ideas in *Poetic Diction*.

See also ORIGINAL PARTICIPATION

Poems of Conformity (CW, 1917)

These early poems of CW were criticized by Theodore Maynard* for their view of evil as having a purpose in serving good: Maynard called CW a satanist, a term he later withdrew. The poems were published at the time of his marriage. Alice Meynell says of them, 'Far from showing how difficult marriage is, how different from courting or being in love, he shows the pattern of his learning, the effort to conform with the life glimpsed in *The Silver Stair.*' The poems, as summarized by Meynell, range over 'sex . . . love . . . marriage . . . dread . . . other subjects include war, friendship, and the earliest printed poems on Sarras, city of the Grail'.

Post-modernism

Post-modernism is a transitional state in the modern world, following the gradual disintegration of modernism. Modernism was shaped and spawned by what is sometimes called the 'Enlightenment project', where human reason was accorded an impossible autonomy, and where there was a blind faith in human progress. A resurgence of religious fundamentalisms, and various spiritualities, including New Age, mark post-modernism. Paradoxically this is linked with a death of God ideology bequeathed by Nietzsche. The writings of JRRT and CSL have found a home in post-modernist culture, perhaps because of their antipathy to modernism, and also perhaps because fantasy is now more acceptable. The preoccupation of post-modernism with language in itself has an affinity with the linguistic concerns of JRRT, OB and CSL, though they emphasized that we see *through* metaphor and language, rather than look *at* it, when knowing. To change the terms to those of Michael Polanyi, we tacitly indwell language as a condition of objective, representational knowledge. Post-modernism had important forerunners in the nineteenth century, in the dissenting thinkers Schopenhauer, Kierkegaard (admired by CW), and Nietzsche.

JRRT and CSL would undoubtedly see post-modernism as much a part of the modern world as their enemy, modernism. This is because for them the important category for describing the modern world is post-Christianity. For CSL the great divide in western history comes with the end of Judeo-Christianity and the classical world as the underlying presupposition of civilization. For him the Old West* had a continuity between the old pagan (including the classical) and Christian virtues, a view shared by JRRT.

See DE DESCRIPTIONE TEMPORUM; THAT HIDEOUS STRENGTH

Prayer

See LETTERS TO MALCOLM

Preface to Paradise Lost, A (CSL, 1942)

Paradise Lost is John Milton's great epic poem, and CSL believed that most recent Milton scholarship had hindered rather than helped a proper reading of the poem. Following the lead given by his friend CW's short Preface to an edition of Milton's poetical works, CSL attempted 'mainly "to hinder hindrances" to the appreciation of Paradise Lost'. He defended the epic form of literature that Milton chose to use, arguing that it had a right to exist, as does ritual, splendour and joy* itself. CSL argued that he differed from the critics of Milton not over the nature of his poetry, but over the nature of humanity and even of joy itself.

See also LITERARY CRITIC, CSL AS A

Prince Caspian (CSL, 1951)

A year after their first adventure in Narnia*, the four Pevensie children are drawn back to help Caspian, the true heir to the throne, whose life is in danger from the tyrant, Miraz, who holds control over Narnia. He has suppressed the Old Narnians who remained loyal to the ancient memory of Aslan* and Narnia's long ago Golden Age, when the children had been kings and queens at Cair Paravel. This story reveals much about the history of Narnia, the rule of humans over the talking animals, and the Telmarines who had stumbled into Narnia long before from our world.

See also CHAPTER 3

Problem of Pain, The (CSL, 1940)

CSL's purpose in writing this book was to 'solve the intellectual problem raised by suffering', not the pastoral issues directly. He had never felt himself qualified 'for the far higher task of teaching fortitude and patience'. In this respect, he said that he had nothing to offer his readers 'except my conviction that when pain is to be borne, a little courage helps more than much knowledge, a little human sympathy more than much courage, and the least tincture of the love of God more than all'. For such a small book, CSL ranged far and wide, discussing God's control over all human events, including suffering, the goodness of God, human wickedness, the fall of humanity, human pain, hell, animal pain and heaven.

The Problem of Pain, like *Miracles**, is among the best of CSL's theological writings. It contains fine passages on heaven, joy*, hell, and the sense of the numinous which is present in so much of CSL's fiction. It argues from the starting point of God's relationship to the universe that he has made, and is uncompromising in its supernaturalism.

For all its strengths, Sir Richard Attenborough's film *Shadowlands* seriously misrepresents CSL's case in *The Problem of Pain* by portraying it as a pastoral as well as an intellectual answer to suffering (and therefore inadequate).

Queen Elizabeth I (CW, 1936)

A volume in Duckworth's 'Great Lives' series, CW's biography of Elizabeth I characteristically explores the theme of temporal power and spiritual authority, set in the wide canvas of sixteenth-century politics. Though ignored by writers of more substantial biographies, the book delivered much more than might be expected from a volume in a popular biography series. As in many of his other books CW places personalities and personal events against the background of large movements of thought; the affairs of the English monarchy are, from the outset, presented in the context of the metaphysics of medieval Europe; yet in the opening pages he offers a glimpse into the mind of Henry VIII that is unusually sensitive. In fact its poetically vivid psychological insights resemble in some respects the later work of Edith Sitwell, who also wrote a remarkable short history of Elizabeth.

Of this book Anne Ridler wrote: 'Much of the historical work is hack work, but at any moment the hack may be become a racehorse. It is always based on careful and wide reading. The sources may be secondary, but the opinions are always original, though the best work is produced, naturally, when the subject – such as witchcraft, or Elizabeth I – is one that has been of permanent interest to him' (Introduction to *The Image of the City and Other Essays*, ed. Ridler 1958). In its review, the Roman Catholic *The Tablet* wrote that CW did not correctly understand the Catholic doctrine of the sacrament.

See also BIOGRAPHIES OF CHARLES WILLIAMS

'Queen Victoria' (CW)

A short biography by CW in *More Short Biographies*, ed. R.C. and N. Goffin (1938). R.C. Goffin was a colleague of CW at the Oxford University Press.

Quest, the

The quest often takes the form of a journey in symbolic literature in fiction such as JRRT's and CSL's. Life and experience have the character of a journey, and this character can be intensified by art. The Christian possibilities of the quest have been explored by Thomas Malory (*Morte d'Arthur*), by John Bunyan (*The Pilgrim's Progress*), as well as by JRRT and CSL – to name a few writers.

The greatest quests in JRRT's fiction are Beren's for the Silmaril (but really for the hand of his beloved, Lúthien), and Frodo and Sam's for the destruction of the one Ring. In JRRT's profound little tale, *Leaf by Niggle**, there is both a quest (to complete the painting of the tree) and a journey – from Niggle's call by the Inspector to his arrival at the beginning of the mountains.

The tales of Middle-earth* abound with quest heroes: Beren, Lúthien, Tuor, Eärendil, Bilbo, Frodo, Sam, Aragorn, to instance a few. For JRRT, the ultimate model of the quest hero is Christ, with his mission to die, and then to turn the cosmic tables by rising again. The life of Christ displays features of the quest tale, such as his final journey to Jerusalem heroically to face the forces of evil and death in his sacrifice for human sin.

The main quest heroes of Middle-earth follow the traditional theme. Each has a specific task or tasks to undertake, some of them taking up much of his or her life. Some of them marry into the elvish race. Each of the quests is different. Beren seeks marriage with Lúthien, his motivation is romantic love*, and the quest for the Silmaril arises out of this. Eärendil seeks the blessed realm of Valinor in order to intercede for the threatened people of Beleriand. Aragorn seeks the return of kingship in the Númenorean tradition, to uphold civilization in a reunited Middle-earth.

As these quests are conducted, all aspects of Christ (love, resurrection, mediation, sacrifice, kingship, conquering of death, healing) are illuminated.

The fiction of Middle-earth essentially begins and ends with a quest. After the awakening of the elves at Cuivienen, they are called on a great journey to the uttermost west, Aman, by the Valar, their guardians. At the end of the Third Age, after the War of the Ring, the Ring-bearers Bilbo and Frodo, and many of the elves, pass from Grey Havens over the Great Sea by the straight road to seek the undying lands beyond the world.

The quest motif is also a hallmark of CSL's writings, both fiction and non-fiction. *The Magician's Nephew** records Digory's double quest for the magic apple and to save his dying mother; *The Voyage of the 'Dawn Treader'** also concerns a double quest, to find the lost lords and to discover Aslan's Country; *Perelandra** features a quest to save the humans of a new world; *The Pilgrim's Regress** documents John's quest for the island of his vision; in parallel, CSL's autobiography *Surprised By Joy** tells of his personal quest for an elusive joy; and *Till We Have Faces** is a tale of Psyche's quest for her lost lover, and Queen Orual's search for the truth about her sister's story of a palace in the mists and a god who loves her.

Reflections on the Psalms (CSL, 1958)

The psalms are an important literary part of the Bible, and CSL felt that he had something he could say about them as a layperson and literary critic. The psalms, he considered, are great poetry, and some, such as Psalms 18 and 19, are perfect poems. Unless the psalms are read as poetry 'we shall miss what is in them and think we see what is not'. The book is particularly good in bringing out how the Hebrews had an appetite and longing for God*, how they appreciated his law (which they saw as rooted in nature as the very structure of reality), and how they viewed nature. There are three key chapters that deal with the inspiration of Scripture and 'second meanings' within it.

Rehabilitations and Other Essays (CSL, 1939)

In his Preface, CSL tells us that all the pieces in this collection are written in defence of things that he loves which have been the object of attack. The first two essays defend great romantic poets such as Shelley and William Morris against 'popular hatred or neglect of Romanticism'. The third and fourth defend the present (i.e. 1939) Oxford English syllabus. The fifth supports the reading of many popular books which have, he believes, greatly increased his power of enjoying more serious literature as well as what is called 'real life'. The sixth essay champions Anglo-Saxon poetry.

See also LITERARY CRITIC, CSL AS A

Religion and Love in Dante (CW, 1941)

Published as the sixth of the 'Dacre Papers' by the Dacre Press, this short booklet by CW identifies marriage as the primary situation for following 'the Dantean way' – though Dante* spoke of it as independent of marriage so that many types of love could be encompassed. The marriage of CW and Florence was much stronger now than in the troubled years following their wedding.

CW explains that the definition of romantic love is not that it is a matter of thrills and excitement, but that it is a technical term; his purpose in the booklet is to examine theology applied to a particular state, that of romantic love. He considers Dante's vision of Beatrice, and points out that it was both a romantic experience and also a call to Dante himself to 'become the thing he has seen'; what, under God, was stirred in him when he saw Beatrice (*caritas*, 'the properties of Almighty Love'), is what he must become. And it is not a solitary exercise; though for some love will not be exercised with a marriage partner, it must always involve other people. He had seen this in his own life. In *Outlines of Romantic Theology** he celebrated romantic love in the context of marriage to his first love, Florence; by the time *Religion and Love in Dante* was published, he had loved and lost his second love, Phyllis Jones*. The later book is a return to his original love, just as in *Paradise* in *The Divine Comedy* Dante re-experiences the rapture of romantic love that he describes in *The New Life*, when Beatrice first smiled upon him.

Return of the King, The (JRRT, 1955)

The third volume of *The Lord of the Rings**, comprising Books Five and Six, and extensive appendices.

Book Five tells of the arrival of Pippin and Gandalf at Minas Tirith; the passing of the Grey Company (those led by Aragorn on the Paths of the Dead); the muster of Rohan; the siege of Gondor; the ride of the Rohirrim; the Battle of the Pelennor Fields (*see THE WAR OF THE RING*); the suicide of Denethor; the restoration of Eowyn and Faramir at the Houses of Healing; the last debate of the Western allies; and the opening of the Black Gate of Mordor, when all seems lost.

Book Six is parallel, for much of its narration, to Book Five. It tells of Sam searching for Frodo at the Tower of Cirith Ungol; their perilous journey into Mordor's land of shadow; their arrival at Mount Doom and the end of the quest* to destroy the Ring; the reunion at the Field of Cormallen; the crowning of Aragorn; the various partings; the hobbits' journey back to the Shire; the scouring of the Shire and the death of Saruman; and the passing of the Ring-bearers from Grey Havens.

The appendices provided a major source of information about the earlier Ages of Middle-earth* until the publication of *The Silmarillion** in 1977.

Return of the Shadow, The (JRRT, 1988)

This is Volume 6 of *The History of Middle-earth**. It is also Part One of *The History of the Lord of the Rings**. The book is made up of JRRT's early drafts of what was to become the first volume of *The Lord of the Rings**, *The Fellowship of the Ring**. Frodo Baggins is here called Bingo, and Strider (Aragorn) has the name of Trotter. The collection provides fascinating insights into JRRT's manner of composition.

Ridler, Anne (b. 1912)

A poet, she worked for Faber and Faber from 1935–40, then became a full-time mother and writer. *Poems* was published 1939, followed by a number of distinguished collections; her *Collected Poems* appeared in 1994. She met CW through his visits to Downe House School, where she was a pupil; a further link is that she was the niece of Humphrey Milford of Oxford University Press. A long correspondence and friendship with CW developed. She edited *Charles Williams: The Image of the City and Other Essays* (1958) for which she provided a critical introduction, and in 1961 compiled *Charles Williams: Selected Writings*.

Her poems have been described as locating spiritual and religious experience in the known and familiar world, a theme that has obvious links with CW and the way of the affirmation of images*.

Road Goes Ever On: A Song Cycle, The (JRRT, 1968, 1978)

Poems by JRRT on the theme of the road*, set to music by Donald Swann. The musical scores are included, along with notes on, and translations of, the elvish poems by JRRT. The first edition included 'The road goes ever on', 'Upon the hearth the fire is red', 'In the Willow-Meads of Tasarinan', 'In Western lands', 'Namarie (Farewell)', 'I sit beside the fire', and 'Errantry'. In the second edition, 'Bilbo's last song' was added. A recording of the poems, sung by William Elvin, and accompanied at the piano by the composer, is available. The recording, *Poems and Songs of Middle-earth*, also contains JRRT reading the poems.

Road, the

The road, which 'goes ever on', is a potent and central image in JRRT, particularly in *The Hobbit** and *The Lord of the Rings**. As in John Bunyan's *The Pilgrim's Progress*, there is the path to be taken by choice, leading to perils and adventures. As Frodo and Sam set off with the Ring, at first 'the road wound away before them like a piece of string'. This road, which leads across rivers, through the underworld, over the dreadful bridge in Khazad-dûm, and finally into Mordor itself through Shelob's lair, is charted in Barbara Strachey's *Journeys of Frodo*.

The road is also a significant motif in CSL's Bunyanesque *The Pilgrim's Regress**, highlighted by its *Mappa Mundi* that charts the road network open to John as he travels in quest* of his visionary island.

Rochester (CW, 1935)

CW was annoyed by the critical reception this book received: the *Listener* described the style as 'sprightly'. It is probably the best of the four biographies commissioned by Arthur Barker. It touches on aspects of love, romance and theology that anticipate his later, more substantial work.
See also BIOGRAPHIES OF CHARLES WILLIAMS

Romantic love

See LOVE; *HE CAME DOWN FROM HEAVEN*; *RELIGION AND LOVE IN DANTE*

Romantic theology

See AFFIRMATION, WAY OF

Roverandom (JRRT, 1998)

A story written and illustrated by JRRT and not published until 1998, over 70 years later. In 1925, while the family was on holiday at Filey in Yorkshire, four-year-old Michael Tolkien lost his toy dog on the beach. In sympathy, his father wrote *Roverandom*, about a real dog Rover, turned into a toy by a wizard. When dropped on the beach by a small boy, the toy is transported to the moon along the path of light the moon makes when it shines over the sea. The Man in the Moon renames him Roverandom and gives him wings. Roverandom and Moondog set out on a series of adventures, encountering the Great White Dragon and other moon fauna such as giant spiders and dragon-moths. Finally, back on earth, Roverandom travels under the sea inside Uim, oldest of the whales, to ask the wizard who changed him into a toy to undo the spell. Though JRRT told many stories to his children, few of his early ones survive. Roverandom became a particular favourite with them, leading JRRT to write it out and illustrate it. The book is introduced by Wayne Hammond and Christina Scull, authors of *J.R.R. Tolkien: Artist and Illustrator*.

Sacramental Way

See AFFIRMATION, WAY OF

Sauron Defeated (JRRT, 1992)

This is Volume 9 of *The History of Middle-earth**. It is also Part Four of *The History of the Lord of the Rings**. The book shows JRRT's developing conception of the final part of the story. It also includes 'The Notion Club Papers'* and 'The Drowning of Anadune'. Anadune is the Adûnaic form of Númenor.

Saving the Appearances (OB, 1957)

This key but difficult book by OB explores the relationship between science and religion. Rather than intending a traditional history of ideas about the momentous rise of modern science, OB is concerned with the evolution of human consciousness*. Changes in how we explore the natural world correspond to changes in consciousness. Today we are the inheritors of an alienation between ourselves and nature as a result of idolatry*. There is a disparity between human consciousness and the mind of the scientist. OB is concerned with human participation* in nature as a historical process. Our need is for a final participation, bringing ourselves to oneness with God and nature.

A sequel, *Worlds Apart* (1963), continues the exploration of its themes in the form of a many-sided dialogue between an OB-like narrator, a rocket research engineer, a theologian, a retired schoolmaster, and a physicist. The participants meet over a weekend with the intention of resolving the gaps between the intellectual disciplines today.

Sayer, George (b. 1914)

A pupil and friend of CSL's who in 1988 published a major biography of his one-time tutor, *Jack: C.S. Lewis and His Times*. CSL often stayed in his home in Malvern. George Sayer was head of the English department at Malvern College from 1949 to 1974. When Sayer first met his tutor he was told by JRRT, 'You'll never get to the bottom of him.' Sayer's biography particularly dwells on CSL's early life, his early poetry, his relationship with Mrs Janie Moore*, his life as a university lecturer, and his domestic life.

Sayers, Dorothy L. (1893–1957)

There is a useful (undated) letter extant to a Miss Falkin, in which Dorothy L. Sayers comments that she (DLS) was not part of any group or circle with CW (so she was not an Inkling); and that she, like CW, knew enough of the occult to be aware of its dangers. CSL, in a letter to *Encounter* (1963), states that he and CW were the only members of the Inklings who knew Sayers. She was, he said, 'the first person of importance' who had ever sent him a fan-letter. She was a friend of CSL and Joy Lewis, and her books were on the Lewises' bookshelves at the Kilns. Douglas Gresham, Joy's son, recalls that the news of Sayers' death was received with great emotion by his mother and step-father.

She admired CW greatly: 'C.S. Lewis is a writer of highly disciplined talent; Charles Williams was a really profound and original mind, with the authentic mark of genius'. His *The Figure of Beatrice** was responsible for her interest in Dante*, and she went on to begin a translation of *The Divine Comedy* for Penguin which was unfinished at her death. She freely acknowledged that it was CW's book that made her read Dante in the first place, and the long correspondence between them as she read contains some of her freshest criticism. CW had read *The Mocking of Christ*, and admired *The Nine Tailors* and *The Zeal of Thy House*; she admired, besides his writings on Dante, *He Came down from Heaven**. She writes a warmly appreciative account of the friendship and the shared interest in Dante in '. . . And Telling You a Story' in *Essays Presented to Charles Williams*. Their friendship was a warm one and full of fun and humour.
See also ALLINGHAM, MARGERY

Scientism

CSL, JRRT and OB were not anti-scientific, but did regard much modern scientific thinking as a form of idolatry*. CSL particularly identified a modern problem of naturalism in *Miracles**. Both CSL and OB argued that a healing in human consciousness is required, due to the alienation of post-Christian humanity from nature, including the moral virtues. CSL explores this theme in *The Abolition of Man** and *That Hideous Strength**. Both, too, explored the period of the rise of modern science, OB in *Saving the Appearances**, and CSL in *The Discarded Image** and *English Literature in the Sixteenth Century (Excluding Drama)**.

Screwtape Letters, The (CSL, 1942)

The Screwtape Letters consists of letters of advice and warning from a senior devil prominent in the lowerarchy of hell to his nephew, Wormwood, a trainee temptor. Wormwood, fresh from the Temptor's Training College, has been assigned a young man. Unfortunately for Wormwood, his client becomes a Christian. Screwtape passes on a number of useful suggestions for reclaiming the young man. *The Screwtape Letters* is one of CSL's most popular books. Although considered by CSL not to be among his best, it stands in a long line of books concerned with angels, demons, heaven and hell, such as *Dante's Divine Comedy*, Milton's *Paradise Lost*, and John Macgowan's* *Infernal Conference; or Dialogues of Devils*.

Screwtape Proposes a Toast (CSL, 1965)

A collection of literary and theological pieces, including several reprinted from *Transposition and Other Addresses** and *They Asked for a Paper**. It contains 'Screwtape Proposes a Toast', 'The Inner Ring', 'Is Theology Poetry?', 'Transposition', 'On Obstinacy in Belief', 'The Weight of Glory', 'Good Work and Good Works' and 'A Slip of the Tongue'.
See also THE SCREWTAPE LETTERS

Secondary world

See SUB-CREATION

Sehnsucht

See JOY IN CSL AND JRRT

Shadow Lands

In the Narnian Chronicle, *The Last Battle**, the name given to England by Aslan* to mark its contrast to the real, new England of his country.

Shadows of Ecstasy (CW, 1933)

The fifth and last of CW's novels to be published by Gollancz, this was the first written, probably completed by 1926. It shows several characteristics of an inexperienced novelist. There is an overworked parallel between its central character, Nigel Considine, and Christ; there is an abundance of authorial prompts to the reader, who is too often reminded how significant events are and the function that particular characters have in the narrative; and CW has not yet found a way of fictionalizing spiritual experience with which he is comfortable. Much more than in the later CW, characters are rigidly identified by their ideas, and key moments of crisis in the narrative are often in danger of being submerged in philosophy. CW's literary influences are very clear: the London riots recall G.K. Chesterton's* *The Napoleon of Notting Hill* (1904), and H.G. Wells and John Buchan* are two authors CW clearly admired (Buchan's *Prester John* is an apparent influence on this novel and on *War in Heaven**). Despite its flaws the novel has an easily followed plot and is well worth reading for CW's many insights and as part of the CW corpus.

The essential themes appear in the first chapters. Roger Ingram, Professor of Applied Literature, and his wife Isabel; the surgeon Sir Bernard Travers, and his son Philip, betrothed to Isabel's sister Rosamunde; the clergyman Ian Caithness; and the wealthy Nigel Considine – all, so to speak, set out their pitch. Ingram's passion is poetry; Travers is a benign sceptic through whose eyes most of the novel's action will be observed; Caithness has a simple faith in the efficacy of the ministrations of the church; Isabel represents married love; and so on. Considine has endowed a lectureship on 'Ritual Transmutations of Energy', which title is the subtext of the speech he makes in the opening pages: the sophisticated, cultured West may (he argues) have missed what African witch-doctors and the like have long known. By dissipating its energies it has lost the hope of defeating death.

Philip works for a large Africa-based engineering company headed by the mysterious Jewish tycoon Simon Rosenberg who commits suicide early in the novel, leaving his vast business empire, fortune and jewels to two grandsons who are devout Jews.

Africa is restless, and its unrest is directed towards the white population. A document issued by 'The High Executive' of Africa announces the imminent expulsion of the white population by a determined and well-armed African alliance. The age of 'intellect' is over. A new world order, of 'profounder experiments of passion . . . the conquest of death in the renewed ecstasy of vivid experience' is to be born.

Conflict deepens between Africa and the West. Racial prejudice and church congregations both grow. There is street violence: Isabel and Roger rescue an African from a white gang. He is Inkamasi, hereditary king of the Zulus. Rosamunde dislikes him immediately, but Sir Bernard and Roger decide he should stay with Sir Bernard. But Considine arrives and insists that the king, over whom he appears to have influence, should stay with him and that Sir Bernard, Roger, Philip and the king dine with him the next night.

At the meal Considine announces his imminent departure for Africa; the intention of the Rosenberg brothers (he is an executor of Simon Rosenberg's will) to liquidize their inherited wealth and rebuild the temple in Jerusalem;

and the fact that he himself is 200 years old. He has transmuted his artistic and spiritual energies – even his need for food, beyond basic subsistence – into 'the conquest of death in the renewed ecstasy of spiritual experience'. Inkamasi, who appears to be deeply under Considine's influence, falls into a coma from which neither shaking nor prayer will rouse him, nor even the sound of gunfire in the distance: London is under attack.

Caithness proposes a Mass be said over Inkamasi at Lambeth; the invocation of the Trinity rouses the king, who in subsequent conversations explains much about Considine. The king's father was a Christian, he himself was baptized, but in infancy was brought under the sway of Considine – who must not be underestimated: 'It is he who holds power over the royalties of Africa.'

Caithness and Sir Bernard are opposed to Considine, and warn the government about him; Roger and Isabel are swayed by his understanding of the ecstatic power of poetry and the potential of the power he commands. Inkamasi hates Considine but longs for Africa to be free. Philip and Rosamunde's romantic relationship deteriorates. In the city, some stability returns, though nobody knows where Considine is.

He turns up at Roger and Isabel's home and invites Roger to come with him to Africa. Roger is very tempted; Isabel consents because she sees how important it is to Roger, but she confronts Considine, arguing that the Christian faith is greater than he, and that the martyred missionaries were in possession of a greater truth than his. Considine responds in messianic language, specifically comparing himself to Christ. As he is about to leave the police arrive to arrest him but he 'passes through the midst of them', leaving much confusion behind.

After a bitter argument with Rosamunde, Philip finds himself near the home of the Rosenberg brothers where he witnesses a mob venting racial hatred and demanding to be given the jewels that are thought to be in the house. One of the brothers is killed and the mob disperses. At Sir Bernard's Kensington home he, Caithness, Isabel and Roger are playing bridge; the king is in his room. As the evening progresses air raids come closer to London, and a government spokesman on the radio announces an increasingly grave situation: enemy forces have landed in London. He is interrupted by the voice of Considine, speaking for the High Executive and warning that the relative leniency so far displayed will not last for ever.

Philip and Ezekiel Rosenberg arrive, followed immediately by Considine who asks who will go with him. Roger says he will; the king attacks Considine but is wounded by a shot from his companion, Mottreux; Considine tells Rosenberg that he has possession of the latter's jewels and remaining in London is futile. Eventually Sir Bernard and Isabel watch the others, willingly or unwillingly, driven away.

The battle against the invaders is fierce but the aftermath reveals relatively little damage. Considine takes his party to a house by the sea, which for Roger represents almost the apotheosis of art and beauty – that incomparable beauty, Considine has promised, that will be made anew once lesser passions for beauty have been transmuted into ecstasy. In this house Roger witnesses the almost successful raising from the dead of one of Considine's associates; the tension grows between Inkamasi's Christian faith and his desire for Considine to free his people; Caithness suspects that Considine intends to keep Rosenberg's jewels; and Mottreux, one of Considine's underlings, becomes obsessed with them; Considine's refusal to consider keeping them provokes Mottreux's defection from his cause; he asks Caithness whether there is a way back.

The novel ends in a welter of violence. Considine, to Mottreux's horror, returns the jewels to Rosenberg; he also announces a 'sacrifice of death'; Inkamasi shall enter into death by Considine's hand and so 'annul it'. Caithness is outraged; Inkamasi resigned. He is poisoned in a scene reminiscent of the Last Supper, and immediately Mottreux shoots Considine, wrests the jewels from Rosenberg, then shoots him too. The body of Considine is carried off by his surviving followers as they escape in a scene of great confusion.

For Roger, these events prompt a revocation of Considine and all his beliefs; 'Let's leave it all.' He will not even collect his coat from the house as he returns to his home and to Isabel – though the prosaic Caithness insists on doing so. With the death of the leader and his inner circle, the attack of the High Executive fails. The estranged characters are reunited. The West launches determinedly into planning a democratic future for Africa. Roger returns to his literary pursuits, but cannot avoid wondering if Considine had succeeded in cheating death, finally achieving that ecstasy of which he spoke; was now waiting, after a sea-change, to return and complete his visionary plans. Perhaps at the moment when his enemies gloated over his fall, Considine might yet 'thrust himself from the place of shades back into immortal and transmuted life'.

Shakespeare, A Myth of (CW, 1929)
See MYTH OF SHAKESPEARE, A (1929)

Shaping of Middle-earth, The (JRRT, 1986)
This is the fourth volume of the series, *The History of Middle-earth**, edited by Christopher Tolkien* from his father's unfinished material. The book is subtitled, *The Quenta, The Ambarkanta and The Annals*. Christopher Tolkien provides an exhaustive commentary on the development of his father's invention.

'The Quenta' is sometimes given the fuller name, 'The Quenta Silmarillion', another name for 'The Silmarillion' (meaning 'The History of the Silmarils'). The book includes the original 'Silmarillion', written by JRRT in 1926, and also the 'Quenta Noldorinwa' of 1930 (the largest section of the book). The latter was the only form of the mythology of the First Age that JRRT ever completed. To it is appended a fragment translated into Old English, sup-posedly by Aelfwine.

'The Ambarkanta' (or 'The Shape of the World'), is the only account found of the nature of JRRT's imagined universe. Though a short work, it throws valuable light on his cosmology, and the effect of the change of the world at the time of the destruction of Númenor.

'The Annals' are in effect annotated chronologies, reflecting JRRT's preoccupation with chronology. This book gives the earliest 'Annals of Valinor' (there were three versions in all), and also the earliest version of the 'Annals of Beleriand' (other versions followed).

The Shaping of Middle-earth shows the development of JRRT's mythology up to sometime in the 1930s. He continued to work on and modify 'The Silmarillion' up to his death in 1973.
See also SILMARILLION, THE

Silmarillion, The (JRRT, 1977)

This was posthumously published, edited by JRRT's son, Christopher*, who is the person closest to his thinking. *The Silmarillion* is based on JRRT's unfinished work, and is not intended to suggest a finished work, though Christopher Tolkien's editorial work is highly skilled, and generally faithful to his father's intentions. The unfinished nature of the book is most apparent in several independent tales that are contained therein, such as 'Beren and Lúthien the elf-maiden'*, 'Túrin Turambar'* and 'Tuor and the Fall of Gondolin'*. These are in fact summaries of tales intended to be on a larger, more detailed, scale, and never completed. The condensed, summary nature of much of the published *The Silmarillion* presents difficulties for many readers, compounded by the plethora of unfamiliar names. When J.E.A. Tyler updated his J.R.R. Tolkien *Companion* to include *The Silmarillion* he had to add about 1,800 new entries!

'The Silmarillion' evolved through all the years of JRRT's adulthood, and strictly is only a part of the published *The Silmarillion*. It chronicles the ancient days of the First Age of Middle-earth. It begins with the creation of the Two Lamps and concludes with the great battle in which Morgoth is overthrown. The unifying thread of the annals and tales of 'The Silmarillion' is, as its title suggests, the fate of the Silmarils.

The published *The Silmarillion* is divided into several sections. The first is the *Ainulindalë* – the account of the creation of the world. This is one of

JRRT's finest pieces of writing, perfectly taking philosophical and theological matter into artistic form. The second section is the *Valaquenta* – the history of the Valar. Then follows the main and largest section, the *Quenta Silmarillion* – 'The Silmarillion' proper (the 'history of the Silmarils'). The next section is the *Akallabeth*, the account of the downfall of Númenor (*see* 'THE NOTION CLUB PAPERS'). The final section concerns the history of the Rings of Power and the Third Age. JRRT intended all these sections to appear in one book, giving a comprehensive history of Middle-earth*. He comments at length on the development of the history of Middle-earth through the Three Ages in the important and lengthy letter 131.

The mythology, history and tales of Middle-earth are, in fact, found in unfinished drafts dating over half a century, with considerable developments and changes in narrative structure. Not least, some of the great tales have poetic and prose versions. The published *The Silmarillion* provides a reasonably stable point of reference by which to read the unfinished publications (collected by Christopher Tolkien in *Unfinished Tales* and *The History of Middle-earth**). Further stability is provided by JRRT's own often lengthy commentaries on *The Silmarillion* in his letters.

FURTHER READING

Clyde S. Kilby, *Tolkien and The Silmarillion* (1976)
Paul H. Kocher, *A Reader's Guide to The Silmarillion* (1980)
Karen Wynn Fonstad, *The Atlas of Middle-earth* (1981)

Silver Chair, The (CSL, 1953)

This Narnia* story is a sequel to *The Voyage of the 'Dawn Treader'**. It concerns Eustace Scrubb and another pupil of Experiment House, a 'modern school', a girl named Jill Pole. They are brought to Narnia by Aslan* to search for the long-lost Prince Rilian, son of Caspian the Tenth, the Caspian of the previous adventure, now in his old age. Their search takes them into the wild lands north of Narnia, and eventually into a realm under the earth called Underland. The two children are accompanied by one of CSL's most memorable creations, Puddleglum the Marshwiggle. They encounter and destroy the Green Witch, murderer of Rilian's mother. Before that, they narrowly escape being eaten by the giants of the city of Harfang, for whom humans are a delicacy, and even marshwiggle is in their cookery book.

Silver Stair, The (CW, 1912)

An 84-sonnet sequence describing first love from the point of view of a young man. There is a substantial discussion in K.L. Henderson, 'It is love that I am seeking', in Brian Horne (ed.), *A Celebration of Charles Williams* (the title is a quotation from W.B. Yeats that CW placed at the beginning of the book). Though not autobiographical, it is significant in respect to CW's later work: love is a dangerous mystery, a profound spiritual journey whose discoveries are as much for the lover as the beloved. And love for CW is not simply the exercise of romantic love*, but is also a participation in the workings of Love itself.

The sequence is divided into three 'books'. CW summarized them thus:

> The 'story', to call it so, is of a young man thoroughly discontented with the world who suddenly and for the first time falls in love – that is the first book. The second is concerned with the development of that experience; and the particular point about it is that he is discontented with the ordinary result of love. He feels it in a way that urges him *away* from marriage as much as towards it; because he feels *love*. Love as a being not a name. He sets aside the ordinary things and enters (he and his lady) on the path of virginal love. And the third book is a kind of ode in praise of Love as God and Man.

Of this sequence and of *Poems of Conformity*, CW wrote to Alice Meynell, 'I cannot recollect any verse in English that does just exactly what they do.'

Silver Trumpet, The (OB, 1925)

OB's only children's book, published by Faber and Gwyer in 1925. It tells the story of twin princesses, Violetta and Gambetta, who have a spell cast over them which makes them love each other even though they constantly disagree about almost everything. A visiting Prince, who has a Silver Trumpet, seeks the hand of a princess, and falls in love with the sweet-tempered Violetta. A servant of the king, a dwarf called the Little Fat Podger, has an emphatic presence in the story. The sound of the trumpet affects all that hear it – Princess Violetta dreams that she is afloat near the bottom of the sea. In an interview for the Wade Center OB described *Silver Trumpet* as 'symbol of the feeling element in life'.

Sir Gawain and the Green Knight (1925)
edited by JRRT and E.V. Gordon

This presentation of the text of the finest of all the English medieval romances helped to stimulate study of this work, much loved by JRRT. It contains a major glossary. His own translation of it was published in 1975. A new edition of JRRT's and Gordon's book came out in 1967, edited by Norman Davis.

Sir Gawain and the Green Knight, Pearl and Sir Orfeo (1975)

These are JRRT's own translations of three major medieval English poems. His verse translations skilfully represent the poetic structures of the original poems. The Sir Gawain and Pearl* poems are by the same author from the West Midlands, an area of England with which JRRT identified, basing the Shire upon it.

Sisam, Kenneth

JRRT's tutor in the English school at Exeter College, Oxford*, when he was an undergraduate. Sisam was a young New Zealander who greatly inspired JRRT in the area of medieval literature. Later the two men collaborated on a book of extracts from Middle English, JRRT painstakingly supplying the glossary. Sisam eventually joined the Clarendon Press (Oxford University Press).

Smith of Wootton Major (JRRT, 1967)

This short story was JRRT's last, and complements his essay, 'On Fairy Stories'* in tracing the relationship between the world of Faery and the Primary World. The story seems deceptively simple at first and, although children can enjoy it, it is not a children's story. JRRT described it as 'an old man's book, already weighted with the presage of "bereavement".'It was as if, like Smith in the story with his elven star, JRRT expected his imagination to come to an end. In a review, JRRT's friend and visitor to the Inklings, Roger Lancelyn Green, wrote of the book: 'To seek for the meaning is to cut open the ball in search of its bounce.'

Like Farmer Giles of Ham*, the story has an undefined medieval setting. The villages of Wootton Major and Minor could have come out of the Shire. As in Middle-earth*, it is possible to walk in and out of the world of Faery (the realm of elves). The story contains an elven-king in disguise, Alf, apprentice to the bungling cake-maker Nokes. Nokes has no concept of the reality of Faery, but his sugary cake for the village children, with its crude Fairy Queen doll, can stir the imagination* of the humble. A magic elven star in the cake is swallowed by Smith, giving him access to Faery. In the village it is the children who can be susceptible to the 'other', the numinous, where their elders are only concerned with eating and drinking.

As in Leaf by Niggle* glimpses of other worlds transform art and craft in human life. The humble work of the village smith is transformed into the sacramental.

The writing of the story was inspired by a growing dislike of some of the fantasy of George MacDonald*, particularly his short story, The Golden Key. That story however is one of MacDonald's great achievements, as Smith of Wootton Major is one of JRRT's, in its deceptive simplicity.

Socratic Club

See OXFORD UNIVERSITY SOCRATIC CLUB

Spenser's Images of Life (CSL, 1967)

CSL's longest piece of literary criticism, as opposed to literary history. It is based upon CSL's Cambridge lectures on Edmund Spenser's great poem, *The Faerie Queene*. CSL's holograph notes were expanded and edited into this book by Alastair Fowler of Brasenose College, Oxford. CSL approaches *The Faerie Queene* as a splendid and majestic pageant of the universe and nature, which celebrates God*, in CSL's own phrase, as 'the glad creator'.
See also LITERARY CRITIC, CSL AS A

Spirits in Bondage: A Cycle of Lyrics (CSL, 1919)

Written while CSL was an atheist, and when he had a strong ambition to be a poet, this collection of poetry was published under the pseudonym of Clive Hamilton (Hamilton was his mother's maiden name). According to CSL, the poems are 'mainly strung around the idea . . . that nature is wholly diabolical and malevolent and that God, if he exists, is outside of and in opposition to the cosmic arrangements'.
See also NARRATIVE POEMS

Steiner, Rudolf (1861–1925)

See ANTHROPOSOPHY

Stevens, Courtnay E. ('Tom', 1905–76)

A member of the Inklings, and Fellow and tutor in Ancient History at Magdalen College, Oxford*, from 1934. He acquired the nickname 'Tom Brown Stevens' while a schoolboy at Winchester.

Studies in Words (CSL, 1960; 1967)

CSL warns in his Preface that the book is not an essay in linguistics; his purpose is merely lexical and historical. His approach, however, differs greatly from that of a dictionary, with a number of advantages. His studies provide an aid to more accurate reading, and the words studied are selected for the light they shed on ideas and sentiments. There is value in considering the relationship between words in a family of meaning, rather than considering words and their roots individually. The history of ideas, CSL believes, is intimately recorded in the shifts of meaning in words (an insight he owed to OB). CSL confesses that he early cultivated the habit of following up the slightest 'semantic discomfort' he felt with a word, a habit now second nature.
See also LITERARY CRITIC, CSL AS A; *HISTORY IN ENGLISH WORDS*

Sub-creation

JRRT believed that the art of true fantasy or fairy story writing is sub-creation: creating another or secondary world with such skill that it has an 'inner consistency of reality'. A fairy story is not a narrative that simply concerns fairy beings. They are in some sense otherworldly, having a geography and history surrounding them.

JRRT's key idea is that Faery, the realm or state where fairies have their being, contains a whole cosmos. It contains the moon, the sun, the sky, trees and mountains, rivers, water and stones, as well as dragons, trolls, elves, dwarves, goblins, talking animals, and even a moral person when he or she is enchanted. Faery is sub-creation rather than either mimetic representation or allegorical interpretation of the 'beauties and terrors of the world'. Just as the reason wishes for a unified theory to cover all phenomena in the universe, the imagination* also constantly seeks a unity of meaning appropriate to itself.

JRRT's concept of sub-creation is the most distinctive feature of his view of art. Though he saw it in terms of inventive fantasy, the applicability might well prove to be wider. Secondary Worlds can take many forms. The philosopher Nicholas Wolterstorff sees 'world-projection' as one of the universal and most important features of art, particularly fiction. It has large-scale metaphorical power. Nicholas Wolterstorff claims: 'by way of fictionally projecting his distinct world the fictioneer may make a claim, true or false as the case may be, about our actual world.' Its metaphorical quality deepens or indeed modifies our perception of the meaning of reality.

See 'ON FAIRY STORIES'; CHAPTER 4; CHAPTER 6

Substitution

See CO-INHERENCE

Surprised By Joy: The Shape of My Early Life (CSL, 1955)

This records CSL's autobiography up to his conversion to Christianity at the age of 31. 'Joy'* is a technical term used by CSL to help to define a distinct tone of feeling which he discovered in early childhood, and which stayed with him on and off throughout his adolescence and early manhood. This inconsolable longing that pointed to joy contradicted the atheism and materialism that his intellect embraced. In first theism and then Christianity both his intellect and his imagination* were fulfilled.

See also LEWIS, CLIVE STAPLES

Tarot pack, the

In The Greater Trumps*, the one perfect Tarot pack and its matching table of golden figures are in correspondence with, and control, the universe.

The Tarot, or Taroc, cards first appeared in fourteenth-century Italy; the name comes from *tarocchi* (derivation unknown). Used in fortune-telling and divination, they are spoken of in medieval, gypsy, Jewish (Kabbalah tradition), Spanish and Egyptian arcane literature. The pack has 78 cards. There are four suits of 14 cards: swords, cups (or chalices), staves (or sceptres, or wands) and coins (or pentacle, or deniers); each suit includes a page, a knight, a queen and a king. The remaining 22 cards are the Greater Trumps* (or Major Arcana): they are numbered from 1 to 21: the Juggler, Emperor, Empress, Hierophant (= High Priest), High Priestess, Chariot, Hermit, Temperance, Fortitude, Justice, Lovers, Wheel of Fortune, Falling Tower, Hanged Man, Sun, Moon, Star, Death, Devil, Last Judgement and the Universe. The last card, the Fool, is numbered zero.

The Tarot pack has intrigued a number of writers, for example T.S. Eliot who used the symbolism in *The Waste Land* (1922). Its use of what Jung called 'synchronicity' (underlying cause joining apparently disconnected events) links it with the *I Ching* (discussed passim in C.G. Jung et al., *Man and His Symbols*, 1964). Aleister Crowley* was an authority on the Tarot pack and the deviser of the Thoth Tarot Deck. Crowley was a fellow initiate of the Order of the Golden Dawn*, which CW later repudiated, though he would have known of the Tarot long before joining the Order; his later fiction (e.g. *All Hallows' Eve**) repudiates the Order and, in the character of Simon Magus, Crowley himself.

That Hideous Strength (CSL, 1945; abridged paperback version 1955)

The final volume of CSL'S science-fiction trilogy, begun in *Out of the Silent Planet**, and *Perelandra** (*Voyage to Venus*). It continues CSL's presentation of the problem of good and evil*. In this 'modern fairy tale for grown-ups', Merlin's ancient magic, linked into the power of the eldila of Deep Heaven, overcomes the threat to humanity of the National Institute for Coordinated Experiments (NICE). This book, as a sequel to the previous stories, set on other planets, brings matters 'down to earth'. It is set on Thulcandra, the silent planet Earth, so called because it is cut off by evil from the beatific language and worlds of Deep Heaven. Borrowing the style of CW's fiction, the supernatural world impinges upon the everyday world of ordinary people. More notably, CSL makes use of the mythical geography of Logres, the Arthurian matter that is the focus of CW's unfinished cycle of poems (*see* ARTHURIAN MYTH).

They Asked for a Paper (CSL, 1962)

A collection of literary and theological pieces, including several reprinted from *Transposition and Other Addresses**. It contains 'De Descriptione Temporum'*, 'The Literary Impact of the Authorized Version', 'Hamlet: The

Prince or the Poem?', 'Kipling's World', 'Sir Walter Scott', 'Lilies that Fester', 'Psycho-analysis and Literary Criticism', 'The Inner Ring', 'Is Theology Poetry?', 'Transposition', 'On Obstinacy in Belief' and 'The Weight of Glory'.

They Stand Together (CSL, 1979)

Letters to one man, Arthur Greeves, a close friend of CSL's over a period of almost 50 years; that is, from his atheistic mid-teens to literally days before CSL died. These letters give rich insight to CSL's life and to the development of his Christian thought and imagination*.

The selection makes up a more complete autobiography than *Surprised By Joy**, where CSL tells his life from a particular point of view – his awareness of joy*, the longing that no earthly philosophy or bodily pleasure could satisfy, and how only Christian theism made sense of it. Also that story finishes at CSL's conversion at the age of 31. This collection, edited by Walter Hooper, contains 296 letters.

We also learn much about the Ulsterman Arthur Greeves from these letters, though CSL kept little of Arthur's side of the correspondence. The foundation of their friendship was a common insight into the joy, with its longing, that was the main constant theme of CSL's life and writings.
See also LETTERS OF C.S. LEWIS

This Ever Diverse Pair (OB, 1950)

This humorous fiction draws upon OB's experience as a London solicitor. Mr Burgeon has a partner, Mr Burden – as an ever diverse pair they inhabit the daily routines of a lawyer's office. Among other routine cases, the office has to deal with an author, Ramsden, who has written books for years. A recent publication, however, has unexpectedly become successful, leading Ramsden unwittingly to fall foul of the Inland Revenue. Ramsden is based on CSL who, in real life, had to be rescued from the taxman by OB.

The subject of the book was described by CSL as 'the rift in every life between the human person and his public *persona*, between, say, the man and the bus conductor or the man and the king.'

Thomas Cranmer of Canterbury (CW, 1936)

See CANTERBURY FESTIVALS

Three Plays (CW, 1931)

This collection included *The Witch* and *The Chaste Wanton*, which Ann Ridler describes as 'better suited for reading than for acting – a kind of drama to which so many distinguished poets have contributed . . . as long as [CW] was writing in blank verse, after the manner of Lascelles Abercrombie (whose work he much admired at the time) he was liable to write in pseudo-Shakespearian metaphors.' John Heath-Stubbs also suggests an influence from the early W.B. Yeats. The third play *The Rite of the Passion* was commissioned for church performance; Heath-Stubbs considers it a 'dramatic quasi-liturgical action' rather than a conventional play. The figure of Satan has been seen as foreshadowing characters in CW's later plays.

All three plays were omitted from the 1963 *Collected Plays*.

Till We Have Faces (CSL, 1956)

In *Till We Have Faces*, CSL retells the ancient story of Cupid and Psyche from Apuleius' *The Golden Ass*. In Apuleius' story, Psyche is so beautiful that Venus becomes jealous of her. Cupid, sent by Venus to make Psyche fall in love with an ugly creature, himself falls in love with her. After bringing her to a palace he only visits her in the dark, and forbids her to see his face. Out of jealousy, Psyche's sisters told her that her lover was a monster who would devour her. She took a lamp one night and looked at Cupid's face, but a drop of oil awoke him. In anger, the god left her. Psyche sought her lover throughout the world. Venus set her various impossible tasks, all of which she accomplished except the last, when curiosity made her open a deadly casket from the underworld. At last, however, she was allowed to marry Cupid.

In *Till We Have Faces*, CSL essentially follows the classical myth, but retells it through the eyes of Orual, Psyche's half-sister, who seeks to defend her actions to the gods as being the result of deep love for Psyche, not jealousy. Psyche's outstanding beauty contrasts with Orual's ugliness (in later life she wore a veil). In Glome the goddess Ungit, a deformed version of Venus, is worshipped. After a drought and other disasters a lot falls on the innocent Psyche to be sacrificed on the Grey Mountains to the Shadowbrute or West-wind, the god of the mountain.

Sometime afterwards, Orual, accompanied by a faithful member of the king's guard, Bardia, seeks the bones of Psyche to bury her. Finding no trace of Psyche, Bardia and Orual explore further and find the beautiful and sheltered valley of the god. Here Psyche is living, wearing rags but full of health. She claims to be married to the god of the mountain, whose face she has never seen. Orual, afraid that the 'god' is a monster or outlaw, persuades Psyche, against her will, to shine a light on her husband's face, while sleeping.

As in the ancient myth, Psyche as a result is condemned to wander the earth, doing impossible tasks. Orual's account goes on to record the bitter years of her suffering and grief at the loss of Psyche, haunted by the fantasy that she can hear Psyche's weeping. Orual then records a devastating undeception she has undergone whereby, in painful self-knowledge, she discovers how her affection for Psyche had become poisoned by possessiveness.

In a letter, CSL explained that Psyche represents a Christ-likeness, though

T

she is not intended as a figure of Christ. Psyche in CSL's novel is able to see a glimpse of the true God himself, in all his beauty, and in his legitimate demand for a perfect sacrifice. A further key to this story lies in the theme of the conflict of imagination and reason, so important to CSL himself throughout his life, and vividly portrayed in *Surprised By Joy**. The final identification of the half-sisters Orual and Psyche in the story represents the harmony and satisfaction of reason and imagination, mind and soul, made fully possible, CSL believed, only within Christianity. The novel explores the depths of insight possible within the limitations of the pagan imagination, which foreshadows the marriage of myth* and fact in the Gospels.

See also FOUR LOVES, THE; CHAPTER 6

Timeless at Heart

See UNDECEPTIONS

Tolkien, Christopher (b. 1924)

The third son of JRRT. He was called Christopher in honour of Christopher Wiseman, one of Tolkien's schoolfriends. Tolkien was especially fond of Christopher, finding a great affinity with him (perhaps captured in the unfinished story, 'The Lost Road'*). During the war years, when Christopher was posted to South Africa with the RAF, JRRT sent him instalments of his work in progress, *The Lord of the Rings**. In a sense, he was the original audience for the work. In earlier years, he had listened intently as his father read to him from the material making up *The Silmarillion**. Christopher also prepared maps for the publication of that work. After his father's death he devoted himself to editing his unfinished work, such as the published *The Silmarillion** (1977), as was JRRT's wish.

Christopher Tolkien was a member of the Inklings. He studied at Trinity College, Oxford* and became a Fellow at New College. He eventually resigned his academic duties to devote himself to editing his father's work.

Tolkien, J.R.R. (1892–1973)

I was born in 1892 and lived for my early years in 'the Shire' in a premechanical age. Or more important, I am a Christian (which can be deduced from my stories), and in fact a Roman Catholic. The latter 'fact' perhaps cannot be deduced . . . I am in fact a Hobbit (in all but size). I like gardens, trees and unmechanized farmlands; I smoke a pipe and like good plain food . . . I like, and even dare to wear in these dull days, ornamental waistcoats. I am fond of mushrooms (out of a field); have a very simple sense of humour (which even my appreciative critics find tiresome); I go to bed late and get up late (when possible). I do not travel much (letter, 25 October 1958).

John Ronald Reuel Tolkien, whose name and distant origins are Germanic, was born in Bloemfontein, South Africa of English parents in 1892. He told his son Christopher that his earliest memory of Christmas was 'of a blazing hot day'. After his father's death his family moved to the West Midlands, living in countryside like the Shire near Birmingham, which he described as his 'home town'. As a child, reading Welsh placenames on coal trucks gave him a love for that language. He attended Birmingham's King Edward VI Grammar School, then located near the city centre, and was familiar with Worcestershire and the Vale of Evesham. It is suggested that the Malvern Hills helped to inspire the mountains of Gondor in Middle-earth.

His mother he remembered as 'a gifted lady of great beauty and wit, greatly stricken by God with grief and suffering, who died in youth [at 34] of a disease hastened by persecution of her faith.' Her non-conformist family were opposed to her move to Roman Catholicism. In her will, she requested that Father Francis Morgan become the guardian of JRRT and his younger brother Hilary. 'It is to my mother,' wrote JRRT, 'who taught me (until I obtained a scholarship . . .) that I owe my tastes for philology, especially of Germanic languages, and for romance.' In 1908, Father Morgan found better lodgings for the orphaned brothers, at Duchess Road, in Birmingham. Here JRRT fell in love with another lodger, Edith Bratt. She was attractive, small and slender, with grey eyes like Lúthien Tinuviel. Concerned that JRRT kept his mind on his education, Father Morgan eventually forbade JRRT to see her until he was 21. They were formally engaged when he was 22, after she had been received into the Roman Catholic Church. His Roman Catholicism was to be a source of tension in their marriage.

After graduating from Exeter College, Oxford, in 1915, and marrying Edith in the next year, he saw bitter action in the First World War, losing all but one of his best friends. With several of these friends he had formed an club, the TCBS. It was during the Great War years that JRRT began working on *The Silmarillion**, writing 'The Fall of Gondolin' in 1917 while convalescing. In fact, in general plot, and in several major episodes, most of the legendary cycle of *The Silmarillion* was already constructed before 1930 – before the writing and publication of *The Hobbit**, the forerunner of *The Lord of the Rings**. In the latter books there are numerous references to matters covered by *The Silmarillion*; ruins of once-great places, sites of battles long ago, strange and beautiful names from the deep past, and elvish swords made in Gondolin, before its fall, for the Goblin Wars.

In a letter written many years later, JRRT outlined to an interested publisher the relationship between his life and his imaginary world. He emphasized that the origin of his fiction was in language. He recalls:

I do not remember a time when I was not building it. Many children make up, or begin to make up, imaginary languages. I have been at it since I could write. But I have never stopped, and of course, as a professional philologist (especially interested in linguistic aesthetics), I have changed in taste, improved in theory, and probably in craft. Behind my stories is now a nexus of languages (mostly only structurally sketched) . . . Out of these languages are made nearly all the names that appear in my legends. This gives them a certain character (a cohesion, a consistency of linguistic style, and an illusion of historicity) to the nomenclature.

JRRT's lifelong study and teaching of languages was the spring and nourishment of his imaginative creations. Just as science-fiction writers generally make use of plausible technological inventions and possibilities, JRRT used his deep and expert knowledge of language in his fantasies. He created in his youth two forms of the elvish tongue, inspired by his discovery of Welsh and Finnish, starting a process which led to a history and geography to surround these languages, and peoples to speak them (and other tongues). He explains: 'I had to posit a basic and phonetic structure of Primitive Elvish, and then modify this by series of changes (such as actually do occur in known languages) so that the two end results would have a consistent structure and character, but be quite different.'

In a letter to W.H. Auden, JRRT confessed that he had always had a 'sensibility to linguistic pattern which affects me emotionally like colour or music.' Equally basic to language in JRRT's complicated make-up from a very early age was a passion for myth* and for fairy story, particularly, he says, for 'heroic legend on the brink of fairy-tale and history'.

JRRT reveals that he was an undergraduate before 'thought and experience' made it dawn on him that story and language were 'integrally related'. His imaginative and scientific interests were not on opposite poles. Myth and fairy story, he saw, must contain moral and religious truth, but implicitly, not explicitly or allegorically (see CHRISTIAN MEANINGS IN THE FICTION OF JRRT).

Both in his linguistic and in his imaginative interests he was seeking constantly 'material, things of a certain tone and air'. Myths, fairy stories and ancient words constantly inspired and sustained the unfolding creations of his mind and imagination – his elvish languages and the early seeds of *The Silmarillion*. The tone and quality that he ever sought he identified with North-Western Europe, particularly England. It could perhaps be called 'northernness'. He sought to embody this quality in his fiction and invented languages.

The stories he invented in his youth – such as the Fall of Gondolin –

came to him as something given, rather than as conscious creation. This sense of givenness and discovery remained with him throughout his life, a spring that never dried up, stopped only by death.

After the Great War, JRRT began university teaching in Leeds, following a period working on the new edition of the *Oxford English Dictionary*. After a few years he moved to Oxford to become Rawlinson and Bosworth Professor of Anglo-Saxon; this was in 1925. In the spring of the next year he met CSL. Their enduring friendship was soon to begin. CSL had not long taken up his post as an English don at Magdalen College for one year. They met at the English faculty meeting on 11 May 1926, and CSL was not amused, recording in his diary: 'He is a smooth, pale, fluent little chap. Can't read Spenser because of the forms – thinks language is the real thing in the English School – thinks all literature is written for the amusement of men between thirty and forty – we ought to vote ourselves out of existence if we are honest . . . No harm in him: only needs a smack or two.' Any initial antipathy, however, was soon forgotten. Within a year or so they were meeting in each other's rooms and talking far into the night.

These conversations proved crucial both for the two men's writings, and for CSL's conversion to Christianity. As the Ulsterman CSL remarked in *Surprised By Joy*: 'Friendship with . . . JRRT . . . marked the breakdown of two old prejudices. At my first coming into the world I had been (implicitly) warned never to trust a Papist, and at my first coming into the English Faculty (explicitly) never to trust a philologist. JRRT was both.' A typical note of the time occurs in a letter from CSL to his Ulster friend Arthur Greeves in December 1929: 'JRRT came back with me to college and sat discoursing of the gods and giants of Asgard for three hours.' JRRT himself recalled sharing with CSL his work on *The Silmarillion*, influencing his science-fiction trilogy. The pattern of their future lives, including the later Inklings, was being formed. JRRT remembered: 'In the early days of our association CSL used to come to my house and I read aloud to him The Silmarillion so far as it had then gone, including a very long poem: Beren and Lúthien.' CSL actually was given the unfinished poem to take home and read, and was delighted by it, offering JRRT suggestions for improvement.

The gist of one of the long conversations between CSL and JRRT was fortunately recorded by CSL in another letter to Arthur Greeves in October 1931. It was a crucial factor in CSL's conversion to Christianity. JRRT argued that human stories tend to fall into certain patterns, and can embody myth. In the Christian Gospels there are all the best elements of good stories, including fairy stories, with the astounding additional factor that everything is also true in the actual, primary world. It combines mythic and historical, factual truth, with no divorce between the two. CSL's conversion deepened the friendship, a friendship only later eclipsed by CSL's acquaintance with CW, and what JRRT called his 'strange marriage' to Joy Davidman Lewis*.

JRRT's academic writings were sparing and rare. In 1937 he published an article entitled, 'Beowulf: The Monsters and the Critics', which, according to Donald K. Fry, 'completely altered the course of Beowulf studies'. It was a defence of the artistic unity of that Old English tale.

In 1939 he gave his Andrew Lang lecture at St Andrews university, 'On Fairy Stories', which was later published in *Essays Presented to Charles Williams* – the Inklings' tribute to the writer who had a great deal in common with JRRT and CSL. It sets outs JRRT's basic ideas concerning imagination, fantasy, and sub-creation*.

The Professor's famous children's story, *The Hobbit*, came out in 1937. He continued with its adult sequel, *The Lord of the Rings*, more and more leaving aside his first love, *The Silmarillion*. It was a long, painstaking task, some of it written in instalments to one of his four children, Christopher, on war-time service with the RAF. At one point, he did not touch the manuscript for a whole year. He wrote it in the evenings, for he was fully engaged in his university work, and other matters. During the Second World War years, and afterwards, he read portions to the Inklings, or simply to CSL alone. He attended almost all the Inklings meetings.

In 1945 JRRT was honoured by a new chair at Oxford, Merton Professor of English Language and Literature, reflecting his by now wider interests. He was not now so cool towards the idea of teaching literature at university as he had been previously. JRRT retained the chair until his retirement in 1959. The scholarly storyteller's retirement years were spent revising the Ring trilogy, brushing up and publishing some shorter pieces of story and poetry, and intermittently working on various drafts of *The Silmarillion*. JRRT also spent much time dodging reporters and youthful Americans, as the 1960s marked the exploding popularity of his fantasies, when his readership went from thousands to millions.

An interviewer at the time of this new popularity, Daphne Castell, tried to capture his personal manner: 'He talks very quickly, striding up and down the converted garage which serves as his study, waving his pipe, making little jabs with it to mark important points; and now and then jamming it back in, and talking round it . . . He has the habits of speech of the true story-teller . . . Every sentence is important, and lively, and striking.' His voice is captured on several recordings of poems and extracts from his fiction.

FURTHER READING

Humphrey Carpenter, *The Inklings: C.S. Lewis, J.R.R. Tolkien, Charles Williams and their friends* (1978)

Humphrey Carpenter, *J.R.R. Tolkien: A Biography* (1977)

Daphne Castell, 'The Realms of J.R.R. Tolkien', *New Worlds SF.* Vol 50, No 168, (1966)
The Letters of J.R.R. Tolkien, edited by Humphrey Carpenter with the assistance of
  Christopher Tolkien (1981)

Transposition and Other Addresses (CSL, 1949)

A selection of addresses given by CSL during the war years and immediately
afterwards, including a famous sermon, one of the most outstanding of such
documents in the history of Christianity. The contents are 'Transposition',
'Learning in War-Time', 'Membership', 'The Inner Ring', and the sermon,
'The Weight of Glory'.

Treason of Isengard, The (JRRT, 1989)

This is Volume 7 of JRRT's *The History of Middle-earth**, and Part 2 of *The
History of the Lord of the Rings**. It helps to show the development of *The
Lord of the Rings** by publishing earlier drafts.

Tree and Leaf (JRRT, 1964; 1988)

This book by JRRT includes his famous essay, 'On Fairy Stories'*, explaining
his view of fantasy and sub-creation*, and an allegory* with autobiographical
elements, 'Leaf by Niggle'*. The new edition of 1988 adds a poem written to
CSL, 'Mythopoeia'*, incorporating ideas about the relationship between
myth* and fact which were influencial in CSL's conversion to Christianity
(*see* CHRISTIAN MEANINGS IN THE FICTION OF JRRT).

'Tuor and the Fall of Gondolin' (JRRT)

JRRT intended this to be a major tale in *The Silmarillion**, standing independently of the history of the ancient days and the First Age. It was never
completed on a grand scale. *The Silmarillion* contains a summary of the
story, while in *Unfinished Tales* there is the first part of a detailed treatment
showing, sadly, the promise of what was never acheived. 'The Fall of
Gondolin' is the first of the tales of the First Age to be composed – during
sick-leave from the Army in 1917. The most complete form of 'The Fall of
Gondolin' is to be found in *The Book of Lost Tales**, but, unfortunately, this
was written early in the development of *The Silmarillion*.

'Túrin Turambar, The Tale of' (JRRT)

The tragedy of Túrin is one of several stories from *The Silmarillion** (the
narrative of the First Age of Middle-earth*) that, according to JRRT, stand
independently of the history and mythology. The tale was conceived early,
when JRRT as a young man wished to make use of elements from the
Finnish *Kalavala*. There is a hint of the story of Oedipus in it, JRRT was
aware. The larger title of the tale is 'The Children of Hurin'.

Hurin, the father of Túrin, had been captured by Morgoth and bound upon the peak of Thangorodrim, where he could better see the outworkings of Morgoth's curse or doom upon his family. The curse bedevils the life of Túrin, and other relations, including Túrin's sister, Nienor, whom Túrin in ignorance eventually marries. Yet the sorrow in Túrin's life comes not only from external causes, though compounded by them, but also because of a 'fatal flaw' that is the stuff of tragedy. Túrin's flaw was a mixture of pride and rashness of action. In the tension between internal motive and external malice in Túrin's life, JRRT explores the problem of evil*. He says that, in the tale of Túrin 'are revealed most evil works of Morgoth', and that it was 'the worst of the works of Morgoth in the ancient world'.

There are several accounts of the tale of Túrin, the dragon-slayer. That in *The Silmarillion* is in fact a summary of a story worked out in great detail by JRRT. A longer, fuller and powerful version, sadly incomplete, appears in *Unfinished Tales** and an unfinished poetic version is recorded in *The Lays of Beleriand**.

FURTHER READING

J.R.R. Tolkien, *The Silmarillion*, chapter 21
Unfinished Tales, Part One, chapter II
The Book of Lost Tales, 2, chapter II
The Lays of Beleriand, chapter I
The Shaping of Middle-earth, 'The Quenta', sections 12–13.

Two Towers, The (JRRT, 1954)

The second volume of *The Lord of the Rings**, comprising Books Three and Four. It tells the adventures of the members of the Company of the Ring after the breakup of their fellowship, up to the beginning of a great darkness from Mordor and the start of the War of the Ring.

Book Three marks a division of the narrative, following the fortunes of the Company other than Frodo and Sam, who had set off for Mordor. The book tells of the confession and death of Boromir, the pursuit of the orcs who had taken Merry and Pippin, the meeting with Eomer and the Riders of Rohan, the escape of the hobbits from the orcs, the reappearance of Gandalf, Merry and Pippin's meeting with the Ent Treebeard, the meeting with King Theoden and Gandalf's removal of the deception upon him, the battle of Helm's Deep, the destruction of Isengard by the Ents, the reunion of Aragorn, Gimli, Legolas and Gandalf with Merry and Pippin, and finally Pippin's look into the Palantir.

Book Four is chronologically parallel to Book Three, telling how Frodo and Sam fared as they made their dangerous way to Mordor. It recounts how Gollum joins the two as their reluctant guide, their passage across the Dead

Marshes, their arrival at the Black Gate, their journey beyond through Ithilien and meeting with Faramir of Gondor, their parting from Faramir at the Cross Roads as they move towards Cirith Ungol, their arrival at Shelob's Lair and the treachery of Gollum, Shelob's attack on Frodo and his capture by orcs of Mordor, and Sam's pursuit into their headquarters, now bearing the Ring.

Undeceptions: Essays on Theology and Ethics (CSL, 1971)

Published in the United States under the title, *God in the Dock*. A large collection of CSL's pieces written over a period of many years. Subsequently, much of the contents of *Undeceptions* has been republished in two small UK paperback collections, *God in the Dock* (1979) and *Timeless at Heart* (1987).

Undeceptions includes a number of articles of interest, including CSL's account of the founding of the Oxford University Socratic Club*, 'Vivisection', 'Cross-Examination' (an interview for *Decision* magazine), and 'The Humanitarian Theory of Punishment'.

Underhill, Evelyn (1875–1941)

Converted to Christianity in 1907, Evelyn Underhill became an Anglican in 1921. She was an influential and extensive writer on religious subjects; her best-known work *Mysticism* (1911) reflects her main interest; *Worship* (1936) is also still read. She was a Christian pacifist. She was greatly influenced by Friedrich von Hugel*, and may have prompted CW's interest in his work. CW edited her *Letters* (1943) and provided a long introduction.

Unfinished Tales of Númenor and Middle-earth (JRRT, 1980)

A collection of JRRT's incomplete or unfinalized tales and narratives supplementing *The Silmarillion**, *The Hobbit** and *The Lord of the Rings**, edited by Christopher Tolkien*.

The book is divided into four parts, three of which are devoted to the First, Second and Third Ages of Middle-earth*, while the fourth concerns the strange Druedain, wizards and the Palantiri, or seeing Stones. There is a useful glossary index.

Part One begins with a beautiful, but sadly unfinished, tale of Tuor and his coming to Gondolin, most probably written in 1951. Had it been completed it would have been a major work, concerning as it does one of the four independent stories of the First Age. Then follows a long, but also unfinished, account of the life of Túrin Turambar*, another of the four major stories of

'The Silmarillion'. This too is marked by great beauty, complemented by the unfinished poetic version in *The Lays of Beleriand**.

Part Two, concerned with the Second Age of Middle-earth, opens with a description of the island of Númenor. This helps to give flesh to the often annalistic accounts of Númenorean history. Then follows a reconstructed story, the only one in existence about Númenor, entitled 'Aldarion and Erendis'. It is also called 'The Tale of the Mariner's Wife', and gives the first hints of the shadow which is to fall, not least in its tone of sadness. After this is a record of the Line of Elros in Númenor, then an account of the history of Galadriel and Celeborn, including a piece on the origin of the Elessar, the brooch eventually bequeathed to Aragorn by Arwen.

Part Three outlines several events from the Third Age: 'The Disaster of the Gladden Fields' and 'Cirion and Eorl and the Friendship of Gondor and Rohan' (both from the earlier history of Gondor and Rohan); 'The Quest of Erebor' (setting out more fully the links between *The Hobbit* and *The Lord of the Rings*); 'The Hunt for the Ring'; and 'The Battles of the Fords of Isen'.

Urbanity, An (CW, 1926)

See VIRGIL

Virgil (70–19BC)

Virgil was part of CW's literary consciousness for a number of reasons. First, of course, was his position as the great epic Latin poet, and his relationship to the medieval concept of romantic love* through *The Aeneid*. Second, he shares with Socrates the reputation of being 'a Christian before Christ' (a title based on his ethics); Virgil's 'messianic' fourth 'Eclogue', written in 40BC, looks forward to the birth of a child who will usher in an age of gold. The poem also appears to contain biblical echoes of, for example, Isaiah. For this reason some medieval writers accepted Virgil as an authentic prophet; Dante* chose him as a guide through hell and purgatory. Third, Virgil was a poetic influence on CW's *Taliessin*, illustrated by references in 'The Last Voyage' in *Taliessin through Logres* and notably, in the same book, 'Taliessin on the Death of Virgil', where Virgil is called 'friend, lover and lord' (*see* ARTHURIAN POEMS).

In lighter mood, in *An Urbanity* (1926), an eight-page set of light verses (printed by Henderson and Spalding, and privately circulated) about several Oxford University staff members then on their summer holidays, CW christened his absent colleagues with names mostly taken from Virgil's 'Eclogues'.

Virgil inspired OB's *Orpheus**, and CSL writes on Virgil's view of the epic

in his *A Preface to Paradise Lost**. CSL also lists Virgil's *The Aeneid* as one of the ten books which most shaped his vocation, attitude and philosophy of life (*Christian Century*, 6 June 1962).
See also AENEID, THE STORY OF THE

Virtuous pagan
See CHAPTER 6; *TILL WE HAVE FACES*

Von Hugel, Friedrich (1852–1925)
Baron von Hugel (he was a Baron of the Holy Roman Empire) was born and partly educated in Florence but made his home in England after 1873. A Roman Catholic and student of natural science, philosophy and history of religion, he became an associate of a wide circle of critical biblical scholars such as Duchesne and Loisy. He became a leader of the Catholic Modernist movement, was a friend of Evelyn Underhill* and George Tyrrell, founded the London Society for Study of Religion, and came to distance himself from many Modernists on the grounds that their work undermined the close communion with and adoration of God that was the hallmark of his own extensive (and often difficult) writings: his major work, on Catherine of Siena, was *The Mystical Element of Religion* (1908).

Von Hugel, in a letter of 7 April 1919, wrote to his niece: 'I wonder whether you realise a deep, great fact? That souls – all human souls – are deeply interconnected? That, I mean, we can not only pray for each other, but *suffer* for each other? That these long, trying wakings [sleepless nights of illness], that I was able to offer them to God and to Christ for my Gwen-child . . . ?' As von Hugel was known to the Inklings through CW and CSL, it is probable that he was an early influence on the idea of Exchange and Co-inherence*.

There is a good introduction to some of the Modernist ideas in Stephen Sykes, *The Identity of Christianity* (1984) passim, and von Hugel's warm humanity and robust piety are well captured in *Letters to a Niece* (ed. Gwendolen Greene, 1928). There is a sympathetic biography by Michael de la Bedoyere, *The Life of Baron von Hugel* (1951).

Voyage of the 'Dawn Treader', The (CSL, 1952)
CSL's sequel to *Prince Caspian**. This is the story of a double quest, for seven lords of Narnia who disappeared during the reign of the wicked King Miraz, and for Aslan's Country at the end of the world over the Eastern Ocean. Reepicheep the mouse is particularly seeking Aslan's Country, and his quest embodies CSL's characteristic theme of joy*. During the sea journey of the *Dawn Treader* various islands are encountered, each with its own kind of adventure. Of the original Pevensie children, only Edmund and Lucy return

to Narnia in this story. Their spoilt cousin, a 'modern boy' called Eustace Scrubb, is also drawn into Narnia. At one stage he turns into a dragon, and he is sorry for his behaviour. Only Aslan*, the great lion, is able to peel off his dragon skin and restore him. After sailing across the final Silver Sea, they reach Aslan's Country, the end of Reepicheep's quest.

Voyage to Venus (CSL, 1943)

See PERELANDRA

Wain, John (1925–94)

A famous pupil of CSL's, and member of the Inklings. His autobiographical *Sprightly Running* records his experiences of wartime Oxford*: 'Once a week, I trod the broad, shallow stairs up to C.S. Lewis' study in the "new building" at Magdalen. And there, with the deer-haunted grove on one side of us, and the tower and bridge on the other, we talked about English literature as armies grappled and bombs exploded.' In 1947 John Wain became lecturer in English at Reading University, staying there until 1955. His novel *Hurry on Down* (1953) was followed by further novels, as well as books of criticism and poetry. From 1973 to 1978 he was Professor of Poetry at Oxford.

War in Heaven (CW, 1930)

Originally completed in 1926 and titled *The Corpse*, this novel – the second to be written by CW – failed to find a publisher until CW was persuaded by a friend to submit it to Victor Gollancz, who read it enthusiastically and published it.

War in Heaven is, like CSL's *Out of the Silent Planet**, a superior contribution to a popular genre – in this case the murder thriller and detective novel. The novel opens with the discovery of a corpse in the small publishing house founded by the now-retired Gregory Persimmons, who has a deep interest in the arcane and occult; he is publishing a book *Historical Vestiges of Sacred Vessels in Literature* by Sir Giles Tumulty. The firm is now run by his long-suffering son Stephen. Several of CW's major concerns are quickly developed, such as the perpetual presence of the concept of Christendom, the absolutes of good and evil, and the definition of people's standing thereunto by reference to what they do with, and make of, objects invested with eternal significance.

Lionel Rackstraw, an editor at the firm, discovers the anonymous corpse in his office. That evening he tells his wife, Barbara; she, their small son Adrian, and the security of his home are a protective barrier of goodness against a universe that has become terrifying to him. Elsewhere, his colleague Lionel Mornington, an ironical, cool man who retains a strong common-sense practicality during the events that are to follow, is visiting his local vicarage where he meets the Archdeacon of the rural parish of Castra Parvorum. A third conversation is taking place in Ealing, London, between the Persimmonses in which Gregory reveals that he is the murderer. CW at this point begins to lose interest in the murder motif, but the conversation is illuminating for its demonstration of Gregory's (mentally) sadistic delight in hurting others, and his contempt for Christianity.

The Archdeacon, shown a copy of Tumulty's manuscript by Mornington, finds a passage marked for deletion that suggests that the Holy Grail* (or Graal, as CW spells it here), is a chalice located in the church at Castra Parvorum. The Archdeacon knows the chalice. The Graal – if such it be – is of little material value in his eyes, but of immense value as a symbol.

Gregory Persimmons, who is the Archdeacon's neighbour, tries to deceive him into selling him the chalice. The Archdeacon declines, but taking the chalice to safety after a break-in at the church, he is attacked and the chalice is stolen. He does not know that his assailant was Persimmons. Convalescing, the Archdeacon is visited by the local vicar, Mr Batesby, who CW represents as a mind set on translating heavenly things into earthly dimensions, and contrasts with the simple trust and dependence that the Archdeacon represents – an intellectual and theological humility.

Persimmons now obtains, with the help of Sir Giles Tumulty, a secret and powerful occult ointment 'rich and scarce and strange'. He enacts a strange midnight ritual by which he enters into a supernatural witches' sabbath and reaches towards 'That' which lies behind the sabbath and all occult lore. But he recognizes that for full and absolute union to be attained a sacrifice must be provided. His thoughts turn to young Adrian Rackstraw.

The Archdeacon, on a visit to Persimmons and Sir Giles Tumulty, recognizes his chalice. His suspicions of Persimmons are now confirmed, but he does not try to recover it. After his departure Persimmons shows Tumulty a room in the house set out for a ritual in which the stolen Graal is to play a key part. The ritual is a kind of inverted Mass, intended to bring Adrian into his power.

The Rackstraw family have come for a holiday as Persimmons' guests in a cottage in his grounds. At the same time Kenneth Mornington arrives, invited for a holiday by the Archdeacon. At the station he meets the Duke of the North Ridings, a Roman Catholic poet.

Kenneth and the Archdeacon discuss the Graal and Persimmons' activities. This is news to Kenneth, who mentions Persimmons' expertise in the occult. The Archdeacon fears that the Graal has been stolen for occult purposes. This motivates him to retrieve it at all costs. Persimmons, however, is subtly discrediting the archdeacon with the local police and establishing a false provenance for the Graal. He has also begun to befriend Adrian and to involve him in 'games' with the Graal. The police are unwilling to become involved. The Archdeacon, the duke and Kenneth Mornington succeed in stealing it back, and take it to the duke's home in London.

The Archdeacon sees the Graal as a holy symbol. The duke sees it as an object to be venerated. Kenneth sees it as integrated with the Arthurian myths. When the Archdeacon senses that a supernatural attack is being made on the Graal, the trio defeat it by prayer.

At the shop (owned by a Greek, Dmitri) where the ointment was bought, Manasseh, a Jew, vows to Gregory that he will destroy the Graal because of its immense power; Gregory is appalled, but reluctantly agrees to help. It is they who made the supernatural attack on the Graal.

A further strange character enters the story: Prester John, a legendary figure charged with the protection of the Graal. Prester John's reactions to the various characters forms part of CW's exposition of the nature of evil*. (*Prester John* is the title of a novel by John Buchan*; there are echoes of his *Greenmantle* and *Three Hostages* in this novel, as there are of M.R. James' story 'Casting the Runes'.) Persimmons continues to befriend Adrian. While playing with him he manages to lightly wound Barbara, and treats the wound with the ointment. Barbara experiences extreme physical and mental trauma. Meanwhile Gregory plays a game of visualizing 'pictures' with Adrian.

A third attempt on the Graal follows. Persimmons succeeds in getting it back by telling Lionel that a doctor friend (Manasseh) can cure Barbara. But when Manasseh arrives, a greater power than his seems to calm her before he has even started.

The role of Prester John develops, both as a foil and challenge to Persimmons' evil and as a rebuke to Mr Batesby's modernist nominalism. He emerges as an explicit herald of Christ, to whom all the 'good' characters relate in different ways. His words to Mornington are simply biblical quotations, prophetic of Mornington's death in the attempt to regain the Graal that follows. The attempt fails, the Duke is captured, and the victors summon the Archdeacon to the shop (which is also being examined by the police, but is proving mysteriously hard to find).

The novel's climax is the supernatural attack on the Archdeacon and the final attempt to use the Graal to achieve occult purposes, to be crowned by the sacrifice of Adrian. The Archdeacon abandons himself to the divine mercy just as Persimmons, in his ritual, abandoned himself to the dark powers. Part of this ritual involves reclaiming the soul of the dead man in chapter 1 – Pattison, who had been a convert to evangelical Christianity – so that it can be placed in the body of the Archdeacon by means of the Graal.

All these rituals, mostly left unexplained by CW, are intended to appease the dark powers. But the scene ends in disaster for the evil characters and salvation for the good, as Prester John comes into his own.

Typically in CW, each character is ultimately defined by what they receive. Persimmons is arrested for murder. There is a celebration of the (Anglican) Mass, with Prester John as celebrant and Adrian serving, and the 'good' protagonists present. In a moving and skilful passage CW translates Prester John into Christ himself, celebrating the Mass and blessing his people. The church is transformed, the Archdeacon dies, 'the Graal and its Lord were gone'; 'normality' returns.

The novel ends with the rational Mr Batesby ascribing most of the foregoing to the Archdeacon's blow on the head during the first attack. Ever the complete modernist, Batesby simply has no understanding at all of what has happened.

War of the Jewels (JRRT, 1994)

Volume 11 of *The History of Middle-earth** traces the evolution of *The Silmarillion** from the completion of *The Lord of the Rings* in 1949 until JRRT's death. Edited by his son Christopher Tolkien, a member of the Inklings, it draws upon unpublished papers to show this development. The task was started in Volume 10, *Morgoth's Ring*. Volume 11 takes the narrative up to the conflict between the elves and the evil Morgoth, containing many of the legends of Beleriand.

War of the Ring, The (JRRT, 1990)

The eighth volume of JRRT's *The History of Middle-earth**, and third volume of *The History of the Lord of the Rings**, edited by Christopher Tolkien*. It is made up of early drafts of what was to become part of *The Lord of the Rings**. The book concerns the battle of Helm's Deep, the destruction of Isengard by the Ents, the journey of Frodo, Sam and Gollum to the Pass of Cirith Ungol, the war in Gondor, and the parley between Gandalf and the ambassadors of Sauron in front of the Black Gate of Mordor. Developments unforeseen by JRRT include the emergence of the Palantir at Isengard and the appearance in the story of Faramir. The book contains illustrations and plans, including Orthanc, Dunharrow, Minas Tirith and the tunnels of Shelob's Lair. Faramir speaks of ancient history, and the languages of Gondor and the Common Speech, material not retained in *The Two Towers**.

Way of Affirmation

See AFFIRMATION, WAY OF

Way of Exchange

See CO-INHERENCE

What the Cross Means to Me (CW, 1943), ed. J. Brierly

See CROSS, THE

Williams, Charles Walter Stansby (1886–1945)

Equally enigmatic as an author and a person, CW was admitted into the Inklings after CSL discovered his supernatural novel, *The Place of the Lion**. He exerted a deep and lasting influence on CSL but not on JRRT. JRRT did respect CW, however, and appreciated his comments on chapters of the unfinished *The Lord of the Rings** as they were read. He contributed his essay, 'On Fairy Stories'* to a posthumous tribute, *Essays Presented to Charles Williams**. At one stage, JRRT wrote an affectionate poem to CW, complaining about difficulty in understanding his writings, but valuing his person nonetheless, and glimpsing his 'virtues' and 'wisdom'. JRRT describes CSL as being under CW's 'spell', and did not entirely approve of this, feeling that CSL was too impressionable a man.

CW's writings become more accessible in the light of the writings of CSL influenced by him. There are many elements consciously drawn from CW in CSL's *That Hideous Strength**, *The Great Divorce**, *Till We Have Faces** and *The Four Loves**. CSL was particularly influenced by CW's novel *The Place of the Lion**, his Arthurian* cycle of poetry (including *Taliessin through Logres*), and his theological understanding of romanticism, especially the experience of falling in love – romantic love*.

CW's writings encompassed fiction, poetry, drama, theology, church history, biography and literary criticism. Anne Ridler perhaps captured the essence of CW when she wrote: 'In Charles Williams' universe there is a clear logic, a sense of terrible justice which is not our justice and yet is not divorced from love.' (George MacDonald similarly spoke of God's 'inexorable love'.) For Anne Ridler 'the whole man ... was greater even than the sum of his works'. Similarly T.S. Eliot – who greatly admired CW – said, in a broadcast talk: 'It is the whole work, not any one or several masterpieces, that we have to take into account in estimating the importance of the man. I think he was a man of unusual genius, and I regard his work as important. But it has an importance of a kind not easy to explain.'

Like JRRT and CSL, CW's thought and writings centred around the three themes of reason, romanticism and Christianity.

Like CSL, he was an Anglican, but theologically he was somewhere between CSL and the Roman Catholic JRRT. His interest in romanticism comes out, in a literary way, in his interest in and use of symbols – or 'images'*, as he preferred to call them. In the business of living, he was interested in the experience of romantic and other forms of love, and the theological implications of human love. As regards reason, he rejected the equation of rational abstraction with reality, and helped to introduce the writings of Søren Kierkegaard to English readers. Yet he felt passionately that the whole human personality must be ordered by reason to have integrity and spiritual health. His least satisfactory novel, *Shadows of Ecstasy** (1933), concerns a conflict between the overintellectualized European races and the deeply emotional, intuitive approach to life of the Africans. CW constantly sought the balance between the abstract and the 'feeling' mind, between intellect and emotion, between reason and imagination*.

CW was in his early forties when his first novel, *War in Heaven**, was published in 1930. Prior to this he had brought out five minor books, four of which were verse, and one of which was a play. His important work begins with the novels; it is after 1930 that his noteworthy works appear, packed into the last 15 years of his life. During these final years 28 books were published (an average of almost two a year) as well as numerous articles and reviews. The last third of these years of maturity as a thinker and writer were spent in Oxford*. They involved CW's normal editorial duties with Oxford University Press, lecturing and tutorials for the university, constant meetings with the Inklings, and frequent weekends in his London home. His wife stayed behind to look after the flat when CW was evacuated to Oxford with OUP.

CW was born in Islington, London, on 20 September 1886. His father was a foreign correspondence clerk in French and German to a firm of importers until his failing eyesight forced the family to move out of London to the countryside at St Albans. There they set up a shop selling artists' materials, and his father contributed short stories to various periodicals. He guided his son's reading, and they went on long walks together. CW dedicated his third book of poems to 'My father and my other teachers'.

The talented boy gained a county council scholarship to St Albans Grammar School. Here he formed a friendship that lasted many years with a George Robinson, who shared his tastes, pursuits and literary inventions. With CW, and his sister Edith, the friends sometimes acted plays to the family circle. The two friends gained places at University College, London, beginning their studies at the age of 15. The family unfortunately were not able to keep up paying the fees, and CW managed to get a job in a Methodist bookshop.

His fortunes changed through meeting an editor from the London office of the Oxford University Press, who was looking for someone to help him with the proofs of the complete edition of Thackeray which, in 1908, was going through the press. CW stayed on the staff until his death, creating a distinctive atmosphere affectionately remembered by those who worked with him, particularly women. He married, was considered medically unfit for the wartime army, and lost two of his closest friends in the Great War. In 1922 his only son, Michael, was born.

In the autumn of that year CW began what was to become a habitual event – giving adult evening classes in literature for the London County Council (*see* ADULT EDUCATION) to supplement the modest family income. He wrote his series of seven supernatural thrillers, including *The Place of the Lion*, for the same reason.

When CW was evacuated with the OUP to Oxford he made a vivid impact there, captured in John Wain's* autobiography, *Sprightly Running*. He comments: 'He gave himself as unreservedly to Oxford as Oxford gave itself to him.' CW's arrival in Oxford, and CSL's friendship with him, was not perhaps entirely welcome to JRRT, as it meant he had less of CSL's attention. In his letters he often mentions seeing CSL 'and CW' rather than CSL alone. When CW died suddenly in 1945 however, he felt deep sorrow over the loss of his friend, writing a letter to his widow.

Oxford University recognized CW in 1943 with an honourary MA. In his *Preface to Paradise Lost**, CSL publically acknowledged his debt to CW's interpretation of Milton. T.S. Eliot praised his work on Dante*, as did Dorothy L. Sayers* (who made a lively translation of *The Divine Comedy*). After his unexpected death, CSL published a commentary on CW's unfinished cycle of Arthurian poetry, *Arthurian Torso**. This poetry has continued to be an influence today in Stephen Lawhead's Pendragon cycle of stories. Several of the Inklings – including CSL, JRRT, OB and W.H. 'Warnie' Lewis – contributed to the posthumous tribute, *Essays Presented to Charles Williams**. *See also* WOMEN AND CW

FURTHER READING

Humphrey Carpenter, *The Inklings: C.S. Lewis, J.R.R. Tolkien, Charles Williams and Their Friends* (1978)
Glen Cavaliero, *Charles Williams: Poet of Theology* (1983)
Alice Hadfield, *Charles Williams: An Exploration of His Life and Work* (1983)
John Wain, *Sprightly Running: Part of an Autobiography* (1962, 1965)

Williams, Florence 'Michal'

Florence Conway, who married CW in 1917, by which time he had christened her Michal, after Saul's daughter who laughed at David for dancing before the Lord (she was embarrassed by his liking for reciting poetry aloud in public places).

Witchcraft (CW, 1941)

Commissioned by T.S. Eliot for Faber and Faber, this book belongs with CW's theological writings. Despite being the author of seven 'supernatural thrillers', CW did not find witchcraft of itself exciting and intriguing. He had, however, been long interested in why people look for power from outside themselves, and his early involvement in the Hermetic Order of the Golden Dawn* had predisposed him to an interest in secret societies (and may have contributed to his evident knowledge of magic, rituals and arcane power).

Having expounded many times the way of the affirmation of images* and the way of the rejection of images, CW in this book addresses the 'Way of the Perversion of Images'. He found it a wearisome book to write, though it was admired by the critics for its readability. He wrote of evil as a real thing, something that far from being exotic or thrilling is actually ordinary and near at hand. Witchcraft is of course the inversion of Christianity, and the second chapter, 'The Arrival of the Devil', provides some of the book's examples of this; the perversion of power, of the city*, of Co-inherence*, of healing ministry. He remains rather ambivalent about the devil himself, pointing out that he appeared at a time that the church needed an adversary.

The book is broadly chronological in scope, and predominantly a psycho-logical study; CW is interested not only in the psychology of the witch but also in the psychological impact on those who witness and judge witchcraft. In this book witchcraft is an affliction, a folly, played out against the theo-logical background against which all CW's books are written; it is a dis-ability of the spirit. Nevertheless, he warns, despite the fact that 2,000 years of Christianity have created a mindset in which witchcraft is no longer an ever-present reality, it is still not so very far away. And the church itself, which in the past has not been wholly detached from it, cannot be complacent.

Women and CW

According to Lois Lang-Sims*, CW (like H.G. Wells) was very attractive to many women, despite his rather ordinary first appearance. He had 'enor-mous personal magnetism' coupled with an acute intellect; and on the lecture podium and in private correspondence he displayed an intensely warm and attractive personality. Added to this, the nature of his writing and the excitement of his metaphysical speculations gave him added charisma.

A number of women are known to have fallen under his spell besides Michal, his wife. Phyllis Jones* joined Oxford University Press in 1924 as librarian. CW called her 'Phyllida' in *An Urbanity** (1926), having by then got to know her well. In that year she began attending his evening lectures and was soon attracted to him, an attraction which was reciprocated, as poems written at that time show; and which flowered when Phyllis acted in CW's *The Masque of the Manuscript* performed in the library in 1927. The friendship deepened into love, though it was a romantic rather than a sexual love; Alice Hadfield, in her biography of CW, suggests that the relationship with Michal may have become static and that CW's capacity for love led him to fall in love with Phyllis (though CW was never unfaithful physically to Michal). In private he called her by another name, Celia, a name that he attached to poetic discoveries and new insights: in 1935 he went so far as to discuss the 'Celian moment' (without mentioning Phyllis) in the introduction to *The New Book of English Verse**, written after Phyllis' marriage and departure to live abroad. By then the relationship had been soured; in 1930 CW had found out that Phyllis had been having a love affair with his colleague Gerry Hopkins, and when she married Billie Somervaille, her subsequent departure to Java caused CW considerable sorrow. The marriage broke down, however, and in 1938 she returned to London. The old relationship and CW's vision of romantic love were neither rekindled nor disowned. When in 1939 the Press moved to Oxford she came too, but she was soon developing a relationship with somebody else. The news that her divorce had been granted and that she would remarry as soon as possible was extremely depressing for CW, who felt that the romantic image he had fallen in love with had been irreparably spoiled and wished only to be free of the 13-year-old love affair. Meanwhile his wife, who had known of her husband's adoration of Phyllis for some time, was forgiving and supportive, though Lois Lang-Sims* recalls that 'total rage against Phyllida burned in her most, but not all, of the time'.

Lois Lang-Sims regards her own relationship with CW as being of a secondary category, that she was one of the many women who were attracted to him and were 'types' of the beloved Lady, to do service when Phyllida and Michal were not there to be adored.

Her cousin attended Downe House School*, and gave her wonderful accounts of CW's visits there, but it was not until she was 26 that she read, in 1943, *The Figure of Beatrice**. She began to write to CW, and he invited her to lunch in Oxford; he was in his mid-fifties. 'For the first few minutes I was so stunned by the total impact of the man that I took in neither the details of his appearance nor the meaning of what he had said.'

The correspondence between Lang-Sims and CW was detailed and far-ranging, and their meetings were highly charged. CW (who christened her 'Lalage') treated her with great courtesy, kissing her hand in farewell on their first meeting; Lang-Sims makes it clear that he never attempted to deepen the physical encounter beyond what was acceptable. Her account of their relationship has caused some controversy due to passages where she describes what seems to be an ascetic, non-sexual disciplining which CW applied to her, involving symbolic beating and prolonged embraces. It has been suggested by Donna Beales, however, that Lang-Sims may have misrepresented or misunderstood what was really going on. Certainly there is no suggestion of sexual impropriety.

Wrenn, Charles (1895–1969)

Member of the Inklings. On his return to England after lecturing in India, Charles Wrenn taught at Leeds University and then in Oxford from 1930, where he assisted JRRT in the Anglo-Saxon course. His wife became one of Edith Tolkien's few friends out of his circle. From 1939 to 1946 Charles Wrenn was Chair of English Language and Literature at the University of London. When JRRT transferred to being Merton Professor of English Language and Literature in 1946 Wrenn took over his post. He was Rawlinson and Bosworth Professor of Anglo-Saxon until 1963.

Wright, Joseph

As a schoolboy JRRT was delighted to acquire a second-hand copy of Joseph Wright's *Primer of the Gothic Language*. As a student at Oxford* JRRT chose Comparative Philology as his special subject (*see* PHILOLOGIST, JRRT AS A), so he had the same Joseph Wright as a lecturer and tutor. This Yorkshireman of humble origins (he started as a woollen-mill worker from the age of six) had, by a long struggle, become Professor of Comparative Philology. The struggle included teaching himself to read at the age of 15. Among the many languages he later studied were Sanskrit, Gothic, Russian, Old Norse, and Old and Middle High German. One of his achievements was the six large volumes of his *English Dialect Dictionary*. Joseph Wright communicated to JRRT his love for philology, and was a demanding teacher.

Bibliography

(NB: Besides printed books and periodicals, the Internet provides much discussion and information concerning the Inklings – either on web pages or in discussion groups (usually referred to as 'newsgroups', in a part of the Internet called 'Usenet'). Rather than list websites and newsgroups that may well change, we suggest using a 'search engine' to locate people and topics that interest you. Currently a good search engine for the World Wide Web is www.google.com, and for newsgroups, dejanews.com.

Major writings of C.S. Lewis, in order of first publication

Spirits in Bondage: A Cycle of Lyrics. William Heinemann: London, 1919. (This book has now entered the public domain and the text can be obtained from Internet sources.)

Dymer. J.M. Dent: London, 1926.

The Pilgrim's Regress: An Allegorical Apology for Christianity, Reason and Romanticism. J.M. Dent: London, 1933.

The Allegory of Love: A Study in Medieval Tradition. Clarendon Press: Oxford, 1936.

Out of the Silent Planet. John Lane: London, 1938.

Rehabilitations and Other Essays. Oxford University Press: London, 1938.

The Personal Heresy: A Controversy (with E.M.W. Tillyard). Oxford University Press: London, 1939.

The Problem of Pain. Geoffrey Bles, Centenary Press: London, 1940.

Broadcast Talks. Geoffrey Bles: London, 1942.

A Preface to Paradise Lost. Oxford University Press: London, 1942.

The Screwtape Letters. Geoffrey Bles: London, 1942. Reprinted with an additional letter as *The Screwtape Letters and Screwtape Proposes a Toast*. Geoffrey Bles: London, 1961. Further new material in *The Screwtape Letters with Screwtape Proposes a Toast*. Macmillan: New York, 1982.

The Weight of Glory. SPCK, Little Books on Religion No. 189: London, 1942.

The Abolition of Man: Reflections on Education with Special Reference to the Teaching of English in the Upper Forms of Schools. Riddell Memorial Lectures, fifteenth series. Oxford University Press: London, 1943.

Christian Behaviour: A Further Series of Broadcast Talks. Geoffrey Bles: London, 1943.

Perelandra. John Lane: London, 1943. Reprinted in paperback as *Voyage to Venus*. Pan Books: London, 1953.

Beyond Personality: The Christian Idea of God. Geoffrey Bles, Centenary Press: London, 1944.

That Hideous Strength: A Modern Fairy Tale for Grown Ups. John Lane: London, 1945. A version abridged by the author was published as *The Tortured Planet* (Avon Books: New York, 1946) and as *That Hideous Strength* (Pan Books: London, 1955).

George MacDonald: Anthology. Compiled, and with an introduction, by C.S. Lewis. Geoffrey Bles: London, 1946.

The Great Divorce: A Dream. Geoffrey Bles, Centenary Press: London, 1946. Originally published as a series in *The Guardian*. Bles inaccurately dated the book as 1945.

Essays Presented to Charles Williams. Edited, and with an introduction, by C.S. Lewis. Oxford University Press: London, 1947.

Miracles: A Preliminary Study. Geoffrey Bles: London, 1947. Reprinted, with an expanded version of Chapter 3, Collins Fontana Books: London, 1960.

Arthurian Torso: Containing the Posthumous Fragment of the Figure of Arthur by Charles Williams and a Commentary on the Arthurian Poems of Charles Williams by C.S. Lewis. Oxford University Press: London, 1948.

Transposition and Other Addresses. Geoffrey Bles: London, 1949. Published in the United States as *The Weight of Glory and Other Addresses*. Macmillan: New York, 1949.

The Lion, the Witch, and the Wardrobe. Geoffrey Bles: London, 1950.

Prince Caspian: The Return to Narnia. Geoffrey Bles: London, 1951.

Mere Christianity. Geoffrey Bles: London, 1952. A revised and expanded version of *Broadcast Talks, Christian Behaviour* and *Beyond Personality*.

The Voyage of the 'Dawn Treader'. Geoffrey Bles: London, 1952.

The Silver Chair. Geoffrey Bles: London, 1953.

English Literature in the Sixteenth Century (Excluding Drama). Volume III of *The Oxford History of English Literature*. Clarendon Press: Oxford, 1954. In 1990 the series was renumbered and Lewis' volume was reissued as Volume IV, *Poetry and Prose in the Sixteenth Century*.

The Horse and His Boy. Geoffrey Bles: London, 1954.

The Magician's Nephew. Bodley Head: London, 1955.

Surprised By Joy: The Shape of My Early Life. Geoffrey Bles: London, 1955.

The Last Battle. Bodley Head: London, 1956.

Till We Have Faces: A Myth Retold. Geoffrey Bles: London, 1956.

Reflections on the Psalms. Geoffrey Bles: London, 1958.

The Four Loves. Geoffrey Bles: London, 1960.

Studies in Words. Cambridge University Press: Cambridge, 1960.

The World's Last Night and Other Essays. Harcourt, Brace and Co: New York, 1960.

An Experiment in Criticism. Cambridge University Press: Cambridge, 1961.

A Grief Observed (published under the pseudonym 'N.W. Clerk'). Faber and Faber: London, 1961.

They Asked for a Paper: Papers and Addresses. Geoffrey Bles: London, 1962.

Posthumous writings and collections

The Discarded Image: An Introduction to Medieval and Renaissance Literature. Cambridge University Press: Cambridge, 1964.

Letters to Malcolm: Chiefly on Prayer. Geoffrey Bles: London, 1964.

Poems. Edited by Walter Hooper. Geoffrey Bles: London, 1964.

Letters of C.S. Lewis. Edited, with a memoir, by W.H. Lewis. Geoffrey Bles: London, 1966. Revised edition, edited by Walter Hooper, 1988.

Of Other Worlds: Essays and Stories. Edited by Walter Hooper. Geoffrey Bles: London, 1966.

Studies in Medieval and Renaissance Literature. Edited by Walter Hooper. Cambridge University Press: Cambridge, 1966.

Christian Reflections. Edited by Walter Hooper. Geoffrey Bles: London, 1967.

Letters to an American Lady. Edited by Clyde S. Kilby. Eerdmans: Grand Rapids, 1967; Hodder and Stoughton: London, 1969.

Spenser's Images of Life. Edited by Alistair Fowler. Cambridge University Press: Cambridge, 1967.

A Mind Awake: An Anthology of C.S. Lewis. Edited by Clyde S. Kilby. Geoffrey Bles: London, 1968.

Narrative Poems. Edited, with a preface, by Walter Hooper. Geoffrey Bles: London, 1969.

Selected Literary Essays. Edited, with a preface, by Walter Hooper. Cambridge University Press: Cambridge, 1969.

God in the Dock: Essays on Theology and Ethics. Edited, with a Preface, by Walter Hooper. Eerdmans: Grand Rapids, 1970. A paperback edition of part of it was published as *God in the Dock: Essays on Theology* (Collins Fontana Books: London, 1979) and as *Undeceptions: Essays on Theology and Ethics* (Geoffrey Bles: London, 1971).

Fern Seeds and Elephants and Other Essays on Christianity. Edited, with a preface, by Walter Hooper. Collins Fontana Books: London, 1975.

The Dark Tower and Other Stories. Edited, with a preface, by Walter Hooper. Collins: London, 1977.

The Joyful Christian: Readings from C.S. Lewis. Edited by William Griffin. Macmillan: New York, 1977.

They Stand Together: The Letters of C.S. Lewis to Arthur Greeves (1914–1963). Edited by Walter Hooper. Collins: London, 1979.

Of This and Other Worlds. Edited by Walter Hooper. Collins Fount: London, 1982.

The Business of Heaven: Daily Readings from C.S. Lewis. Edited by Walter Hooper. Collins Fount: London, 1984.

Boxen: The Imaginary World of the Young C.S. Lewis. Edited by Walter Hooper. Collins: London, 1985.

First and Second Things: Essays on Theology and Ethics. Edited, with a preface, by Walter Hooper. Collins Fount: Glasgow, 1985.

Letters to Children. Edited by Lyle W. Dorsett and Marjorie Lamp Mead. Collins: New York and London, 1985.

Present Concerns. Edited by Walter Hooper. Collins Fount: London, 1986.

Timeless at Heart. Edited by Walter Hooper. Collins Fount: London, 1987.

Letters: C.S. Lewis and Don Giovanni Calabria: A Study in Friendship. Edited, with an introduction, by Martin Moynihan, 1988, Collins: Glasgow, includes Latin text. First issued as *The Latin Letters of C.S. Lewis*, paperback edition Crossway Books: Westchester, 1987, without Latin text.

The Collected Poems of C.S. Lewis. Edited by Walter Hooper. HarperCollins: London, 1994.

C.S. Lewis: Collected Letters, Volume 1, Family Letters 1905–1931. Edited by Walter Hooper. HarperCollins: London, 2000.

Major writings of J.R.R. Tolkien, in order of first publication

A Middle English Vocabulary. The Clarendon Press: Oxford, 1922. Prepared for use with Kenneth Sisam's *Fourteenth Century Verse and Prose* (The Clarendon Press: Oxford, 1921) and later published with it.

Sir Gawain and the Green Knight. Edited by J.R.R. Tolkien and E.V. Gordon. The Clarendon Press: Oxford, 1925 (new edition, revised by Norman Davis, 1967).

The Hobbit, or There and Back Again. George Allen and Unwin: London, 1937.

Farmer Giles of Ham. George Allen and Unwin: London, 1950.

The Fellowship of the Ring: Being the First Part of the Lord of the Rings. George Allen and Unwin: London, 1954.

The Two Towers: Being the Second Part of the Lord of the Rings. George Allen and Unwin: London, 1954.

The Return of the King: Being the Third Part of the Lord of the Rings. George Allen and Unwin: London, 1955.

The Adventures of Tom Bombadil and Other Verses from the Red Book. George Allen and Unwin: London, 1962.

Ancrene Wisse: The English Text of the Ancrene Riwle. Edited by J.R.R. Tolkien. Oxford University Press: London, 1962.

Tree and Leaf. George Allen and Unwin: London, 1964.

The Tolkien Reader. Ballantine Books: New York, 1966.

The Road Goes Ever On: A Song Cycle. Poems by J.R.R. Tolkien, music by Donald Swann. Houghton Mifflin Company: Boston, 1967. (Enlarged edition, 1978).

Smith of Wootton Major. George Allen and Unwin: London, 1967.

Posthumous writings

Sir Gawain and the Green Knight, Pearl and Sir Orfeo. Translated by J.R.R. Tolkien; edited by Christopher Tolkien. George Allen and Unwin: London, 1975.

The Father Christmas Letters. Edited by Baillie Tolkien. George Allen and Unwin: London, 1976.

The Silmarillion. Edited by Christopher Tolkien. George Allen and Unwin: London, 1977.

Pictures by J.R.R. Tolkien. Edited by Christopher Tolkien. George Allen and Unwin: London, 1979.

Unfinished Tales of Númenor and Middle-earth. Edited by Christopher Tolkien. George Allen and Unwin: London, 1980.

The Letters of J.R.R. Tolkien. Edited by Humphrey Carpenter, with the assistance of Christopher Tolkien. George Allen and Unwin: London, 1981; Houghton Mifflin Company: Boston, 1981.

Old English Exodus. Text, translation and commentary by J.R.R. Tolkien; edited by Joan Turville-Petre. The Clarendon Press: Oxford, 1981.

Finn and Hengest: The Fragment and the Episode. Edited by Alan Bliss. George Allen and Unwin: London, 1982.

The Monsters and the Critics and Other Essays. Edited by Christopher Tolkien. George Allen and Unwin: London, 1983.

Mr Bliss. George Allen and Unwin: London, 1982; Houghton Mifflin Company: Boston, 1983.

The History of Middle-earth. Edited by Christopher Tolkien. Published in 12 volumes between 1983 and 1996, by George Allen and Unwin, Unwin Hyman and HarperCollins.

Roverandom. Edited by Christina Scull and Wayne G. Hammond. HarperCollins: London, 1998.

Major writings of Charles Williams, in order of first publication

(NB: Adapted from Alice Mary Hadfield, *Charles Williams: An Exploration of His Life and Work.* New York: Oxford University Press, 1983. For fuller bibliographies, the reader should consult Anne Ridler's *The Image of the City*, Oxford University Press, 1958; and Lois Glenn, *Charles W.S. Williams: A Checklist.* The Kent State University Press, 1975)

The Silver Stair. Herbert and David: London, 1912.

Poems of Conformity. Oxford University Press: London, 1917.

Divorce. Oxford University Press, 1920.

Poems of Home and Overseas. Compiled by Charles Williams and V.H. Collins. Clarendon Press: Oxford, 1921.

'*Outlines of Romantic Theology*'. Manuscript, 1924. Published as *Outlines of Romantic Theology*. Edited by Alice M. Hadfield. W.B. Eerdmans: Grand Rapids, 1990.

Windows of Night. Oxford University Press, 1925.

An Urbanity. Privately printed, 1926.

E.A. Parker, compiler, *A Book of Longer Modern Verse*. Prefatory note by Charles Williams. Clarendon Press: Oxford, 1926.

A Book of Victorian Narrative Verse. Chosen and introduced by Charles Williams. Clarendon Press: Oxford, 1927.

A Carol of Amen House. Privately printed, 1927. Words by Charles Williams, music by Hubert Foss.

A Masque of the Manuscript. Privately printed, 1927.

The Oxford Book of Regency Verse. Edited by H.S. Milford in collaboration with Charles Williams and F. Page. Clarendon Press: Oxford, 1928.

A Masque of Perusal. Privately printed, 1929.

A Myth of Shakespeare. Oxford University Press, 1929.

Heroes and Kings. Sylvan Press: London, 1930.

The Masque of the Termination of Copyright. Unpublished, 1930.

Poems of Gerard Manley Hopkins. Edited by R. Bridges, 2nd ed. Critical introduction by Charles Williams. Oxford University Press: London, 1930.

Poetry at Present. Clarendon Press: Oxford, 1930. (Literary criticism, with interspersed verses by Charles Williams.)

War in Heaven. Victor Gollancz: London, 1930.

Many Dimensions. Victor Gollancz: London, 1931.

The Place of the Lion. Mundanus (Victor Gollancz): London, 1931.

Three Plays (The Witch, The Rite of the Passion, The Chaste Wanton). Oxford University Press: London, 1931.

The English Poetic Mind. Clarendon Press: Oxford, 1932.

The Greater Trumps. Victor Gollancz: London, 1932.

A Myth of Francis Bacon. Privately printed, 1932.

Bacon. Arthur Barker: London, 1933.

Reason and Beauty in the Poetic Mind. Clarendon Press: Oxford, 1933.

Shadows of Ecstasy. Victor Gollancz: London, 1933.

A Short Life of Shakespeare with the Sources. Abridged by Charles Williams from Sir William Chambers' *William Shakespeare*. Oxford University Press: London, 1933.

W.S. Landor, *Imaginary Conversations*, edited by F.A. Cavenagh et al. Introduction by Charles Williams. Oxford University Press: London, 1934.

James I. Arthur Barker: London, 1934.

Browning, Robert, *The Ring and the Book*. Retold by Charles Williams. Oxford University Press: London, 1934.

The New Book of English Verse. Edited, with an introduction, by Charles Williams. Victor Gollancz: London, 1935.

Rochester. Arthur Barker: London, 1935.

Queen Elizabeth. Duckworth: London, 1936.

The Story of the Aeneid. Retold by Charles Williams. Oxford University Press: London, 1936.

Thomas Cranmer of Canterbury. Oxford University Press: London, 1936.

Descent into Hell. Faber and Faber: London, 1937.

Henry VII. Arthur Barker: London, 1937.

Stories of Great Names. Oxford University Press: London, 1937.

He Came down from Heaven. William Heinemann: London, 1938.

Taliessin through Logres. Oxford University Press: London, 1938.

The Descent of the Dove: A Short History of the Holy Spirit in the Church. Longmans: London, 1939.

Judgement at Chelmsford. Oxford University Press: London, 1939.

The Passion of Christ. Anthology compiled by Charles Williams. Oxford University Press: London, 1939.

The English Poems of John Milton. Introduction by Charles Williams. Oxford University Press, World's Classics: London, 1940.

Søren Kierkegaard, *The Present Age*. Introduction by Charles Williams. Oxford University Press: London, 1940.

The New Christian Year. Anthology compiled by Charles Williams. Oxford University Press: London, 1941.

Religion and Love in Dante. Dacre Press: London, 1941.

The Way of Exchange. James Clarke: London, 1941.

Witchcraft. Faber and Faber: London, 1941.

The Forgiveness of Sins. Geoffrey Bles: London, 1942.

'The Cross', in a symposium entitled *What the Cross Means to Me*, edited by J. Brierley. James Clarke: London, 1943.

The Figure of Beatrice. Faber and Faber: London, 1943.

Letters of Evelyn Underhill. Edited, with an introduction, by Charles Williams. Longmans: London, 1943.

To Michal: After Marriage. The Grasshopper Broadsheets, third series, no. 10, 1944.

The Region of the Summer Stars. Editions Poetry London: London, 1944.

All Hallows' Eve. Faber and Faber: London, 1945.

The House of the Octopus. Edinburgh House Press: London, 1945.

Wilfred Gibson, *Solway Ford and Other Poems*. Selection by Charles Williams. Faber and Faber: London, 1945.

Evelyn Underhill, *The Letters of Evelyn Underhill*. Edited, with an introduction, by Charles Williams. Longmans: London, 1945.

John Webster, *The Duchess of Malfi*. Introductions by George Rylands and Charles Williams. Sylvan Press: London, 1945.

Flecker of Dean Close. Canterbury Press: London, 1946.

Posthumous writings and collections

Arthurian Torso (containing the first five chapters of the unfinished *The Figure of Arthur*). With commentary on the Arthurian poems by C.S. Lewis. Oxford University Press: London, 1948.

Seed of Adam and Other Plays (*Seed of Adam, The Death of Good Fortune, The House by the Stable, Grab and Grace*). Edited by Anne Ridler. Oxford University Press: London, 1948.

The Image of the City and Other Essays. Edited, with an introduction, by Anne Ridler. Oxford University Press: London, 1958.

Selected Writings. Edited by Anne Ridler. Oxford University Press: London, 1961.

Collected Plays by Charles Williams. Edited by John Heath-Stubbs. Oxford University Press: London, 1963. (Verse plays previously published, and also *Terror of Light* in prose and the broadcast verse play *The Three Temptations*.)

Letters to Lalage: The Letters of Charles Williams to Lois Lang-Sims. With commentary by Lois Lang-Sims and introduction and notes by Glen Cavaliero. Kent State University Press: Kent and London, 1989.

Arthurian Poets: Charles Williams. Edited by David Llewellyn Dodds. The Boydell Press: Woodbridge, Suffolk, 1991. (Contains *Taliessin through Logres, The Region of the Summer Stars* and previously unpublished and uncollected Arthurian poetry by Charles Williams.)

Major writings of Owen Barfield, in alphabetical order

'Anthroposophy and the Future'. *Towards* 3.1 (1987): 32–35, 49–50.

'Coleridge Collected' (review of *Collected Works of Coleridge*, edited by Kathleen Coburn). *Encounter* 35 (November): 74–83.

'Coleridge in the 21st Century' (review of Trevor H. Levere's *Poetry Realized in Nature: Samuel Taylor Coleridge and Early Nineteenth Century Science*). *Towards* 2.2 (1982): 38–41.

'The Concept of Revelation'. *Seven: An Anglo American Literary Review* (March 1980): 117–25.

'East, West and Saul Bellow' (review of *The Dean's December*). *Towards* 2.3 (1983): 26–28.

'Either: Or' in *Imagination and the Spirit: Essays in Literature and the Christian Faith Presented to Clyde S. Kilby*. Edited by Charles Huttar. W.B. Eerdman: Grand Rapids, 25–42.

'The Evolution Complex'. *Towards* 2.2 (1982): 6–16.

'Foreword'. *Orpheus: A Poetic Drama*: 7–10.

'Giordano Bruno and the Survival of Learning'. *The Drew Gateway* 42 (Spring): 147–59.

'Greek Thought in English Words'. *Essays and Studies* 3 (1950): 69–81.

History in English Words. London: Faber and Faber, 1926.

'History of English Poetry in the Second Half of the Twentieth Century'. *Towards* 1.5 (1979): 22–23.

History, Guilt and Habit. Wesleyan University Press: Middletown, 1979.

'Human Relationships'. *Towards* 1.7 (1980–81): 15–16.

'Imagination and Science'. *Journal of the American Academy of Religion* 52 (1984): 585–89.

'Introducing Rudolf Steiner'. *Towards* 2.4 (1983): 42–44.

'Introduction'. *Light on C.S. Lewis*. Edited by Jocelyn Gibb. Harcourt, Brace and World: New York, 1966, ix–xxi.

'Language, Evolution of Consciousness, and the Recovery of Human Meaning'. *Teachers College Record* 82 (1981): 427–33. Reprinted in *Toward the Recovery of Wholeness: Knowledge, Education, and Human Values*. Edited by Douglas Sloan. Teachers College Press: New York, 1984: 55–61.

'Meaning, Revelation, and Tradition in Language and Religion'. *Towards* 2.7 (1986): 11–16.

'Meaning, Revelation and Tradition in Language and Religion'. *The Missouri Review*, 5.3 (1982): 117–28.

'The Nature of Meaning'. *Seven: An Anglo American Literary Review* (March 1981): 32–43.

'Night Operation'. *Towards* 2.4 (1983): 10–19 and 2.5 (1984): 14–27.

'A Note on the Production'. *Orpheus: A Poetic Drama*: 11–12.

Orpheus: A Poetic Drama. Edited by John C. Ulreich, Jr: Lindisfarne Press West: Stockbridge, MA, 1983.

'Owen Barfield and the Origin of Language'. *Towards* 1.2 (1978): 1, 3–7 and 1.3 (1978): 12–15.

Owen Barfield on C.S. Lewis. Edited by G.B. Tennyson. Wesleyan University Press: Middletown, 1989.

An Owen Barfield Sampler. Edited by Thomas Kranidas and Jeanne Clayton Hunter. State University of New York Press: Albany, 1993.

Poetic Diction: A Study in Meaning. 2nd ed. Faber and Faber: London, 1962; McGraw Hill: New York, 1964.

'Poetry in Walter De La Mare'. *Denver Quarterly* 6 (Winter): 69–81.

'The Politics of Abortion'. *Denver Quarterly* 6 (Winter): 18–28.

'Preface'. *The Taste of the Pineapple: Essays on C.S. Lewis as Reader, Critic, and Imaginative Writer.* Edited by Bruce L. Edwards. Popular: Bowling Green, OH, 1988.

'The Presence of Subterranean Springs (review of Douglas Sloan's *Insight-Imagination*)'. *Towards* 2.5 (1984): 36–38.

'Program Notes for the Original Production'. *Orpheus: A Poetic Drama*: 113–16.

The Rediscovery of Meaning and Other Essays. Wesleyan University Press: Middletown, 1977.

'Reflections on C.S. Lewis, S.T. Coleridge, and R. Steiner: An Interview with Owen Barfield'. *Towards* 2.6 (1985): 6–13.

'Review of *Coleridge, the Damaged Archangel*, by Norman Fruman'. *Nation* 214 (12 June): 764–65.

'Review of *The Origin of Consciousness in the Breakdown of the Bicameral Mind*, by Julian Jaynes'. *Teachers College Record* 80 (1979): 602–4.

Romanticism Comes of Age. 2nd ed. Wesleyan University Press: Middletown, 1967.

Saving the Appearances: A Study in Idolatry. Harcourt, Brace Jovanovich: New York, 1957.

'The Self in Vogue' (review of Peggy Rosenthal's *Words and Values*). *Towards* 2.7 (1986): 33–35.

The Silver Trumpet (1925); rpt. Bookmakers Guild: Boulder, 1986.

'Solovyev and the Meaning of Love'. *Towards* 2.6 (1985): 14–15, 23.

Speaker's Meaning. Rudolf Steiner Press: London, 1967.

This Ever Diverse Pair. Gollancz: London, 1950.

'*Towards* Interviews Owen Barfield'. *Towards* 1.6 (1980): 6–10.

'Two Kinds of Forgetting'. *The Nassau Review* 4 (1981): 5–6.

Unancestral Voice. Wesleyan University Press: Middletown, 1965.

What Coleridge Thought. Wesleyan University Press: Middletown, 1971.

Worlds Apart: A Dialogue of the Sixties. Wesleyan University Press: Middletown, 1977.

Bibliography of Selected Writings About the Inklings

Adey, Lionel. *C.S. Lewis's 'Great War' with Owen Barfield.* University of Victoria: Canada, 1978.

Adey, Lionel. *C.S. Lewis: Writer, Dreamer and Mentor.* Eerdmans: Grand Rapids and Cambridge, 1998.

Aeschliman, Michael D. *The Restitution of Man: C.S. Lewis and the Case Against Scientism.* Eerdmans: Grand Rapids, 1983.

Allan, James (ed). *An Introduction to Elvish and to Other Tongues and Proper Names and Writing Systems of the Third Age of the Western Lands of Middle-earth as Set Forth in the Published Writings of Professor John Ronald Reuel Tolkien.* Bran's Head Books: Hayes, Middlesex, 1978.

Andrews, Bart with Bernie Zuber. *The Tolkien Quiz Book: 1001 Questions About Tolkien's Tales of Middle-earth and Other Fantasies.* Signet Books: New York, 1979.

Armstrong, Helen. *Digging Potatoes, Growing Trees: 25 Years of Speeches at the Tolkien Society's Annual Dinners.* Volumes 1 and 2. The Tolkien Society, 1997–98.

Arnott, Anne. *The Secret Country of C.S. Lewis.* Hodder: London, 1974.

Battarbee, K.J. (ed). *Scholarship and Fantasy: Proceedings of the Tolkien Phenomenon, May 1992, Turku, Finland.* University of Turku: Turku, Finland, 1993.

Becker, Alida (ed). *The Tolkien Scrapbook.* Grosset and Dunlap: New York, 1978.

Becker, Alida (ed). *A Tolkien Treasury.* Courage Books: Philadelphia, 1989.

Beversluis, John. *C.S. Lewis and the Search for Rational Religion.* The Paternoster Press: Exeter, 1985.

Blackwelder, Richard E. *Tolkien Phraseology: A Companion to a Tolkien Thesaurus.* Tolkien Archives Fund: Marquette University, 1990.

Blount, Margaret. *Animal Land: The Creatures of Children's Fiction.* Hutchinson: London, 1974; William Morrow: New York, 1975.

Burson, Scott and Jerry Walls. *C.S. Lewis and Francis Schaeffer.* InterVarsity Press: Downers Grove, 1998.

Carnell, Corbin S. *Bright Shadows of Reality.* W.B. Eerdmans: Grand Rapids, 1974.

Carpenter, Humphrey. *J.R.R. Tolkien: A Biography.* George Allen and Unwin: London, 1977; Houghton Mifflin: Boston, 1977.

Carpenter, Humphrey. *The Inklings: C.S. Lewis, J.R.R. Tolkien, Charles Williams and Their Friends.* George Allen and Unwin: London, 1978; Houghton Mifflin: Boston, 1979.

Carter, Lin. *Tolkien: A Look Behind the Lord of the Rings.* Ballantine: New York, 1979.

Cavaliero, Glen. *Charles Williams: Poet of Theology.* Macmillan: London, 1983.

Christensen, Michael J. *C.S. Lewis on Scripture.* Hodder: London, 1980.

Christopher, Joe R. *C.S. Lewis.* G.K. Hall and Co: Boston, 1987.

Christopher, Joe R. and Joan K. Ostling. *C.S. Lewis: An Annotated Check List of Writings About Him and His Works*. Kent State University Press: Ohio, 1974.

Clute, John and John Grant. *The Encyclopedia of Fantasy*. Orbit: London, 1997.

Como, James T. (ed). *C.S. Lewis at the Breakfast Table and Other Reminiscences*. Macmillan: New York, 1979.

Cunningham, Richard B. *C.S. Lewis, Defender of the Faith*. The Westminster Press: Philadelphia, 1967.

Day, David. *A Tolkien Bestiary*. Mitchell Beazley: London, 1979; Ballantine: New York, 1979.

Dorsett, Lyle. *Joy and C.S. Lewis*. HarperCollins: London, 1988 and 1994.

Downing, David. *Planets in Peril: A Critical Study of C.S. Lewis's Ransom Trilogy*. University of Massachusetts Press: Amherst, 1992.

Duriez, Colin. *The C.S. Lewis Handbook*. Monarch: Eastbourne, 1992; Baker Book House: Grand Rapids, 1992.

Duriez, Colin. *The J.R.R. Tolkien Handbook*. Baker Book House: Grand Rapids, 1992.

Duriez, Colin. *The Tolkien and Middle-earth Handbook*. Monarch: Eastbourne, 1992; Angus and Robertson: Pymble, NSW, 1992.

Duriez, Colin. 'Sub-creation and Tolkien's Theology of Story' in *Scholarship and Fantasy*. University of Turku: Turku, Finland, 1994.

Duriez, Colin. 'Tolkien and the Other Inklings' in Patricia Reynolds and Glen H. Good-Knight. *Proceedings of the J.R.R. Tolkien Centenary Conference: Keble College, Oxford, 1992*. The Tolkien Society: Milton Keynes and The Mythopoeic Press: Altadena, 1995.

Duriez, Colin. 'J.R.R. Tolkien' in *British Children's Authors 1914–1960*, a volume of the *Dictionary of Literary Biography*. Bruccoli Clark Layman: Columbia, 1996.

Duriez, Colin. '"Art Has Been Verified . . .": The Friendship of C.S. Lewis and J.R.R. Tolkien' in Helen Armstrong. *Digging Potatoes, Growing Trees: 25 Years of Speeches at the Tolkien Society's Annual Dinners*. Volume 2. The Tolkien Society, 1998.

Duriez, Colin. 'C.S. Lewis' Theology of Fantasy' in *The Pilgrim's Guide*. Edited by David Mills. W.B. Eerdmans: Grand Rapids, 1998.

Duriez, Colin. 'The Theology of Fantasy in C.S. Lewis and J.R.R. Tolkien' in *Themelios*, Vol. 23, No. 2 (February), 1998.

Duriez, Colin. 'Tolkien and the Old West' in Helen Armstrong. *Digging Potatoes, Growing Trees: 25 Years of Speeches at the Tolkien Society's Annual Dinners*. Volume 2. The Tolkien Society, 1998.

Duriez, Colin. 'In the Library: Composition and Context' in *Reading Literature with C.S. Lewis*. Edited by Thomas Martin. Baker Book House: Grand Rapids, 2000.

Duriez, Colin. *The C.S. Lewis Encyclopedia*. Crossway Books: Wheaton, Illinois, 2000.

Duriez, Colin. *Tolkien and 'The Lord of the Rings'*. Azure: London, 2001.

Edwards, Bruce L. *A Rhetoric of Reading: C.S. Lewis's Defense of Western Literacy*. Brigham Young University, 1986.

Edwards, Bruce L. (ed). *The Taste of the Pineapple: Essays on C.S. Lewis as Reader, Critic, and Imaginative Writer*. Bowling Green State University Popular Press, 1988.

Elgin, Don D. *The Comedy of the Fantastic: Ecological Perspectives on the Fantasy Novel*. Greenwood, 1985.

Ellwood, Gracia Fay. *Good News from Tolkien's Middle-earth: Two Essays on the 'Applicability' of the Lord of the Rings*. W.B. Eerdmans: Grand Rapids, 1970.

Etkin, Anne (ed). *Eglerio! In Praise of Tolkien*. Quest Communications: Greencastle, Pennsylvania, 1978.

Evans, Robley. *J.R.R. Tolkien*. Crowell: New York, 1976.

Every, George. 'Charles Williams – I. The Accuser'. *Theology* li 333 (1948): 95–100.

Every, George. 'Charles Williams – II. The City and the Substitutions'. *Theology* li 334 (1948): 145–50.

Filmer, Kath. *The Fiction of C.S. Lewis: Mask and Mirror*. Macmillan: New York, 1993.

Flieger, Verlyn. *Splintered Light: Logos and Language in Tolkien's World*. W.B. Eerdmans: Grand Rapids, 1983.

Fonstad, Karen Wynn. *The Atlas of Middle-earth*. Houghton Mifflin: Boston, 1981.

Ford, Paul F. *Companion to Narnia*. Harper and Row: San Francisco, 1980.

Foster, Robert. *The Complete Guide to Middle-earth: From the Hobbit to the Silmarillion*. George Allen and Unwin: London, 1978; Ballantine Books: New York, 1978.

Fuller, Edmund. *Books with Men Behind Them*. Random House: New York, 1962.

Garbowski, Christopher. *Recovery and Transcendence for the Contemporary Mythmaker: The Spiritual Dimension in the Works of J.R.R. Tolkien*. Maria Curie-Sklodowska University Press: Lublin, 2000.

Gardner, Helen. 'Clive Staples Lewis 1898–1963'. *Proc. British Academy* li (1965): 417–28.

Gibb, Jocelyn (ed). *Light on C.S. Lewis*. Geoffrey Bles: London, 1965.

Gibson, Evan. *C.S. Lewis: Spinner of Tales*. Christian University Press: Washington DC, 1980.

Giddings, Robert (ed). *J.R.R. Tolkien: This Far Land*. Vision: London; Barnes and Noble: Totowas, New Jersey, 1983.

Giddings, Robert and Elizabeth Holland. *J.R.R. Tolkien: The Shores of Middle-earth*. Eletheia Books: Maryland, 1981.

Gilbert, R.A. *The Golden Dawn: Twilight of the Magicians*. Aquarian Press: Wellingborough, 1983. (Useful background on the Hermetic Order of which Charles Williams was a sometime member.)

Glaspey, Terry. *Not a Tame Lion: The Spirit and Legacy of C.S. Lewis*. Highland Books, 1996.

Glover, Donald E. *C.S. Lewis: The Art of Enchantment*. Ohio University Press, 1981.

Goffar, Janine. *C.S. Lewis Index: Rumours from the Sculptor's Shop*. La Sierra University Press: Riverside, 1995; and Solway: Carlisle, 1997.

Green, R.L. and Walter Hooper. *C.S. Lewis: A Biography*. Collins: London, 1974.

Gresham, Douglas. *Lenten Lands: My Childhood with Joy Davidman and C.S. Lewis*. Collins: London, 1989.

Griffin, William. *Clive Staples Lewis: A Dramatic Life*. Harper and Row: San Francisco, 1986.

Griffin, William. *C.S. Lewis: The Authentic Voice*. Lion: Tring, 1988.

Grotta, Daniel. *The Biography of J.R.R. Tolkien: Architect of Middle-earth*. Running Press: Philadelphia, 1978.

Hadfield, Alice Mary. *Charles Williams: An Exploration of His Life and Work*. Oxford University Press: Oxford, 1983.

Hammond, Wayne G. with the assistance of Douglas A. Anderson. *J.R.R. Tolkien: A Descriptive Bibliography*. St Paul's Bibliographies: Winchester and Oak Knoll Books: New Castle, 1993.

Hannay, Margaret. *C.S. Lewis*. Ungar: New York, 1981.

Harris, Richard. *C.S. Lewis: The Man and His God*. Collins Fount: London, 1987.

Hart, Dabney A. *Through the Open Door: A New Look at C.S. Lewis*. University of Alabama Press: Alabama, 1984.

Harvey, David. *The Song of Middle-earth: J.R.R. Tolkien's Themes, Symbols and Myths*. Allen and Unwin: London, 1985.

Helms, Randel. *Tolkien's World*. Houghton Mifflin: Boston, 1974.

Helms, Randel. *Tolkien and the Silmarils*. Houghton Mifflin: Boston, 1981.

Hillegas, M.R. (ed). *Shadows of Imagination*. Feffer and Simons Inc: London and Amsterdam, 1969.

Hillegas, Mark R. (ed). *Shadows of Imagination: The Fantasies of C.S. Lewis, J.R.R. Tolkien and Charles Williams*. Southern Illinois University Press: Carbondale, 1969; new edition, 1979.

Holbrook, David. *The Skeleton in the Wardrobe: C.S. Lewis's Fiction, A Phenomenological Study*. Bucknell University: Lewisburg and Associated University Press: London, 1991.

Holmer, Paul L. *C.S. Lewis: The Shape of his Faith and Thought*. Harper and Row: New York, 1976; Sheldon Press: London, 1977.

Hooper, Walter. *Past Watchful Dragons*. Collins Fount: London, 1979.

Hooper, Walter. *C.S. Lewis: A Companion and Guide*. HarperCollins: London, 1996.

Horne, Brian (ed). *Charles Williams: A Celebration*. Gracewing: Leominster, 1995.

Howard, Thomas. *The Achievement of C.S. Lewis: A Reading of His Fiction*. Harold Shaw: Wheaton, 1980.

Howard, Thomas. *The Novels of Charles Williams*. Oxford University Press: London, 1983; repr. Ignatius Press: San Francisco, 1991.

Huttar, Charles A. (ed). *Imagination and the Spirit: Essays in Literature and the Christian Faith*. W.B. Eerdmans: Grand Rapids, 1971.

Isaacs, Neil D. and Rose A. Zimbardo (eds). *Tolkien: New Critical Perspectives*. The University Press of Kentucky: Kentucky, 1981.

Karkainen, Paul A. *Narnia Explored*. Revell: Old Tappan, 1979.

Keefe, Carolyn (ed). *C.S. Lewis: Speaker and Teacher*. Hodder: London, 1974.

Kilby, Clyde S. *The Christian World of C.S. Lewis*. W.B. Eerdmans: Grand Rapids, 1965, 1996.

Kilby, Clyde S. *Tolkien and the Silmarillion*. Harold Shaw: Wheaton, Illinois, 1976; Lion: Tring, 1977.

Kilby, Clyde S. *Images of Salvation in the Fiction of C.S. Lewis*. Harold Shaw: Wheaton, 1978.

Kilby, Clyde S. and Douglas Gilbert. *C.S. Lewis: Images of His World*. W.B. Eerdmans: Grand Rapids, 1973.

Kilby, Clyde S. and Marjorie Lamp Meade (eds). *Brothers and Friends: The Diaries of Major Warren Hamilton Lewis*. Harper and Row: San Francisco, 1982.

Knight, Gareth. *The Magical World of the Inklings*. Element Books: Longmead, 1990.

Kocher, Paul H. *Master of Middle-earth: The Fiction of J.R.R. Tolkien*. Houghton Mifflin: Boston, 1972; British edition: *Master of Middle-earth: The Achievement of J.R.R. Tolkien*. Thames and Hudson: London, 1972.

Kocher, Paul H. *A Reader's Guide to the Silmarillion*. Thames and Hudson: London, 1980.

Kranz, Gilbert. *C.S. Lewis: Studien zu Leben und Werk*. Bouvier: Bonn, 1974.

Kreeft, Peter. *C.S. Lewis*. W.B. Eerdmans: Grand Rapids, 1969.

Kreeft, Peter. *C.S. Lewis for the Third Millennium: Six Essays on the Abolition of Man*. Ignatius: San Francisco, 1994.

Lawlor, John (ed). *Patterns of Love and Courtesy: Essays in Memory of C.S. Lewis*. Edward Arnold, 1966.

Lawlor, John. *C.S. Lewis: Memories and Reflections*. Spence Publishing: Dallas, 1998.

Lichański, Jakub (ed). *J.R.R. Tolkien: Recepcja Polska*. Wydawnictwa Uniwersytetu Warszawskieso: Warsaw, 1996. (Includes abstracts in English.)

Lindskoog, Kathryn. *C.S. Lewis: Mere Christian*. Gospel Light: Glendale, 1973.

Lindskoog, Kathryn. *The Lion of Judah in NeverNeverLand: God, Man and Nature in C.S. Lewis's Narnia Tales*. Eerdmans: Grand Rapids, 1973.

Lindskoog, Kathryn. *The C.S. Lewis Hoax*. Multnomah Press: Portland, 1988.

Little, Edmund. *The Fantasists: Studies in J.R.R. Tolkien, Lewis Carroll, Mervyn Peake, Gogol and Kenneth Grahame.* Avebury, 1984.

Lobdell, Jared. *A Tolkien Compass.* Open Court Publishing: La Salle, 1975; Ballantine: New York, 1980.

Lobdell, Jared. *England and Always: Tolkien's World of the Rings.* W.B. Eerdmans: Grand Rapids, 1981.

Lochhead, Marion. *Renaissance of Wonder: The Fantasy Worlds of C.S. Lewis, J.R.R. Tolkien, George MacDonald, E. Nesbit and Others.* Canongate: Edinburgh, 1973; Harper and Row: San Francisco, 1977.

Lochhead, Marion. *The Renaissance of Wonder in Children's Literature.* Canongate: Edinburgh, 1977.

Lowenberg, Susan. *C.S. Lewis: A Reference Guide, 1972–1988.* Maxwell Macmillan International, 1993.

Manlove, C.N. *Modern Fantasy.* Cambridge University Press: Cambridge, 1975.

Manlove, C.N. *C.S. Lewis: His Literary Acheivement.* St Martin's Press: New York, 1987.

Manlove, C.N. *Christian Fantasy: From 1200 to the Present.* The Macmillan Press: Basingstoke and London, 1992.

Martin, Thomas L. (ed). *Reading the Classics with C.S. Lewis.* Baker Academic: Grand Rapids; Paternoster Press: Carlisle, 2000.

Matthews, Richard. *Lightning from a Clear Sky: Tolkien, the Trilogy and the Silmarillion.* Borgo: San Bernardino, 1978.

Meilaender, Gilbert. *The Taste for the Other: The Social and Ethical Thought of C.S. Lewis.* Eerdmans: Grand Rapids, 1978.

Melmed, Susan Barbara. *John Ronald Reuel Tolkien: A Bibliography.* University of Witwatersrand Department of Bibliography, Librarianship and Typography: Johannesburg, 1972.

Menuge, Angus (ed). *Lightbearer in the Shadowlands: The Evangelistic Vision of C.S. Lewis.* Crossway Books: Wheaton, 1997.

Miesel, Sandra. *Myth, Symbol and Religion in the Lord of the Rings.* TK Graphics: Baltimore, 1973.

Miller, Stephen O. *Middle-earth: A World in Conflict.* TK Graphics: Baltimore, 1975.

Mills, David (ed). *The Pilgrim's Guide: C.S. Lewis and the Art of Witness.* Eerdmans: Grand Rapids, 1998.

Montgomery, John W. (ed). *Myth, Allegory and Gospel.* Bethany Fellowship: Minneapolis, 1974.

Montgomery, John Warwick (ed). *Myth, Allegory and Gospel: An Interpretation of J.R.R. Tolkien, C.S. Lewis, G.K. Chesterton and Charles Williams.* Bethany Fellowship: Minneapolis, 1974.

Moorman, Charles. *Arthurian Triptych: Mythic Materials in Charles Williams, C.S. Lewis and T.S. Eliot.* University of California Press: Berkeley, 1960.

Moorman, Charles. *The Precincts of Felicity: The Augustinian City of the Oxford Christians.* University of Florida Press: Gainesville, 1966.

Morrison, Louise D. *J.R.R. Tolkien's the Fellowship of the Ring: A Critical Commentary.* Monarch: New York, 1976.

Morse, Robert E. *Evocation of Virgil in Tolkien's Art.* Bolchazy Carducci Publishers: Oak Park, Illinois, 1987.

Moseley, Charles. *J.R.R. Tolkien.* Northcote House: Plymouth, 1997.

Myers, Doris. *C.S. Lewis in Context.* Kent State University Press: Kent, 1994.

Nitzsche, Jane Chance. *Tolkien's Art: A 'Mythology for England'.* St Martin's Press: New York, 1979.

Noel, Ruth S. *The Mythology of Middle-earth*. Houghton Mifflin: Boston, 1977; Thames and Hudson: London, 1977.

Noel, Ruth S. *The Languages of Tolkien's Middle-earth*. Houghton Mifflin: Boston, 1980.

O'Neill, Timothy R. *The Individuated Hobbit: Jung, Tolkien and the Archetypes of Middle-earth*. Houghton Mifflin: Boston, 1979.

Palmer, Bruce. *Of Orc-rags, Phials and a Far Shore: Visions of Paradise in the Lord of the Rings*. TK Graphics: Baltimore, 1976.

Patrick, James. *The Magdalen Metaphysicals: Idealism and Orthodoxy at Oxford 1901–1945*. Mercer University Press, 1985.

Payne, Leanne. *Real Presence: The Holy Spirit in the Works of C.S. Lewis*. Monarch Publications: Eastbourne, 1989.

Pearce, Joseph (ed). *Tolkien: A Celebration, Collected Writings on a Literary Legacy*. Fount: London, 1999.

Peters, John. *C.S. Lewis: The Man and His Achievement*. The Paternoster Press: Exeter, 1985.

Petty, Anne Cotton. *One Ring to Rule Them All: Tolkien's Mythology*. University of Alabama Press, 1979.

Purtill, Richard L. *Lord of the Elves and Eldils: Fantasy and Philosophy in C.S. Lewis and J.R.R. Tolkien*. Zondervan: Grand Rapids, 1974.

Purtill, Richard. *C.S. Lewis's Case for the Christian Faith*. Harper and Row: San Francisco, 1982.

Purtill, Richard L. *J.R.R. Tolkien: Myth, Morality and Religion*. Harper and Row: San Francisco, 1985.

Ready, William. *The Tolkien Relation*. Regnery: Chicago, 1968.

Reilly, Robert J. *Romantic Religion: A Study of Barfield, Lewis, Williams and Tolkien*. University of Georgia Press: Athens, 1971.

Reynolds, Patricia and Glen H. GoodKnight. *Proceedings of the J.R.R. Tolkien Centenary Conference: Keble College, Oxford, 1992*. The Tolkien Society: Milton Keynes and the Mythopoeic Press: Altadena, California, 1995.

Rogers, Deborah Webster and Ivor A. Rogers. *J.R.R. Tolkien*. Twayne Publishers: Boston, 1980.

Rossi, Lee D. *The Politics of Fantasy*. UMI Research: Epping, 1984.

Sale, Roger. *Modern Heroism: Essays on D.H. Lawrence, William Empson and J.R.R. Tolkien*. University of California Press: Berkeley and Los Angeles, 1973.

Salu, Mary and Robert T. Farrell (eds). *J.R.R. Tolkien, Scholar and Storyteller: Essays in Memoriam*. Cornell University Press: Ithaca, 1979.

Sammons, Martha C. *A Guide through Narnia*. Hodder: London, 1979.

Sammons, Martha C. *A Guide through C.S. Lewis's Space Trilogy*. Cornerstone Books, 1980.

Sayer, George. *Jack: C.S. Lewis and His Times*. Macmillan: London, 1988.

Schakel, Peter J. (ed). *The Longing for a Form: Essays on the Fiction of C.S. Lewis*. Kent State University Press: Ohio, 1977.

Schakel, Peter J. *Reading with the Heart: The Way into Narnia*. W.B. Eerdmans: Grand Rapids, 1979.

Schakel, Peter J. *Reason and Imagination in C.S. Lewis: A Study of 'Till We Have Faces'*. Paternoster Press: Exeter, 1984.

Schakel, Peter J. and Charles A. Huttar (eds). *Word and Story in C.S. Lewis*. University of Missouri Press: Columbia, 1991.

Schofield, Stephen (ed). *In Search of C.S. Lewis*. Bridge Publications, 1984.

Schultz, Jeffrey D. and John G. West, Jr (eds). *The C.S. Lewis Readers' Encyclopedia*. Zondervan: Grand Rapids, 1998.

Shideler, Mary McDermott. *The Theology of Romantic Love: A Study in the Writings of Charles Williams*. W.B. Eerdmans: Grand Rapids, 1962.

Shippey, T.A. *The Road to Middle-earth*. George Allen and Unwin: London, 1982; Houghton Mifflin: New York, 1983.

Shippey, T.A. *J.R.R. Tolkien: Author of the Century*. HarperCollins: London, 2000.

Shorto, Russell. *J.R.R. Tolkien: Man of Fantasy*. (Foreword by G.B. Tennyson.) The Kipling Press: New York, 1988.

Sibley, Brian. *Shadowlands*. Hodder: London, 1985.

Sibley, Brian. *The Land of Narnia*. Collins Lions: London, 1989.

Smith, Robert H. *Patches of Godlight: The Pattern of Thought of C.S. Lewis*. University of Georgia Press: Athens, 1981.

Starr, Nathan Comfort. *C.S. Lewis 'Till We Have Faces': Introduction and Commentary*. Seabury Press, New York, 1968.

Strachey, Barbara. *Journeys of Frodo*. Unwin Paperbacks: London, 1981.

The Filmbook of J.R.R. Tolkien's 'The Lord of the Rings'. Ballantine Books: New York, 1978.

Tolkien, Christopher. *The Silmarillion by J.R.R. Tolkien: A Brief Account of the Book and Its Making*. Houghton Mifflin: Boston, 1977.

Tolkien, John and Priscilla. *The Tolkien Family Album*. Unwin/Hyman: London, 1992.

Tyler, J.E.A. *The Tolkien Companion*. Macmillan: London, 1976.

Tyler, J.E.A. *The New Tolkien Companion*. St Martin's Press: New York, 1979.

Urang, Gunnar. *Shadows of Heaven: Religion and Fantasy in the Writing of C.S. Lewis, Charles Williams and J.R.R. Tolkien*. SCM Press: London, 1970; United Church Press: Philadelphia, 1971.

Vanauken, Sheldon. *A Severe Mercy*. Hodder: London, 1977; Harper and Row: New York, 1979.

Wain, John. *Sprightly Running: Part of an Autobiography*. Macmillan: London, 1962.

Walker, Andrew and James Patrick (eds). *A Christian for all Christians: Essays in Honour of C.S. Lewis*. Hodder: London, 1990.

Walsh, Chad. *C.S. Lewis: Apostle to the Skeptics*. Macmillan: New York, 1949.

Walsh, Chad. *The Literary Legacy of C.S. Lewis*. Harcourt Brace Jovanovich: New York, 1979.

Watson, George (ed). *Critical Thought 1: Critical Essays on C.S. Lewis*. Scholar Press: Aldershot, 1992.

West, Richard C. *Tolkien Criticism: An Annotated Checklist*. Kent State University Press: Kent, Ohio, 1970.

White, William L. *The Image of Man in C.S. Lewis*. Hodder: London, 1970.

Willis, John. *Pleasures for Evermore: The Theology of C.S. Lewis*. Angel Press/Loyola University Press: 1989.

Wilson, A.N. *C.S. Lewis: A Biography*. Collins: London, 1990.

Wilson, Colin. *Tree by Tolkien*. Covent Garden Press: London, 1973; Capra Press: Santa Barbara, 1974.

Zipes, Jack. *Breaking the Magic Spell: Radical Theories of Folk and Fairy Tales*. University of Texas Press: Austin, 1979.